More
Words

Still More Words of Wall Street

Allan H. Pessin
Joseph A. Ross

BUSINESS ONE IRWIN
Homewood, Illinois 60430

This publication is designed to provide accurate and
authoritative information in regard to the subject matter
covered. It is sold with the understanding that neither the
author nor the publisher is engaged in rendering legal, accounting,
or other professional service. If legal advice or other expert
assistance is required, the services of a competent
professional person should be sought.

*From a Declaration of Principles jointly adopted by a Committee
of the American Bar Association and a Committee of Publishers.*

Acquisitions Editor: Amy Hollands
Project editor: Rita McMullen
Production manager: Bette K. Ittersagen
Interior design and art: Image House
Compositor: Precision Typographers
Typeface: 10/12 Century Schoolbook
Printer: Arcata Graphics/Kingsport

Library of Congress Cataloging-in-Publication Data

Pessin, Allan H.
    Still more words of Wall Street / Allan H. Pessin, Joseph A. Ross.
        p.   cm.
    ISBN 1-55623-329-9
    1. Investments—Dictionaries.   2. Securities—Dictionaries.
3. Finance—Dictionaries.   I. Ross, Joseph A.   II. Title.
HG4513.P467   1990
332.6′03—dc20   90–3667

Preface

We have been proud of the support that you, our readers, have given to *Words of Wall Street* and *More Words of Wall Street*. Thank you very much.

With this present addition of *Still More Words of Wall Street*, we have completed our original intent: to provide the students of our industry with three volumes that would serve as:

- an introduction to the financial services industry (*Words of Wall Street*)
- an intermediate text for industry professionals (*More Words of Wall Street*)
- an advanced text for institutional and inter-national executives (*Still More Words of Wall Street*)

As with the previous books, this present book is not a how-to-do-it book. Instead, this book concentrates on the myriad of new terms—many of them from Britain and Japan—that have come into our industry in the past decade as both Britain and Japan have begun to trade more shares daily than we do in the United States.

This internationalization of securities markets will mark the 1990s and will continue into the 21st century, and you will see the addition of more terms as we update these three volumes.

Although we aimed these volumes to the beginner, the intermediate, and the advanced professional in our industry, we would not want you, our valued reader, to limit yourself to just one of these volumes. As they stand, the three volumes taken together form *one dictionary* of our industry.

As with all dictionaries, the meanings of words come from usage. Used words are correct words. Thus, we invite the reader—as we did in the prefaces to the previous books—to send us entries that should be included in future revisions of these books. We appreciate your help in the subsequent editions of these books—just as we appreciate your support in the past.

Allan H. Pessin
Joseph A. Ross

Still More Words of Wall Street

A

A
First letter of the English alphabet, used:
1. Lowercase in newspaper stock transaction tables after dividend report to designate extra cash dividends in that year; for example, 2.40a. Formerly used in option transaction tables to designate no trades that day.
2. Uppercase in corporate newspaper reports to designate that the American Stock Exchange is the principal marketplace for a security; for example, Atlas Van (A).
3. In NASDAQ market system as the fifth letter of a stock symbol if there are various classes of common stock outstanding; for example, BISHA to designate Biscayne Holdings Class A common stock.
4. Uppercase to designate American Medical Buildings, Inc., common stock. This stock is traded on the American Stock Exchange.

ABANDONMENT
The failure of an owner to claim property that is rightfully his or hers over a long period. Such property then becomes subject to escheat (pronounced ess–cheet) laws of the individual states or country. For example, a brokerage client has on deposit with the broker 100 shares of fully paid stock and fails to claim that stock or to communicate with the broker over a prestated time period. In such a case, the property may be considered abandoned and reverts to the state.

ABS
The Automated Bond System (ABS) is a subscription service whereby member firms can be linked to the bond trading floor of the NYSE. This

automated system replaced the inactive (cabinet) bond crowd formerly in use. Through ABS, previously entered limit orders to buy or sell can be automatically paired off and reported to subscribing members.

ABOUT-AMOUNT TRADE
In the English marketplace, customer orders may be entered for an amount in pounds, rather than for a specific number of shares. Thus, an order for shares of an English insurance company stock for 5,000 pounds sterling can be accepted. When the share price is set, the actual number of shares will be determined accordingly. The English marketplace gives marketmakers flexibility in accommodating such customer instructions.

ABUSIVE TAX SHELTER
Popular name for an investment without economic merit. Such an investment, for example, would be one that provides subscribers with tax deductions of questionable applicability with little or no probability of profit on the enterprise.

The Tax Reform Act of 1986 (TRA 86) permits the IRS to challenge the tax deductions on abusive tax shelters.

ACAPULCO SPREAD
Tongue-in-cheek expression for a long and short option position which, when closed, automatically creates four commissions for the broker. Although the customer may profit, the broker always will enjoy risk-free commission income. Theoretically, the broker will use the money to vacation in sunny Acapulco, Mexico.

Also called "Cadillac spread."

ACCRUAL BOND
See Z-BOND.

ACE
An acronym for:
1. American Commodities Exchange. This is a corporate affiliate of the American Stock Exchange where certain futures contracts for interest-rate sensitive financial instruments are traded.
2. The cooperative confirmation, comparison, and settlement systems initiated by AIBD, Cedel, and Euroclear, three independent associations that specialize in the handling of non-US securities transactions.
3. "Approximate certainty equivalent," which is a portfolio valuation concept. ACE measures and anticipates changes in the risk premium associated with equity portfolios as changes in the economy's inter-

est rate environment occur. Generally, the more stable a company's earnings, the greater its ACE predictability.

ACES
Acronym for Advanced Computerized Execution System. This is an NASD market system that enables dealers to execute both proprietary and customer orders in quantities in excess of 1,000 shares, which is the upper limit on the Small Order Execution System (SOES).

Through ACES, preapproved members or customers can trade electronically and immediately with the marketmaker whose quotations and sizes are displayed on the CRT screen. In this way, the marketmaker can control its market risk exposure.

ACHA
Acronym: Associate Clearing House of Amsterdam, a wholly owned subsidiary of the European Stock Options Clearing Corporation. ACHA acts as an intermediary clearing point for OCC in the comparison and settlement of XMI options trading on the European Option Exchange.

ACKNOWLEDGMENT
Term used to designate the signature verification on a certificate or on an assignment and power of substitution form. To transfer ownership of a certificate (stock or registered bond), or to transfer an account from one broker to another, the owner must have his or her signature validated (guaranteed, or acknowledged) by a recognized broker/dealer or a commercial bank.

Popular synonym: signature guarantee.

ACROSS THE BOARD
Used to describe all stocks (bonds) in the same industry or with similar credit characteristics. For example, "Tobacco stocks were up across the board following a favorable ruling by a New York District Court," or "Long corporate bonds were down sharply across the board as the yield curve flattened this week."

ACRS
See MACRS.

ACT SYSTEM
See AUTOMATED CONFIRMATION TRANSACTION

A-DAY
English designation of Authorization Day. This was the specific day in 1988 when the 1986 Financial Services Act became fully operative in

the United Kingdom. On that date, as determined by the Department of Trade and Industry (DTI), any firm or person intent on doing business in the financial industry in the UK must have been licensed by the Securities Investment Board (SIB) or by one of the self-regulatory organizations (SRO) empowered to grant such licenses.

ADJUSTED GROSS INCOME (AGI)
The bottom line of the front page of Form 1040 for individual taxpayers.

AGI includes all forms of taxable income—including net items from Schedules B, C, D, and E—minus contributions to IRA (deductible) and Keogh plans, and alimony paid.

AGI, except for personal exemptions and deductions (either standard or itemized), is the main determinant of the taxpayers bracket and ultimate tax obligation.

It is the goal of tax-free and tax-deferred investing to keep items off the front page of Form 1040.

ADJUSTED NET CAPITAL
See ANC.

ADJUSTED TRADING
An NASD term used to designate a broker/dealer swap with a customer at prices not reasonably related to the current market value of the securities; that is, a purchase at a price above the current market, and a sale below the current market. Such transactions may impact the customer's tax liability and represent a fraud.

Also called "linked transactions."

ADR INDEX OPTION
See INTERNATIONAL MARKET INDEX.

ADS
Acronym: American Depository Shares.

ADS differs from ADR in that ADS are shares created for the American market by the issuer. ADRs, in turn, are created by a commercial bank as receipts for the underlying shares.

Both ADRs and ADSs facilitate the sale and transfer of foreign security ownership.

ADVANCED COMPUTERIZED EXECUTION SYSTEM
See ACES.

AFBD
Acronym: Association of Futures Brokers and Dealers. AFBD is an SRO in the United Kingdom. It is authorized to regulate firms dealing or brokering in futures or options or who provide advice or management about this business.

AFFILIATED CORPORATION
1. In the United States, a term similar in meaning to affiliated person, as used in the Investment Company Act of 1940. In general, any officer, director, employee, or partner of an investment company or its advisor. It also includes anyone who holds 5% or more of the voting stock of such companies, or who is controlled by anyone who holds 5% or more of the voting stock.
2. In Japan, because of interlocking corporate relationships, this term applies only to institutions that control 20% or more of a corporation's stock. Such companies are "insiders" and may not buy equity securities of the issuer controlling them during the announcement and stabilization periods preceding financings.

AGENTS DE CHANGE
French title for brokerage firm. Until 1992, these firms have a government authorized monopoly to conduct a securities business in France. Only *agents de change* are authorized to become members of the Paris Bourse. All *agents de change* in France must be specifically approved by the French Ministry of Finance.

AGM
In Japan, an acronym for a corporation's annual general meeting. Such meetings are required under Japanese law. Anyone holding 1,000 or more shares may attend and participate in the annual discussion of corporate affairs and objectives.

AIBDQ
Acronym: Association of International Bond Dealers Quotations. AIBDQ is a computerized CRT system for trading Eurodollar debt issues among its European members. The system is designed to provide trade and market information among dealers. Some members of AIBD fear that AIBDQ provides too much information to competitors and customers and thus gives them an advantage over dealers.

AICPA
Acronym: American Institute of Certified Public Accountants. AICPA is a trade association for members of the accounting profession. Its purpose is to represent the business interests of its members, to serve for the

exchange of ideas and information, and to improve the accounting skills of its members.

AID CALL
See ANY-INTEREST-DATE CALL.

AIM
Acronym: Amsterdam Interprofessional Market. AIM is an experimental block trading system for equities listed on the Amsterdam Stock Exchange. The system consists of 40 video display terminals distributed to members and institutional investors. Timely quotations and trade reports are displayed. Those who use the terminals for executions receive lower than usual commission rates.

AIR
See ANTICIPATED INVESTMENT RETURN.

AIR POCKET
Term used if a stock, or the market, suffers a sudden and precipitous drop. Term is an analogy based on the sudden drop when an airplane hits an air pocket (a down current). The term itself describes the fact, but not the reason, for the drop.

Similar terms: *downward spike, freefall.*

ALFRED BERG NORDIC INDEX
A daily index of performance of the Swedish, Norwegian, Finnish, and Danish stock markets. Named after a Swedish brokerage firm, this index is comprised of 136 issues, with each country weighted according to marking capitalization. In effect, the Alfred Berg Nordic Index tracks Scandinavian market performance.

ALL IN
Trader's slang for "all included." The term is used to give the issuer's interest cost after all other costs; for example, commissions, are included. Thus, an issuer's bonds may be offered at 8.30%, but after the payment of expenses its all-in cost may be 8.375%.

ALL ORDINARIES INDEX
An index of 85% of the domestic issues traded on the six floors of the Australia Stock Exchange.

See AUSTRALIA STOCK EXCHANGE.

ALL SUBSEQUENT COUPONS ATTACHED
This characteristic, popularly initiated as ASCA or simply SCA, means that a bearer municipal bond has the current and all subsequent coupons attached. If the bond has been in default, the initial passed coupon is listed and ASCA follows. For example, the Highland County Sewer Revenue Bonds, 7 5/8s due 5/1/09, with coupon #4 and ASCA.

ALL THE EIGHTHS
Order room and exchange floor slang for orders and transactions at 7/8ths; that is, with all the eighths before a new digit is used.

ALPHA (COEFFICIENT)
The calculation of a (alpha in Greek) in the formula for the slope of a line: $a + bx = y$. If b (beta in Greek) is set at zero, thereby eliminating market price volatility, alpha will measure the investment return for a particular security when compared to the baseline of the Standard & Poor's Index.

Alpha measurements that are positive (e.g., plus 10) mean that the particular stock will yield dividend returns 10% greater than the average of the S&P. An alpha of 0 is equal to the S&P dividend return; an alpha of minus 5 is 5% lower than the S&P. Thus, alpha measures investment return and beta measures price volatility of individual stocks versus a commonly accepted baseline. These concepts are extensively used.

ALPHABET STOCK
Slang for any of the variously lettered stock introduced by General Motors as it acquired different companies. These shares have different voting features and varying dividends that are dependent on the financial success of the acquired companies. Thus, there is General Motors "E" stock issued to acquire Electronic Data Systems, and General Motors "H" stock issued to acquire Hughes Aircraft.

ALTERNATIVE MINIMUM TAX (AMT)
An alternative tax computation method (minimum tax = 21%) whereby certain taxpayers who have lowered their tax by the use of certain "preference items" must pay the larger tax. About 1% of U.S. taxpayers are subject to AMT.

Preference items include the appreciation on charitable gifts, the bargain element on incentive stock options, certain deductible losses from passive investments, certain deductions from amortization and depletion, itemized deductions of state and local taxes, and the like. Tax advice is needed. Of particular importance is the fact that the interest income on some private activity bonds is considered preference income.

ALTERNATIVE NET CAPITAL REQUIREMENT
The SEC has established net capital requirements for broker/dealers.
The formulas are complex. The alternate net capital requirement is particularly appealing for U.S. broker/dealers who maintain proprietary accounts (trading positions). Here, the net capital must be equal to the greater of $100,000 or 2% of the aggregate debit items as computed in the SEC's Rule 15c3-3 formula for customer protection.

AMBULANCE STOCK
Tongue-in-cheek term, used primarily in Japan, to describe stock that is about to be manipulated upward—thus, an advantage to those who buy before the upward movement. Allusion: if you are losing money in the market, this stock will make you well—financially speaking—in a hurry.

AMERICAN DEPOSITORY SHARES
See ADS.

AMERICAN INSTITUTE OF CERTIFIED PUBLIC ACCOUNTANTS
See AICPA.

AMERICAN-STYLE EXERCISE
Quality of most listed option contracts traded in the United States. If an option permits American-Style exercise, the option holder may exercise the option at anytime during its effective life.

Antonym: European-Style Exercise. Some index options may only be exercised in a short period before their expirations.

AMPS
Acronym: auction market preferred stock. A Merrill Lynch proprietary term for certain preferred shares. This product was originated to compete with First Boston's STARS and Salomon Brothers' DARTS.

In effect, an issuer's preferred dividend is reset every 49 days to mirror prevailing money market conditions. Securities thus purchased are held more than the statutory 46-day holding period required for corporate holders to be eligible for the 70% "dividend received" exclusion under the IRS Code.

AMSTERDAM INTERPROFESSIONAL MARKET
See AIM.

AMSTERDAM STOCK EXCHANGE
The Amsterdam Stock Exchange is located in Holland (Netherlands) and, having been founded in 1602, is the oldest in the world. The ex-

change is international in scope and more than half its listed securities are of foreign-based companies. Trading is from 10:00 A.M. until 4:30 P.M., but Dutch issues may be traded for an additional six hours. Settlement terms are quite liberal and payment/delivery are to be made on the 10th business day following the trade

AMT
See ALTERNATE MINIMUM TAX.

ANC
Acronym: Adjusted Net Capital. A term used by the Commodities Futures Trading Commission (CFTC) to set minimum financial requirements for futures commission merchants (FCM) registered with the CFTC. The general formula is: Specified current assets minus Adjusted liabilities, minus Capital charges. The adjusted liabilities include customer funds that must be segregated. ANC, by CFTC rule, must be at least 4% of such segregated funds.

ANGEL
Slang for an investment grade debt security; that is, a debt security with one of the top four ratings. The term arises from the fact that such bonds are favored by institutional investors anxious to avoid criticism for their portfolio management.

Synonym: investment grade or bank grade.
Antonym: junk bond.

ANNUALIZED DISCOUNT
Term used of the dollar valuation of T-bills and contingent T-bill options.

The discount is stated as a percent and is based on a 360-day year. The dollar amount of the discount is based on the formula:

$$\frac{\text{Days to}}{\text{maturity}} \times \frac{\text{Price in}}{\text{basis points}} \times 0.277778 = \frac{\text{Face value}}{\text{in dollars}}$$

This formula is accurate for trades of $10 million or less. For larger trades, introduce another 7 into the constant repeating decimal of 0.2777778. This decimal represents 0.01 divided by 0.01 × 360 (in other words, the decimal factor for a basis point for 1 day).

ANTIPODEAN ISSUER
The term is heard most frequently in Europe. It refers to an offering of securities in Australia or New Zealand.

Derived from the Greek-rooted word, antipodes, meaning the other side of the world.

ANSERM
Acronym: Association of Nagoya Stock Exchange Regular Members. ANSERM is a nonregulatory organization whose purpose is to promote mutual friendship, the exchange of ideas, and philanthropy. Its surveillance activities are strongly influenced by the JASD.

ANTICIPATED INVESTMENT RETURN
Term used in conjunction with the performance of annuity units of a variable annuity. When an owner of investment units of a variable annuity elects to annuitize and selects one of the annuity options (single life, one life and survivor, and the like) the insurance company assigns the annuitant a fixed number of annuity units. Because these annuity units will vary in performance, it is necessary to assign an arbitrary anticipated investment return (AIR). According to the annuity contract, the owner will receive monthly payment based on this AIR. The AIR, in turn, will be adjusted on a monthly, quarterly, or semiannual basis to conform to the actual experience of the separate account. It is in this sense that the annuity is said to vary.

ANY-INTEREST-DATE CALL
A feature of some municipal bonds whereby the issuer reserves the right to redeem the obligation on any date on which an interest payment is due. The redemption privilege may be at par, or at a premium, as outlined in the indenture.

AOSERM
Acronym: Association of Osaka Stock Exchange Regular Members. Like ANSERM, AOSERM is a nonregulatory organization whose purpose is to promote mutual friendship, the exchange of ideas, and philanthropy. Its surveillance activities are strongly influenced by JASD.

APPRECIATION
1. Any increase in investor equity. For example, a client purchases a security for $25 per share and sells it at $32 per share.
2. Any increase over the "ratable cost" of an investment. For example, a zero-coupon bond has an adjusted cost of $450 and the bond is sold at $522.
3. In a broad sense, any increase in net worth resulting from an investment. In this sense, it is used as a synonym for total return. For example, "We anticipate that your total return on this investment, includ-

ing reinvested cash flows, will be 15% per year over the next 10 years."

As a general rule, meanings 1 and 2 do not include dividends and interest; meaning 3 does.

APPROVED LIST
A list of investment vehicles considered acceptable for bank trust departments, financial institutions, and fiduciaries. The criteria for acceptability varies from jurisdiction to jurisdiction, but—in general—securities are either selected by statute or by a commissioner of securities for that state.

Also called the "legal list."

APS
Acronym: Auction Preferred Stock. APS were created by Goldman Sachs to compete with First Boston's STARS and Salomon Brothers' DARTS. These preferred issues have a dividend whose rate is reset each 49 days to mirror prevailing money market rates. In this way the holder has fulfilled the statutory 46-day holding period required for the 70% "dividend received" exclusion for corporate holders.

APT
Initials stand for Automated Pit Trading, an electronic trading system developed by the London International Financial Futures Exchange (LIFFE) for implementation after normal trading hours. It competes directly with Chicago's major commodities exchange's GLOBEX system, although it is currently capable of accommodating futures contracts in only Euromarks and German Bunds.

ARCDELTA RISK
The risk a futures portfolio incurs at specific price intervals, based on changes in trading ranges of commodities products. The risk can be measured and plotted.

ARIEL
A computerized trade matching program in the United Kingdom that enabled institutional holders to trade directly with one another, thereby bypassing the London Stock Exchange's system of fixed commissions, in use before October 27, 1986. The custom was similar to the Fourth Market in the United States. Its use has been virtually abandoned.

AR-OP
See ASSISTANT REPRESENTATIVE-ORDER PROCESSING.

ARMS INDEX
Technical indicator named for Richard Arms, a journalist with *Barron's* in 1967.

Popularly known as TRIN.

ARRS
See AUTOMATED REGULATORY REPORTING SYSTEM.

ARTICLE 65
A section of Japanese securities law that prohibits a bank, trust company, or similar financial institutions from engaging in most aspects of securities business. Agency orders and principal transactions for its own investment account are permissible exceptions. It is similar in scope to the Glass-Steagall Act in the United States.

ASAM
Acronym: Automated Search & Match System. ASAM is a NYSE data base of persons affiliated with issuers of stocks traded on the exchange. The data base is culled from financial manuals, directorships, and so on. It is so arranged that the system can be searched for opportunists, sources of, or circulators of, "inside" market information if there is evidence of price influencing of listed securities.

ASCA (A.S.C.A.)
See ALL SUBSEQUENT COUPONS ATTACHED.

ASE
1. Acronym: American Stock Exchange. Sometimes referred to as the "Curb." Located in New York, the ASE is one of the largest exchanges in the United States. In recent years, the exchange has preferred to be initialed as the AMEX.
2. Acronym: Amsterdam Stock Exchange. The largest securities exchange in Holland. It is a leading European marketplace and it deals in many international issues. It also sponsors trading of the AMEX's Major Market Index (XMI).

ASPIRIN
Acronym: Australian Stock Price Riskless Indexed Notes. These government-guaranteed notes are backed by the Treasury of New South Wales. They guarantee repayment of the face value in four years. They pay no current interest; thus, they are zero-coupon. In exchange, the noteholder will receive—in addition to par value—the percentage increase by which the Australian Stock Index of All Ordinaries (common stock) rises above 1,372 points during that period. In effect, they are

bonds with no downside risk, no regular return, but a percentage return that is coupled to the performance of the Australian stock market during their lifetime.

ASSESSABLE STOCK
An equity participation in a corporation; for example, common or preferred stock, which allows the issuer to require further cash infusions from the stockholders.

The concept has not been applicable for many years in the sale and transfer of publicly traded shares. Such shares are inscribed as follows:

> Fully paid and nonassessable shares
> of such-and-such corporation

The concept can be important in the interpretation of state securities laws, where the "gift" of assessable stock is actually considered a "sale," because of this further requirement for funds from the holder.

ASSET ALLOCATION
The distribution of cash, stocks, bonds, real estate, and other assets in an institution's portfolio. The percentage of each component is a function of the portfolio manager's assessment of market and interest-rate risk—and other factors—at the present time. The distribution may also reflect the institution's investment objectives and its present and future cash flow needs.

Nothing prevents the term from being used of the portfolio mix of an individual investor. For example, a security research service may recommend that portfolios be 10% cash, 45% bonds, and 45% stocks under present market conditions.

ASSET-BACKED SECURITY
Generic term for any security whose underlying collateral or cash flow is dependent on an item of value. Such items of value are often receivables of corporations; thus, we see names like CARS (for car loans), CARDS (for credit card loans), and so on.

As a general rule, while the concept is the same, the term *asset-backed security* is not used of securities backed by mortgages. Instead, such securities are popularly called "mortgage-backed securities" (MBS) or "collateralized mortgage obligations" (CMOs).

ASSET PLAY
Expression associated with the upward movement of an actively traded stock when no other fundamental reason is apparent. The concept: If there is no apparent reason for the upswing, technicians and salespersons suspect that a group of investors see undervalued assets on the cor-

poration's balance sheet and are buying the stock in anticipation of an appreciation of these assets by other investors.

In effect, accounting aberrations or certain assets, tangible or intangible, are being carried below their actual worth. Thus, such a company may be worth more dead than alive—especially to a corporate raider.

ASSET STRIPPER
This is the English term for a corporate raider who assumes significant debt to acquire a target company. Once in control, the asset stripper sells off parts of the company to pay down or liquidate the liability. Many leveraged buyouts (LBOs), whether done by an outside corporate raider or by company management, are characterized by such "stripping."

US expression: corporate raider, or predator.

ASSISTANT REPRESENTATIVE-ORDER PROCESSING (AR-OP)
An NASD registration status applicable to a member firm employee who regularly accepts unsolicited customer orders. This employee, it is presumed, does nothing else that would require qualification as a general securities registered representative.

Qualification as an AR-OP is obtained by application and passage of an examination.

ASSOCIATION OF COMPENSATION FUND FOR CONSIGNED LIABILITIES IN COMMODITY FUTURES, INC.
See HOSHO-KIKIN SYSTEM.

ASSOCIATION OF FUTURES BROKERS AND DEALERS, THE
See AFBD.

ASSOCIATION OF INTERNATIONAL BOND DEALERS
See AIBD.

ATHENS STOCK EXCHANGE
A relatively small exchange—even for Greece. The market is open each weekday from 10 A.M. until noon, although after-hour trading is permitted until 2 P.M. Contract settlement is due for a fortnightly accounting on regular way transactions; thus, it copies the procedure of the ISE. It is a verbal marketplace, with no restriction on foreign membership.

ATP
Acronym: Arbitrage Trading Program. Term used to describe investors who attempt to lock in market profits through the simultaneous purchase of stock index futures and the sale of the underlying stocks in that

index or vice versa. Speed of execution is necessary to capture the profits available because of price variations.

Such arbitrage traders are often simply called "program traders."

ATSERM

Acronym: Association of Tokyo Stock Exchange (TSE) Regular Members. ATSERM is a nonregulatory organization in Japan comprised of all members of the exchange. Its purpose is the promotion of mutual friendship, the exchange of ideas, and philanthropy. Its surveillance responsibilities are strongly influenced by the JASD.

AUDIT TRAIL

This term identifies the attempt by the NASD and the major stock and option exchanges to track trade executions and to eliminate broker errors (DKs). To do this, each participating member must submit immediately such basic information as buy/sell, quantity, issue, price, contra party, time of execution, and firm capacity on-line to the NASD or exchange. In this way, errors are quickly identified.

AUNT AGATHA

See AUNT MILLIE.

AUNT MILLIE

This term is representative of the small shareholder; that is, the unsophisticated retail investor who relies on the professional broker/dealer as a financial physician and advisor. The expression is often used to emphasize suitability when making investment recommendations to less-knowledgeable customers; that is, those unable to distinguish risk from opportunity.

In the United Kingdom, known as Aunt Agatha; in Brussels as the Belgian Dentist.

AUSTRALIA STOCK EXCHANGE (ASX)

The exchange is comprised of six trading floors linked by a computerized trading system (SEATS). The exchange is physically located in Sydney, Melbourne, Brisbane, Perth, Adelaide, and Hobart (Tasmania). Official trading hours are 10:00 A.M. to 12:15 P.M. and from 2:00 P.M. until 3:15 P.M. Settlements are scheduled on a once-a-month basis, but shorter-term trade completions are not unusual.

The exchange's "All Ordinaries Index" provides investors with an accurate view of the performance of this market, because the index contains about 85% of all of the domestic issues traded on the marketplace.

AUSTRALIAN STOCK PRICE RISKLESS INDEXED NOTES
See ASPIRIN.

AUTOM
Acronym: Automated Option Market system, an on-line system developed by the Philadelphia Stock Exchange. AUTOM allows electronic delivery of option orders from member firms directly to the specific specialist in an option series. Execution information from the specialist is speeded back to the member firm as well as to the OPRA tape.

AUTOM is independent from PACE, the electronic system used by PHLX for stock orders.

AUTOMATED BOND SYSTEM
See ABS.

AUTOMATED CONFIRMATION TRANSACTION SYSTEM (ACT)
An NASD electronic system that enables members to submit, compare, and automatically clear their transactions through the National Securities Clearing Corporation (NSCC). Through a linkage of computer terminals in member firm offices, a marketmaker participating in a transaction can submit trade information immediately, have it automatically compared (with its terms "locked in" on T+1), and completed successfully at NSCC on the settlement date.

AUTOMATED OPTIONS MARKET SYSTEM
See AUTOM.

AUTOMATED PIT TRADING
See APT.

AUTOMATED REGULATORY REPORTING SYSTEM (ARRS)
An NASD service that enables members to access the NASD immediately through a computer interface. ARRS can be used for ongoing reporting requirements of members as well as for petitions for extensions of time under Regulation T, or SEC Rule 15c3-3.

AUTOMATED SEARCH AND MATCH
See ASAM.

AUTRANET
AUTRANET specializes in marketing "soft dollar" services in the European investment community; that is, it pays for computer, research, and systems services for institutional customers in exchange for commission business from that customer. The ratio of expense for commis-

sion revenues is negotiable between the customer and AUTRANET. The corporation is an affiliate of US broker/dealer Donaldson Lufkin & Jenrette.

B

B

Second letter of the English alphabet, used:
1. Lowercase in stock tables to designate that the annual dollar dividend was accompanied by the payment of a stock dividend in addition; for example, 2.45b.
2. Lowercase in older option tables to designate that an option series was not offered. Current usage: s.
3. Used uppercase as the fifth letter in certain NASDAQ symbols to designate that more than one class of common stock is outstanding; for example, EBNCB is for Equitable Bancorporation, Class B common stock.
4. Uppercase as the NYSE symbol for the Barnes Group, Inc., a manufacturer and distributor of precision mechanical springs.

BABY BELL(S)
Used individually and collectively as a nickname for the seven operating telephone companies divested by American Telephone & Telegraph under terms of a federal court decree. Each of these companies dominates a particular region of the United States. The baby bells are: Bell Atlantic, Ameritech, NYNEX, Pacific Telesis, BellSouth, U.S. West, and Southwestern Bell.

"BACK DOOR" SUBSCRIPTION
In connection with the NASD's interpretations for "hot issue" allocations, this term refers to a broker/dealer's sale to a conduit-type customer; that is, an institution's action for a buyer whose identity is not revealed to the firm. The NASD requires that the member obtain a representation from the institution that it is not circumventing the association's rules by acting as an agent for someone who is ineligible to subscribe to the issue. In effect, that the ineligible person is not coming in through the "back door."

BACK-END BONUS
An expression used to describe additional compensation to certain salespersons in the securities industry. The term refers to an increased aggregate percentage commission payable to registered representatives (RR). For example, a broker/dealer uses a tiered compensation payout grid. Each time an RR reaches a preset production breakpoint—let's say

$250,000—all old production is aggregated with the new to award the salesperson the new percentage payout. In this way, first dollars are equal to last dollars in terms of commission payout.

BACK-END LOAD
1. Term used to describe early redemption penalties paid by holders of certain mutual funds registered under 12b-1 of the Investment Company Act. Holders of these no-load funds who cash in at prevailing asset value during the first few years after purchase are subject to a penalty fee.
   Also called "deferred contingent sales charge."
2. A slang term for any hidden sales charge by a mutual fund that does not charge an up-front sales charge. The charge is hidden, in that the investor pays the charge indirectly; that is, through a higher operating charge against the assets of the fund.
   See also DISTRIBUTION PLAN or 12b-1 PLAN.

BACK MONTHS
Expression used in futures and option trading for the later months of trading. For example, if contracts are available for July, August, September, October, and January, October and January would be considered "back months."

BACK-TO-BACK LOANS
Swap arrangement whereby parties in different countries borrow money from each other in the other's currency. For example, a U.S.-domiciled company has Swiss francs, and a Swiss company has U.S. dollars, and they borrow from one another. These simple, direct arrangements avoid the expense of a third party and the resulting transaction fees.

If the borrowing entities are subsidiaries, the loans are also said to be parallel. Back-to-back loans imply that the lender/borrowers are independent companies.

BADEN
Tokyo Stock Exchange term for a telephone booth on its trading floor. The baden (pronounced baa–den) forms a communication link between the trading floor and the office of the member firm entering the order.

BAGGING A DEALER
Expression used to denote deception by a marketmaker or portfolio manager. "Bagging" indicates that a sale of stock is made to a block positioner at a price that is higher than the current market level. Concept: The issue is highly volatile and the dealer is not alert to the rapid

change and thus buys the stock at an inflated price. The dealer is thus "bagged" as an investor, unless the dealer is willing to sell immediately at a loss.

BAGGING THE OFFERING
The practice of selling short an issue in registration, with the intent of covering the short with shares (or bonds) acquired from the new offering. The practice is based on the fact that the new offering may depress the price. In this way, the "bagger" can sell short above the offer price and cover with new shares at a profit.

The practice is now illegal under SEC Rule 10b-21.

BAG-TRADING
Colorful expression for the illegal act of prearranged trading on behalf of two customers in the futures marketplace. Using an intermediary (the "bag" man), the dealer sells one customer's contract at the low end of the trading range while, at about the same time, the dealer buys the same contract through the same intermediary at the high end of the range. The dealer (FCM) and the bag man then split the profit.

BAIKAI
See CROSS TRADING.

BAILOUT BONDS
Popular term for the long-term bonds of the Resolution Funding Corporation, an adjunct of the Resolution Trust Company (RTC), empowered under FIRREA (q.v.) to resolve the financial insolvencies of savings institutions.

Semiannual interest is U.S. guaranteed and free of state and local taxes. The first bonds were issued in 1989.

BAILING OUT
Trading expression for the sale of a security quickly and without regard for the price. If the market turns and the trader is caught "long and wrong," the trader will often sell out—often at a severe loss. This is in line with the Street jingle: "He who lives to run away, lives to trade another day."

B&B
English slang for "bed and breakfast" as applied to the securities market. This English technique—often also applied in a U.S. context—endeavors to lessen tax liability without sacrificing a security position.

The technique involves a sale as late as possible in the day and a repurchase as early as possible the next day. Because there is minimal market risk between the two days, the customer, in effect, maintains the same security position. On the other hand, the sale/purchase commissions and a one-day cost of carry on the security should offset one another. The customer, however, is flat overnight against adverse news and has offsetting tax considerations.

BANIF
Short name for Banif de Inversiones Finanzaz, S.A., a wholly owned subsidiary of Banco Hispano-Americano, S.A., one of the largest banks in Spain.

BANIF serves as an investment manager for the largest pool of funds in that country, and it is also an advisor to the First Spanish Investment Trust, plc, a closed-end fund concentrated in issues traded on the Spanish stock market.

BANK
1. Any institution that accepts time and demand deposits and makes loans.
2. If such loans are to individuals and businesses, the term *commercial bank* is used.
3. If such loans are primarily made in the form of mortgages, the term *savings and loan* is used.
4. If the bank is primarily engaged in the raising of capital, both short- and long-term, for corporations, municipalities, or governments, the bank is called an "investment bank."
5. In the United Kingdom, banks involved in corporate investing or bills of trade are called "merchant banks."

BANK INSURANCE FUND (BIF)
An arm of the Federal Deposit Insurance Corporation (FDIC). It was created to insure depositor's savings accounts up to $100,000 at member banks. The enabling legislation for BIF is abbreviated FIRREA.

BANK INVESTMENT CONTRACT
See BIC.

BANKRUPTCY
The state of being insolvent; that is, liabilities exceed assets, with little hope of a reversal of this situation.

Under the laws of the United States, persons who are in the state of bankruptcy may petition to be declared bankrupt and to be protected from the immediate claims of their creditors. This same petition may be made by corporations and other business enterprises.

BARCLAYS SHARE PRICE INDEX
A popular capitalization-weighted index of 40 stocks traded in New Zealand. This special index reflects the market performance of the most important companies—although it is oriented toward natural resource companies domiciled in New Zealand. The index also serves as the basis of a futures contract traded there by means of a computerized order matching system.

BAREFOOT PILGRIM
A derogatory term for a public customer in the securities industry. It is supposed to identify a naive investor who has lost his or her shirt—and often his or her shoes—in the harsh world of securities trading.

"BARROW BOYS"
A derisive term used in the English financial industry to distinguish securities traders from bankers. Allusion: traders are often working-class in both background and schooling and are from the lower social order. Bankers, on the other hand, traditionally stem from the aristocracy, have public school educations, and are from a higher stratum of society.

BASE
Acronym: Brokerage Accounting System Element. BASE is a computerized operations department that processes all transactions executed on the floor of the Boston Stock Exchange. When added to the exchange's BEACON system, it will immediately confirm executions, update specialist positions, and provide average inventory costs on a continuing basis.

BASE LENDING RATE
This is the percentage interest rate charged to a bank's best customers in the United Kingdom. It is similar to the prime rate in the United States. Just as the Federal Reserve influences the prime rate in the United States, so the Bank of England influences the United Kingdom base lending rate.
   Also called the "base rate."

"BASH AND TRASH"
Slang for the endeavor of analysts to deride the merits of another investment banker's takeover deal. "Bash" refers to the deriding of the junk bonds that will be issued, and "trash" refers to their deriding of the deal in general. For example, "There was a chorus of 'bash and trash' reports from Street analysts when AJAX proposed the takeover of COMET by the use of junk bonds."

BASIS SWAP

A transaction arrangement whereby contra parties exchange floating-rate obligations that are calculated on different indices. For example, Company A has a variable-rate liability based on the six-month T-bill rate. Company B has a variable-rate liability based on LIBOR. The companies may be inclined to swap liabilities if they feel that the other's rate index would save interest dollar expenses over the near term.

Also known as a FLOATING SWAP.

BASKET BOOK BROKER

See BBB.

BBB

1. NYSE designation for a Basket Book Broker. A BBB is similar in function to an order book official (OBO) on the CBOE. In effect, a BBB is a "passive marketmaker," in that the BBB accepts limit orders for ESP (Exchange Stock Portfolio) options and executes them—always as agent!—when it is feasible to do so.
2. Standard & Poor's credit designation for a bond that is at the lower edge of investment grade. Such bonds are either severely influenced by changes in the economy or have minimal bond debt service coverage in the investment grade category.
3. NYSE ticker tape symbol for Baltimore Bancorp, a large bank holding company in Maryland.

BB SYSTEM

Abbreviation for "broker's brokerage," a futures trading system in Japan that enables nonmembers of commodities exchanges to solicit and enter orders for exchange-listed contracts through members, with both organizations receiving compensation for their services.

BCC

1. Among Self-Regulatory Organizations (SRO) the initials commonly used to denote Business Conduct Committee.
2. The NYSE stock symbol for the Boise Cascade Corporation, a large lumber and paper processor.

BEACON

Acronym: Boston Exchange Automated Communication Order routing Network. BEACON is an electronic system available for the entry and execution of market and marketable limit orders up to 1,299 shares. This system can also provide for execution at prices based on primary market openings, or the consolidated tapes, at the preference of the customer.

BEAR BONDS
A Eurodebt issue with its redemption amount linked to the downward movement of a specific foreign stock index, such as the Nikkei Japanese stock index or the FAZ (Frankfurter Allgemeine Zeitung) German stock index.

Bear bonds are designed to appeal to Japanese and German investors in whose countries options and futures trading were considered illegal and are now considered unsuitable for domestic citizens. These issues offer holders a long-term put on the stock markets of these nations. Holders receive a premium over par value at maturity if the benchmark index declines below a predetermined figure.

See also BULL BONDS for opposite concept.

BEARDS
Slang for the illegal practice of using "dummy" customer accounts as a repository for stocks purchased. In effect, the purchase is disguised and the identity of the beneficial owner is hidden. This practice, which is illegal, is used to avoid federal filing requirements or to avoid premature disclosure of merger or acquisition intentions.

BEAR HUG LETTER
A written communication with an issuer threatening to buy control of that company unless certain specified measures are taken. It is a form of corporate blackmail done by a raider seeking a favorable reorganization or an offer of "greenmail." Bear hug letters have proven to be effective when management has a minimal ownership in the corporation.

BEAR POSITION
Euphemistic term used in England to identify a short security position. One who has sold short and who does not own the underlying stock is positioned to profit from a drop in the price of the stock when the short position is covered. Term *bear* is from the 18th century London Exchange slang: to sell a bear(skin). Allusion: the skin was sold before the bear was caught, because the dealer considered that bear skin prices would fall. Today, in England, stock is often a "bear skin."

BEARS
Acronym: Bonds Enabling Annual Retirement Savings. BEARS are investment instruments designed to appeal to retirement plans and other financial institutions. BEARS holders receive the maturity value of bonds underlying calls not exercised by holders of CUBS, or by aggregate exercise price itself if those calls are actually exercised.

See also CUBS.

BEAR TRAP
Slang for a market situation where falling prices encourage short selling by speculators who believe that further declines are imminent. Soon after the short sales, the market reverses itself and prices start to rise rapidly. The bears are thus forced to cover the short positions at substantial losses. The speculators were literally trapped by the ensuing bull market rise in the underlying securities.

BELGIAN DENTIST
See AUNT MILLIE.

BELG-INDEX FUND
The Belg-Index is based on the performance of stocks listed and traded only on the Brussels Stock Exchange. In practice, there are 40 different Belgian companies in the index and these represent about 91% of the market's total valuation. This investment company (mutual fund) is sponsored and sold by Reyers Timmermans, a small Brussels stock brokerage company.

BES
See BUSINESS EXPANSION SCHEME.

"BET THE JOCKEY NOT THE HORSE"
Saying among horse racing fans that is echoed on Wall Street. The analogy suggests that traders should copy successful investors and insiders and not be concerned about individual companies. The philosophy is predicated on the opinion that such successful investors and insiders have superior timing patterns of purchases and sales because of their proximity to the situation.

BIC
Acronym: Bank Investment Contract. A BIC is an interest in a portfolio that guarantees subscribers a specific yield over a predetermined period. BICs are guaranteed by a bank; in this way, they are similar to a GIC (guaranteed investment contract) issued by an insurance company.

BIF
See BANK INSURANCE FUND.

BIG
See BOND INTERNATIONAL GOLD.

"BIG BANG"

A colorful term associated with the revision of operating rules of London's (*now* ISE) Stock Exchange on October 27, 1986. Under these rule changes, fixed commission charges became fully negotiable; members were allowed to function in a dual capacity (agent/principal); new and more comprehensive capital rules were adopted for member organizations; and some principals of member organizations could now be non-U.K. nationals.

BIG DRAGON

Term often used of Japan in its role as the most important financial power in the Asiatic sphere of influence. Following World War II, Japan quickly gained international prominence in the production and sale of automobiles, textiles, electronic and photographic equipment, and computer components. Ironically, Japan is now facing challenges from the "Little Dragons" of Asia, who are using the same strategies, particularly low-cost labor, that helped Japan to reach its prominence.

THE BIG FIVE

Term often applied to the five largest securities/commodities firms in Japan. Generally, they account for more than 50% of the total trading volume on each day. The five firms are: Nomura, Daiwa, Nikko, Yamaichi, and Kokusai.

"THE BIGGER THE TOP, THE BIGGER THE DROP"

Jingle used by technical analysts to presage a large drop in the price of a stock if there is a large top formation without significant corrections.

A top formation is represented by a horizontal price movement following a relatively long rise in the price of a stock. The longer the horizontal price movement (the top formation itself), the greater the probability of a subsequent and significant downward price movement if there is a penetration of the support level for the top movement.

BIG INDEX SWAP

A product initiated by Salomon Brothers to compete with Merrill Lynch's Dollar BILS. The product is a synthetic asset for institutional customers, whereby they can match or beat the return on the Salomon Brothers Broad Investment Grade (BIG) bond index.

Under a BIG INDEX SWAP a customer is guaranteed a monthly return on a specified principal amount for a three to five-year period. In return, the customer guarantees to pay Salomon monthly the LIBOR rate less 20 basis points. The difference is settled by checks based on the two rates. In effect, the swap is between two floating rates, which the customer can hedge by investing the principal in a LIBOR-based instrument during the calculation period.

BIG PRODUCER
Expression used of a registered representative who generates substantial revenues for a broker/dealer. Although the differentiation between little, medium, and large producer will differ from firm to firm, and during differing periods in the market cycle, it is generally admitted that registered representatives in the $500,000 to $1,000,000, and up range in annual revenues are big producers.

BIG TELEPHONE
See MA BELL.

BIG THREE, THE
1. In the United States, the three largest automakers, namely General Motors, Ford, and Chrysler.
2. In Switzerland, the three largest banking institutions, namely Credit Suisse, Swiss Bank Corporation, and Union Bank of Switzerland. The Big Three control about 70% of the new issue market in Switzerland.

BIG TICKET
1. Slang for any high-priced stock, particularly if the stock is felt to be overpriced.
2. Any large customer order for stocks or bonds that results in significant compensation for the salesperson who enters the order.

BIG UGLIES
Slang for issues currently out of favor with the investing public. This disfavor may be perception on the part of the public, or it may be based on the fundamentals of the underlying industries or companies. As a result, the "big uglies" often sell at significant discounts to their underlying asset value.

"BLACK" FCMs
In Japan, black FCMs are unregistered futures commission merchants who seek domestic futures business and execute it on overseas commodities exchanges. Such FCMs operate on the fringe of illegality, and they are generally ostracized by local members of the securities and commodities exchanges.

BLACK FRIDAY
Expression used to designate any financial debacle. The origin of the term occurred in 1869 at the time of the gold panic and depression, but it was used in later years for any sharp market drop which, coincidentally, often occurred on Fridays.

In practice, the expression is used for any large market sell-off, no matter on which day of the week it happened.

BLACK MONDAY
Media-coined term used to designate the financial events of October 19, 1987. On that day, both price and volume record changes occurred as the Dow Jones Industrial Average plunged 508 points and NYSE volume skyrocketed to more than 600 million shares. Many used the term as a parallel to the Black Friday of the 1929 crash and felt that it presaged the start of another depression.

BLANK CHECK OFFERING
Expression used of an initial public offering (IPO) of the stock of a company that does not have an established business. In effect, subscribers give management discretion over the use and application of their money. In general, such offerings are successful only when speculation predominates the marketplace.

BLIP
Term used to identify any deviation from what is considered normal or routine.
1. Used by analysts when a company announces quarterly earnings that were unexpected, but it is expected that the next quarter's earnings will be back to normal.
2. Used by chartists when a stock's price spikes up or down for no explainable reason. It is anticipated that the chart pattern will resume its normal movement in the near future.

BLITZKRIEG TENDER OFFER
From the German: lightning-like war. The term is used in mergers and acquisitions to describe a raider's attempt to take over a company in a quick military-like fashion. Using great speed and offering higher than market prices, the raider asks shareholders to quickly sell their stock to facilitate control of the company.

BLOOD LETTER
Quaint British term for a European underwriter's letter to a law firm asking for a legal opinion about an issue's exemption from the U.S. Security Act of 1933. If the underwriter is willing to state that the offering

27

will be sold exclusively to non-US investors, and that care will be exercised to ensure that the security will not "leak back" into the United States, the law firm will generally state that the security qualifies as a private placement under Section 4(2) of the '33 act.

BLOWOUT
1. Term used to describe the immediate sellout of a new issue of securities. You will often see the term used as a verb form; for example, the issue was blown out the window.
2. Slang expression to describe the dissipation of a customer's assets through frequent trading or poor investments. The combination of frequent trading—with concomitant commissions—and poor investments will quickly reduce the client's assets.
Synonym: CHURNING or TWISTING.

BLUE-COLLAR WORKER
Expression used to designate nonmanagement, nonadministrative personnel in industry. Because such workers often wear heavy-duty clothing—usually blue—they were dubbed with this name.

BLUE LIGHT
NYSE trading floor term for an official request to registered competitive market makers (RCMMs) to help with a block trade. The Blue Light is an electronic message alert asking RCMMs to assist the specialist in taking the contra side of a block trade. In this way, the RCMM(s) and the specialist give liquidity to the marketplace on block trades.

BLUE MONDAY
Term originated by the media to describe the phenomenon that—more often than not—the DJIA goes down on Mondays. The unexplainable statistics may arise from the fact that unfavorable news often occurs over the weekend.

BLUE SHEET INFORMATION
Securities and Exchange Commission (SEC) enquiries of selected broker/dealers requiring identification of trade participants, pertinent details of their transactions, and possible affiliation with the issuer. The request is so called because of the color of the paper containing the SEC's solicitation of information. At present, there is a project underway whereby this information can be sent directly to the SEC by electronic means.

BLUE-SKY REGISTRATION

1. The qualification of a broker/dealer to do securities business in one of the 50 states.
2. The qualification of an agent of a broker/dealer to solicit buy and sell orders for securities from the residents of one of the 50 states. Many states require the Series 63 USASLE Exam (Uniform Security Agent State Law Examination) as a qualification.
3. The qualification of a nonexempt security by the issuer for sale within one of the 50 states. This qualification may be by notification, coordination, or qualification. As a general rule, Treasuries, agencies, municipals, and securities registered on a national exchange do not need separate blue-sky qualification.

BNL

1. NYSE ticker tape symbol for Beneficial Corporation, which is devoted to consumer loan activities.
2. Initials for the Banco Nationale del Lavoro, Italy's largest commercial bank.

BOARD OFFICIAL

Those employees on the floor of the London Stock Exchange (*now* ISE) who accept and record public orders for options in a special book and who, at the first practical opportunity, execute such orders. Their function is similar to that of the order book official (OBO) on the CBOE.

"BO DEREK STORY"

Term for a company that is perceived to be of the highest quality; that is, similar to the movie *10* in which Bo Derek was starred and was depicted to be the most perfect (a "10") woman in terms of physical qualities.

BOARD ROOM

1. The place where corporate directors periodically meet to set policy, declare dividends, and make executive management decisions.
2. In the parlance of the Street, the place in which brokers' desks are located and where they can meet with, or phone, customers to transact business. The board room often contains a ticker tape and other information sources for the use of the broker and customers.

BODY RAIN

The term has received two relatively tasteless meanings:
1. A time of profuse perspiration as displaced executives look for jobs because of layoffs, takeovers, and mergers.

2. The period following the crash of 1929 when many speculators were financially ruined and committed suicide by leaping from the windows of tall buildings.

BOERSENZEITUNG INDEX
A popular index of performance of the German stock market. The index is composed of 30 blue-chip issues, all equally weighted. The index uses September 1959 as its base and it is updated every 30 minutes.

BOGEY
Trader's terminology for a particular target, whether it be a price or yield objective. For example, "That customer has a bogey of 8½% for the sale of the commercial paper in his portfolio." Term probably arises from military slang: a bogey; that is, an unidentified flying object on a radar screen.

BOILERPLATE
1. Used of pro forma information that is provided to conform to certain laws, but that—in general—has little positive content. For example, the red herring caveat on a preliminary prospectus.
2. A pejorative term for any form of professional cant or other insincere printed statement whose value is relatively meaningless. The term is not used of false statements.

BOLSA
The Spanish word for a purse. By long-term attribution, this term is applied to a stock exchange and thus parallels the French (bourse) and Italian (borsa) usage for an exchange.

There are four stock exchanges in Spain, with the exchange in Madrid being the largest and having the most trading activity.

BOMBAY STOCK EXCHANGE (BSE)
The largest stock exchange in India. Although the BSE is open for business for only a short time during the day, it does have an index of 30 stocks that serves as a barometer of economic activity in India.

BOND DADDIES
Also referred to as "Memphis Bond Daddies," these organizations were high-pressure telephone sales boiler rooms that specialized in the sale of municipal, government, and agency securities. Operating in Memphis, Little Rock, and Palm Beach, these boiler room operations gained their reputation from high-pressure selling, large markups, and account churning.

BOND INTERNATIONAL GOLD (BIG)

An investment vehicle for gold trading founded by Alan Bond, a wealthy Australian entrepreneur. Under the umbrella of Mr. Bond's international gold interests, this corporation invited public subscription for its shares which—in turn—were collateralized by gold bullion, the main assets of his concern. In effect, an investment in this company was a play on the value of gold bullion in world markets.

BON VOYAGE BONUS

This is the original designation for what has subsequently become known as "greenmail"; that is, the payment of a premium for shares held by a prospective predator to avoid a proxy contest for control of a company. Such an agreement is always accompanied by another agreement whereby the predator promises not to acquire additional shares for an extended period.

BOOK ENTRY (SYSTEM)

A recordkeeping process for securities whereby the names of registered holders—for either stocks or bonds—is maintained in a computerized or other recordkeeping procedure. The central concept is this: no certificate is available. Book entry systems are used for listed options, U.S. Treasuries, and agency securities.

BOOKRUNNER

English term for the lead (managing) underwriter of the syndicate involved in the distribution of securities. The bookrunner keeps a record of each member's allocation, the "pot" for institutional investors, and so forth. As in the United States, the bookrunner receives an additional fee for its services.

BOOT

1. In capital letters, an acronym for Branch Office Operations Training. BOOT is a formal system of instruction used by brokerage firms with decentralized branch offices. BOOT is designed to teach new employees the fundamentals of order entry, recordkeeping, and cashiering procedures.
2. This term is also used to identify start-up procedures needed to activate computerized programs and to load those programs into the system.

BORROWING POWER

In general, the amount of money that may be borrowed against securities pledged as collateral.

Under Regulations T, U, G, and X of the Federal Reserve, broker/dealers and banks may lend up to 50% of the purchase amount on such securities, provided they are listed on an exchange or traded on the NASDAQ National Market system. Other equity securities and listed options have no borrowing power.

Separate rules apply to other securities. In general, the borrowing power on corporate bonds, municipals, and governments is set by the exchanges, the NASD, or the MSRB.

BOSTON STOCK EXCHANGE (BSE)
The BSE is an important regional stock exchange located in Boston, Massachusetts. The BSE has a trading linkage to both the NYSE and the Montreal Stock Exchange.

BOTTOM FISHER
Slang for a prospective buyer who is looking to buy a security at its lowest price.

Bottom fishers appear after an extended decline, or during bankruptcy proceedings, and attempt to buy at distressed prices.

BOTTOMING OUT
A market technician's term used to signify that the decline in a stock (or the market in general) is apparently coming to an end. Needless to say, such a cessation of a drop in prices does not necessarily mean that the price will rise. If demand equals supply, there could be an extended accumulation of the stock. Only when the accumulation is completed, or underlying fundamentals change and demand increases, will the stock begin to rise. Indeed, instead of stabilizing, (i.e., reversing its trend), it may consolidate—which means, return to its former pattern of falling lower.

BOUNCE
1. Whenever delivery of a security by the seller, or the seller's agent, is refused by the purchaser—for whatever reason—it is said to be "bounced."
2. Whenever a security's price falls precipitously downward and then soon recovers its old price level, the security is said to have "bounced."
   Synonym: downward spike.

BOUNCED STOCK
Slang for a rejected delivery from one dealer to another.

The official term is *reclamation*. A reclamation may result from a bad delivery; that is, a certificate in wrong form or denomination, a certificate without a proper assignment, a certificate that is stolen, or a certificate that is forged or counterfeit.

BOX SPREAD
An option position that has four components. There is a long call—short put position with identical expiration dates and exercise prices; this establishes the bullish side of the position. Then, there is a long put—short call position with its own exercise prices and expiration dates. In effect, the investor has set all four corners of the possible market activities.

From the bettor term, *to box,* whereby the bettor selects four opposing positions—and bets on each—on the presumption that the reward will exceed all of the bets made.

BREAKFAST OPTION
Slang expression to describe the fact that Standard & Poor's Index options were referenced to the opening, rather than the closing, of the market on the third Friday of the expiration month. This was done by the SEC to mute the extreme market volatility on "triple witching days." Breakfast referred to the fact that the major marketplaces began trading at 8:30 A.M. Central Time.

BRIDGE FINANCING
Short-term corporate borrowings used as an interim step before the issuance of securities. Commercial banks are the usual providers of this form of financing prior to the completion of an underwriting, although some brokerage firms also provide such loans.

Also called "bridge loans."

BRITISH FUNDS
The common terms for English government bonds. In exchange dealings, these bonds are subdivided into "shorts" (up to 5 years), "intermediates" (from 5 to 15 years), and "longs" (more than 15 years.)

British funds are also called "gilts" or "government stock."

BROKEN AMOUNT
English terminology for what we would call an "odd lot." For stocks, this is a trade for less than 50 shares (on 50-share traders) or 100 shares (on 100-share traders); for bonds, any debt security with a par value of less than 100 pounds.

Also called a "broken number."

BROKERAGE ACCOUNTING SYSTEMS ELEMENT
See BASE.

BROKER'S BROKERAGE
See BB SYSTEM.

BROKING
English securities industry term for acting as an agent and charging a client a commission for services performed. The American equivalent is called "brokering."

Webster considers the word to come from the Spanish *alboroque*, meaning to give a drink to the other party upon completion of a trade.

BROUGHT OVER THE WALL
Term used to describe the finance department's confidential use of research persons to enhance a particular investment banking deal. Technically, the research person is now privy to "inside information" and thus may no longer provide opinions about the underlying company.

Allusion: the use of the research person's expertise by corporate finance has breached the "Chinese Wall" that should separate investment banking from sales and trading within a member organization.

BRUSSELS STOCK EXCHANGE
One of the four stock exchanges located in Belgium, the Brussels Stock Exchange is the largest and the most active. The exchange is open for trading from 12:30 P.M. until 2:30 P.M.—although there is no limitation on trading after that time. Trades are done on a cash and forward basis, with cash trades settling on the next business day and forwards settling on a fortnightly basis.

BSE
1. Boston Stock Exchange (q.v.).
2. Bombay Stock Exchange (q.v.).
3. Brussels Stock Exchange (q.v.).

BUBA
Derivative from the German word for a grandmother or a guardian angel. Buba has become the quaint term used by Germans for the Bundesbank, the regulator of national banks in Germany. The Bundesbank controls banks, all financial activities, and—in practice—the value of the principal unit of currency, the deutsche mark.

BUCKSHOT BUYING
Term used of programmed transactions in low-capitalized over-the-counter stocks. In an "enhanced" index, an institution may buy enough of a low-capitalization company to remove the float from market. This, in turn, will cause the price to rise and thus show good results for the program. The big risk is that the holdings may not be able to be sold, because of lack of demand or an illiquid market.

BUG

1. Noun: slang—an unanticipated problem in the programming of a computer that does not show up until processing begins.
2. Verb: slang—to pester or annoy others to do an action that they have previously refused to do. Example: "He is a successful salesperson because he bugs his clients until they buy."

BUKKO

Japanese word for manager. In Japan, where a person's training can entail most of one's working life, it is not unusual for someone to rotate through all departments of a firm before appointment as manager. This may take years and provide a broad spectrum of knowledge about every aspect of the firm. This practice has serious drawbacks in the financial industry, where individuals quickly become specialists in complex products and intricate trading techniques.

BULGE BRACKET

Slang for the major participants in an underwriting syndicate, so called because they subscribe to and sell the largest portion of the offering. The firms in the "bulge bracket" are typically listed at the top of the tombstone advertisement.

An underwriter with slightly smaller subscriptions is said to be in the "mezzanine bracket."

BULL BONDS

A Eurodebt issue with the redemption amount linked to the upward movement of a specific foreign stock index, such as the Nikkei or the FAZ (Frankfurter Allgemeine Zeitung) stock index.

Bull bonds are designed to appeal to Japanese and German investors in whose countries options and futures trading was deemed illegal. It is now just "unsuitable" for domestic customers. In effect, bull bonds are a long-term call on the stock market and holders receive a premium over par value at maturity if the benchmark index rises over a predetermined figure that was established at the time of issuance.

See also BEAR BONDS for the opposing concept.

BULL PEN

Nickname applied to the area in a typical member firm where the registered representatives (RRs) work and meet their clients. The area may have cubicles for the individual RRs, or it may be quite open. Generally, the larger producers have individual offices.

The term is also used of a similar area in the investment banking function where interns and newly hired financial personnel work.

BULL POSITION
English term used to signify a long position in a security. Thus, the person is able to physically deliver the security if sold and thereby profit from a rise in the security's price.

BUMP-UP CD
An innovative product of the Crossland Savings Bank. It is a certificate of deposit with a fixed rate of interest for the length of the deposit. However, if interest rates rise during the period of the deposit, the holder has a one-time right of requesting that the new rate apply to the remainder of the term. A drop in interest rates, on the other hand, does not lower the original rate.

BUNNY BONDS
Slang for a rather unusual bond, in that the holder may hop back and forth upon any interest-rate payment date to a larger investment (at par) or to cash, at the option of the investor.

"BURNED OUT" TAX SHELTER
Slang for an investment vehicle that no longer produces tax-deductible write-offs for subscribers, but which—in turn—now begins to return declarable income.

More formal expression: the tax shelter has reached its cross-over point and the participants now receive fully taxable income.

BUSINESS CONDUCT COMMITTEE (BCC)
A group of industry professionals appointed by each of the self-regulatory organizations (SROs) to continuously monitor the members' compliance with that organization's rules and regulations. Generally, this organization has the authority to censure, fine, suspend, or even expel a member who violates the rules and regulations. Such decisions may be appealed to the SEC.

BUSINESS EXPANSION SCHEME (BES)
A plan adopted by the British government to attract venture capital to start-up and buyout companies. It offers individuals tax relief for a number of years following such investments.

BUSINESS MIX TEST
A term used in SEC Rule 11a 1-1(T) that relates to the ability of stock exchange members and member organizations to trade as principal on an exchange. Under the rule, a member is qualified to act as principal if, during the preceding year, more than 50% of gross revenues were derived from such activities as underwriting, acting as broker for cus-

tomers' securities transactions, or distributing securities issued by other persons.

BUSTED CONVERTIBLE
A convertible bond or preferred stock that is selling at or near the price at which it would sell were it not convertible. For example, at a time when general interest rates are 10%, a convertible bond with a 6% coupon is selling at 62; that is, to have a current yield at approximately 10%. In effect, the marketplace has given up—at least for the present—on the convertibility of the bond and prices it as though it were not convertible.

Synonym: BROKEN CONVERTIBLE. Such bonds are said to trade at their "investment value" as a bond. There is no special premium for convertibility.

BUST-UP TAKEOVER
A corporate finance technique often used in mergers and acquisitions. A corporation is bought out by the use of borrowed money, either bridge loans or junk bonds. Subsequently, the debt is paid down by the sale of portions of the acquired corporation.

BUY-BACK
Term used in conjunction with the repurchase by an issuer of its own securities. Such securities will then either be retired or placed "in the treasury."

The buy-back of bonds is often in conjunction with a sinking fund or a refinancing.

The buy-back of equities, to avoid any allegation of manipulation, is usually done in accord with SEC Rule 10b-18, or the tender regulations 14D or 14E.

BUYING THE SPREAD
Expression used both in the options and futures marketplaces to identify the simultaneous sale of a near-term contract and the purchase of a long-term contract. Because the strike price is the same, the long-term contract will cost more. Thus, the transactor of this spread position pays the difference between the sale and purchase prices.

BY-PASS TRUST
A testamentary trust that permits a surviving spouse to receive income from the assets in trust during his or her lifetime. After the survivor's death, the property passes to the grantor's other heirs, as designated in the by-pass trust agreement.

C

C

The third letter of the English alphabet, used:

1. As a Roman numeral designation for 100. Often used in parlance for a $100 bill; thus, a "C note."
2. As the fifth letter in the stock symbol of certain NASDAQ/NMS stocks as an identifier that the particular stock no longer meets the NASD's qualifications for trading on NASDAQ. For example, WSTXC stands for Westronix, Inc., an issuer with total assets of less than $750,000 or fewer than 300 shareholders. It is subject to delisting at the next NASDAQ meeting.
3. Uppercase by the NYSE as the symbol for Chrysler Corporation, a major automotive manufacturer.

CAC INDEX

An index of the 241 common stocks listed on the Paris Bourse. The index is based on the opening price of these stocks. The index is not updated throughout the day; instead, a new index price is computed on the opening of each subsequent business day.

CAC 40 INDEX

An index of the 40 most popular issues traded on the Paris Bourse. Unlike the CAC Index, the CAC 40 Index is updated throughout the market day and is the basis for index futures and index options contracts. The 40 stocks comprise about 50% of the total FF (French franc; also Fr.F.) capitalization of the Paris Bourse.

CALLABLE SWAP

An exchange of interest-rate obligations (fixed or floating rate, or vice versa) in which the counterparty has an option to cancel the swap arrangement after a prescribed time. The subscriber pays a significant premium for the option to cancel.

CALVET

Composite word used for the California Department of Veterans Affairs. CALVET was created under California state law to look after important public affairs. CALVET has legal status to issue municipal revenue bonds.

CAMPS

Acronym: Cumulative Auction Market Preferred Stock. CAMPS were created by Oppenheimer & Co. to compete with First Boston's STARS and Salomon Brothers' DARTS. CAMPS are basically preferred shares whose dividend is reset every 49 days to mirror prevailing money conditions. Holders are entitled to the "dividend received" exclusion if they are corporations and hold the shares more than 46 days.

CANADIAN INTEREST COST
See TRUE INTEREST COST.

CANADIAN/U.S. PRINCIPAL SECURITIES
See CUPS.

CANDLE CHART
See ROSOKU-ASHI.

CAPITAL BUILDER ACCOUNT (CBA)
A Merrill Lynch Servicemark for its margin account with a debit card and check writing privileges. CBA accounts are geared to the young professional who is just beginning to accumulate capital. Security purchases may be made in CBA accounts. CBAs are similar to the highly successful CMA (Cash Management Account) of Merrill Lynch but require only $5,000 in cash or securities to be opened, rather than $20,000 as required in CMA accounts.

CAPITAL GEARING
An English term for what in the United States is called the "capitalization ratio" of a corporation. Thus, capital gearing measures the percentage of bonds, preferred stock, and common stocks in the capital of a corporation, thereby measuring the company's ability to finance and carry debt or equity in its day-to-day operations.

CAPITAL INTERNATIONAL INDICES
A series of measurements of worldwide stock performances owned and maintained by the Morgan Stanley Group, Inc.
 The indexes cover 2,000 equities domiciled in 21 countries outside the United States. As such, the indexes reflect stock market performance on a global scale. The indexes have great appeal to international investors who are endeavoring to gauge their own portfolio performance.

CAPITAL INTERNATIONAL WORLD INDEX (MSCI)
A Morgan Stanley-owned product that tracks price performance of selected equities throughout world markets. MSCI was acquired in 1986 from Capital International S.A (Geneva). MSCI was started in 1968 and it contains about 1,400 companies in 19 countries. It represents about 60% of the total capitalization of the stock exchanges on which these issues are traded.

CAPITALISATION ISSUE
See SCRIP ISSUE #2

CAPITAL MARKETS
General term used for both primary and secondary markets that deal in securities with maturities of more than one year.

For example, stocks and long-term bonds are traded in the capital markets. Or, LMN Corporation, because of financial difficulties, has had difficulty in entering the capital markets.

It is also a general term for the institutional market in the securities industry; that is, the stock and bond market transactions made by fiduciaries. The term tends to include broker/dealer proprietary trading, transactions by mutual funds, pension and profit-sharing plans, bank trusts, corporate investors, and many eleemosynary institutions.

Antonym: money markets; that is, markets for securities that will mature in one year or less. Longer-term securities with variable rates and put features are considered to be part of the money market.

CAP ORDERS
Acronym: Convert And Participate Orders. In effect, CAP orders are "percentage orders" left with exchange specialists. Such orders are not reflected in prevailing quotations; they do, however, become market or limit orders after a specified percentage of volume occurs in a designated security.

CAPITAL SHARES
1. It is the English term for common stock; that is, the basic unit of equity ownership in a corporation. Some American corporations use the term also; for example, the capital shares of American Telephone & Telegraph.
2. A class of shares issued by dual-purpose investment companies, as opposed to income shares. Capital shares entitle the owner to any appreciation in value plus all gains on transactions in any shares of the company. Capital shares may also go down in value due to market activity or because they are liquidated to provide the minimum prearranged income for the income shares. In effect, the income shares are similar to cumulative preferred shares.

CARDS
A servicemark of Salomon Brothers standing for certificates for amortizing revolving debts (CARDs). In effect, the holder of credit card receivables (i.e., the financing bank) used the receivables as collateral for short-term debt instruments. In this way, the bank lessens its need for reserves to protect assets that are now "off its books."

CARIBBEAN VACATION
A euphemism in the financial industry for an SEC-imposed short suspension from the securities business. The term arises from the 30–60 day suspensions that the SEC frequently imposes on individuals for violations of securities laws. The allusion is that such suspended persons—since they are not permitted to work nor be on the premises of their employers—spend the "down time" on an island in the Caribbean.

CARROT EQUITY
An English euphemism for a capital contribution to a corporation that permits an even larger purchase of equity if the corporation reaches certain financial targets. In effect, it is an investment with an option to buy more (the carrot) of the company.

CASH & NEW
A speculative practice on the London Stock Exchange, *now* ISE, whereby a customer can roll a position from one account period (ordinarily two weeks in length) into the next one. The rollover is effected by selling for cash on the last day of the period and reestablishing the position on the following Monday. The practice, by exchange rules, may not be repeated for more than seven account periods.

CASHBOX COMPANY
Term applied to an issuer who raises cash for the purpose of making nonspecific investments in the stock market. In effect, investors put their money in a blind pool and have no effective control over the company's business or investments. Shareholders, since they have no product or service to rely upon, are placing their trust in management's capabilities as investors.

CASH CALL
An English euphemism for a rights offering. Thus, in the English marketplace, if an issuer wants to increase its equity capital, it offers subscriptions to new stock. Present stockholders, therefore, are required to contribute more cash—hence the name—to maintain their present proportionate ownership in the company.

CASH COMMODITY
A completed commodity contract that requires immediate settlement and delivery. A cash commodity is used in contrast to a futures contract. A futures contract is a completed contract that requires settlement and delivery sometime in the future. As time passes, a futures contract becomes a cash (or spot) commodity.
  Synonym: SPOT COMMODITY.

CASH COW

1. Slang for any company that has a substantial operating surplus without any immediate need for reinvestment of the surplus in the business. Thus, the company often pays a large dividend to its stockholders.
2. Slang for a municipal bond that pays a large amount of tax-free interest to its bondholders.

CASH INDEX PARTICIPATION

See CIP.

CASH-ON-CASH

A method of computing return (yield) on an investment whereby the return is simplified in the following formula:

$$\frac{\text{Annual return in dollars}}{\text{Total dollar amount invested}}$$

The formula avoids the pitfalls of both current yield and yield to maturity (call, if applicable), but it oversimplifies the problem of "opportunity value" derived from the resale value of the asset. Used principally of limited partnerships where the resale value is difficult to compute but basis is easy to compute.

CASH-OUT TIME

Term used in conjunction with CIPs, EIPs, and VIPs. It is a specific date each quarter when the holder of that particular index participation option can receive its closing index value upon exercise of the accompanying privilege.

CIPs, EIPs, and VIPs are currently the subject of an injunction requested by the major commodities exchanges because of their similarity to futures contracts.

CASH SETTLEMENT

1. In the United States, the description of a transaction that requires delivery and settlement on the trade date.
2. In the United Kingdom, the description of a transaction that requires delivery and settlement on the first business day following the trade date. Typically, British government bonds, options, new issues, and rights subscriptions settle for cash on the next business day.

CASUAL PASS

Term for an innocent and informal contact by a raider of a target corporation's management. If management is not frightened into submission, the raider can back away without further announcement or adverse publicity.

Also called a "teddy bear pat."

CATASTROPHE CALL

The term is used in conjunction with most municipal revenue bonds. In effect, the provision in the bond indenture requires redemption (issuer call) if natural events (a catastrophe) take place and impede the flow of revenues that should be realized from the project financed by the revenue bonds. Because the project is generally insured by commercial carriers, the issuer's issuance coverage will be sufficient to implement the redemption requirement.

For example, the collapse of a bridge from a hurricane would be a catastrophe. In law, this is called a *force majeure*; that is, an unanticipated event that can excuse performance on a contract.

CATS

1. Acronym: Certificate of Accrual on Treasury Securities. A form of security that is proprietary to Salomon Brothers. CATS represent ownership in a payment of future interest or principal on selected U.S. Treasury securities. In effect, CATS are zero-coupon bonds with underlying governments as the investment. The bonds themselves (both principal and interest coupons) are held in trust by a commercial bank.
2. Acronym: Computer Assisted Trading System. An electronic trading system of the Toronto Stock Exchange. Under this program, certain stocks can be traded without first going to the auction floor.

CB

Initials for convertible bond; that is, a debt security exchangeable for a fixed number of common shares. In practice, convertibles are considered as equity securities for regulatory purposes.

CB is used primarily in the Japanese marketplace; the US marketplace generally uses the initials CV.

CBA

See CAPITAL BUILDER ACCOUNT.

CBMM

Acronym: Competitive Basket Market Maker. A CBMM is a NYSE member registered to make bids and offers in ESP (exchange stock portfolios), a market basket of stocks worth about $5 million each. Since the CBMM makes bids and offers for his personal trading account, he gives liquidity to this special security product developed for institutional investors.

C-BONDS

Used for long-term obligations of corporate issuers. The usage is analogous with the expression "T-bonds" to signify long-term Treasury issues.

CBS STOCK TREND INDEX
A market index comprised of the values for most stocks traded on the Amsterdam Stock Exchange. It is calculated seven times daily during exchange trading hours. The information is supplied by the Dutch Central Bureau of Statistics—hence the initials CBS. The index excludes investment funds, property funds, and holding companies because their underlying securities are already part of the index.

CCA
Initials for Current Cost Accounts, an English accounting term used to provide a realistic valuation of a firm's balance sheet.

By recognizing the distorting effect that inflation can have on a balance sheet, this valuation approach assigns current market costs to specified balance sheet assets. It thereby avoids the use of actual costs, which in practice may be considerably lower, and which could be misleading in evaluating the company.

CDSL
See CONTINGENT DEFERRED SALES LOAD.

CEILING
This expression is used to designate the highest price, or highest interest rate, that is acceptable to the purchaser (or issuer) of a security. It always refers to a maximum number needed to arrange a transaction between a buyer and seller. For example, "The issuer has placed a ceiling of 9% on the issue."

The term *ceiling* is used interchangeably with *cap*.

CEMETERY SPREAD
A tongue-in-cheek expression used by option traders when spread premiums move in the wrong direction. Normally a spread trader who puts on a spread at a debit expects premiums to so widen that the spread can be taken off at a profit. The opposite is true if a spread is put on at a credit. When the premiums go in the wrong direction, the spread trader is getting "killed"—financially, of course—and this gives rise to the expression "cemetery" spread.

CENTRAL SCHOOL DISTRICT
See CSD.

CENTRAMART
The silent broadcast system used to tie Philadelphia Stock Exchange executions into the national trade reporting system; that is, the consolidated tape.

The system has been in operation since 1988 and is currently manually operated, although it should soon be linked to the ITS trade system employed by all domestic stock exchanges.

Popularly called the "ticker" by exchange members.

CERTIFICATES FOR AMORTIZING REVOLVING DEBTS
See CARDS.

CERTIFICATE OF LAND APPRECIATION NOTES
See COLAS.

CERTIFIED FINANCIAL MANAGER
A Merrill Lynch designation for financial consultants (RRs) who have completed an in-house course. This course is a series of continuing education programs and includes instruction in financial planning, risk management, insurance, wills and estates, fixed-income securities, communication. The course was designed to compete with the courses of the College for Financial Planning. Successful completion of the assigned courses gives the RR the right to be called a "certified financial manager" and to use the initials CFM on business cards.

CERTIFIED FINANCIAL PLANNER
A certificate awarded to persons who have successfully completed a course prepared by the College for Financial Planning located in Englewood, Colorado. The courses are administered both in residence or via correspondence, and completion is tested by examination. The course includes financial concepts, terminology, strategies, and, in effect, as a form of continuing education for RRs employed by member firms.

Persons who successfully complete the six portions of the program are permitted to designate themselves as a certified financial planner (CFP) on their business cards and other correspondence.

CFP
See CERTIFIED FINANCIAL PLANNER.

CGT
An English abbreviation for capital gains tax; that is, a special rate for this type of income as opposed to ordinary earned income.

The expression is not used in the United States.

CHANGE OF MODE PAYMENTS
See CMOP.

CHAPDELAINE AUTOMATIC TRADING SYSTEM

Abbreviation: CHATS. An automated order entry and execution system for government securities developed by Chapdelaine and Co., a government and municipal securities dealer in New York City. Although its availability was initially restricted to primary dealers, the system also permits nonprimary dealers and institutional investors to use it. A transaction fee is levied upon users of this computerized system.

CHAPTER 10

A reference to a section of the federal bankruptcy statutes whereby an insolvent entity may petition the court for protection from its creditors and for the appointment of an independent manager (trustee in bankruptcy) to reorganize the company. If granted, the company continues its operations free from immediate obligations to its creditors while it undergoes restructuring and recapitalization.

Often written "Chapter X."

CHAPTER 11

A reference to a section of the federal bankruptcy statutes whereby an insolvent entity may petition the court for protection from its creditors while present management attempts to reorganize the company. If granted, the corporation will be freed from immediate obligations and management will try to restructure the company, debt payments, and the like.

Also written "Chapter XI."

CHARM

A computer information processing system used by the International Stock Exchange of the United Kingdom and the Republic of Ireland to compare daily transactions (also called "bargains") made between members. CHARM is similar to the NYSE's SIAC system for trade comparisons, and it works in tandem with the Talisman system to complete settlements.

CHASING THE MARKET

An expression used of a customer who originally entered a limit, rather than a market, order and who then watches the market move away from the limit: if a buyer, the price moves up; if a seller, the price moves down. Finally, the customer has to enter a market order to complete the transaction. Needless to say, the execution price is at a level that is different from that originally intended by the customer. In effect, the customer has chased the market.

CHASTITY BONDS
These are nonconvertible corporate debt securities with built-in protection for the holder in the event of a corporate takeover attempt. In the event of a takeover, a tender offer, or a LBO, the holders of these bonds are authorized to turn in the bonds for redemption at par value. In effect, the bondholders are protected from the probable decline in bond rating that will occur if the company substantially increases its debt-to-equity ratio.

CHATS
See CHAPDELAINE AUTOMATIC TRADING SYSTEM.

CHICKEN CONVERTS
Humorous term coined by traders to identify the Holly Farms 6% subordinated convertible debentures due February 15, 2017. "Chicken" refers to the principal business activity of the issuer. Each $1,000 bond is convertible into 16.84 shares of common stock of Holly Farms.

CHINESE PAPER
The name given to new securities that are used in lieu of cash to acquire a company. The value of these securities is often questionable, because the newly merged company ends up with diluted equity or overburdening debt. Whether or not a pun was intended, "Chinese paper" in the current environment is also known as "junk bonds."

CHINESE WALL
A slang expression to designate the communication barrier that should exist between the finance/research areas of a member firm and the trading/sales areas. The term signifies that the finance area possesses "inside information" that must not be communicated to others until such time as the fact becomes public.

The barrier is moral, rather than physical; but it usually involves the use of code names and other subterfuges to prevent premature leaking of material information.

CHUMMING
A slang expression for the creation of artificial transactions on one exchange to equalize the price with transactions made on another exchange. When options were traded on multiple exchanges, this was sometimes done to make sure that prices were the same on both exchanges.

The analogy is to the practice of commercial fishermen who use chum (chopped up fish or refuse from fish canning factories) to attract fish to the fishing boat.

Chumming violates SEC rules.

CHUNNEL

A popularized English term that combines "channel" and "tunnel" to identify the Euro-Tunnel plc. This enterprise is engaged in the development and construction of a tunnel from England to France below the English Channel. The tunnel will permit direct train and auto traffic from England to the Continent.

C.I.C.

Acronym: Canadian Interest Cost.
See TRUE INTEREST COST.

CICI

The expression is an acronym for Computer-to-Computer Interface. CICI is an NASD term for an automated communication relationship between marketmakers or between marketmakers and selected customers. In effect, CICI enables marketmakers to receive and execute orders electronically in OTC securities.

CINS

See CUSIP INTERNATIONAL NUMBERING SYSTEM.

CIP

Acronym: Cash Index Participation. CIP was developed by the Philadelphia Stock Exchange. CIP was designed to enable the average investor to participate pricewise in the whole market by purchasing this one security. CIP is similar to a mutual fund in that its value is based upon a structured portfolio similar in concept to the DJIA or the S&P Index. On the other hand, CIP trades freely in the open market. It is similar to a mutual fund, also, in that dividends from the underlying securities in the portfolio are passed through to the CIP holder. Unlike mutual funds, CIP does not assess a management fee. It is now the subject of a court-issued injunction because of its similarity to a futures instrument.

CIRCUIT BREAKER

A generic term used by industry leaders and regulators of some proposed solutions to the price volatility that may be caused by various kinds of programmed trading, particularly index arbitrage. Circuit breakers would apply when certain market conditions occurred. Among the solutions proposed as circuit breakers are: trading halts, higher margin requirements, denial of the use of automated trading systems, or price movement limits on index futures contracts. It is envisioned that one or more of these controls should cushion the impact of market volatility and thus quiet small investor concerns.

CIRCUS

Acronym: Combined Interest Rate and Currency Swap. CIRCUS involves an exchange between two parties of fixed- and floating-rate obligations in different currencies. In effect, the swap is made because the two parties have diametrically opposed opinions of currency and interest-rate trends. For example, if a person swaps fixed interest obligations in one currency for floating obligations in another currency, that person is engaging in a CIRCUS transaction, and he or she believes that short-term rates will rise on the "floater" and that the fixed-income currency will depreciate versus the currency of the floater. Obviously, the other party to the swap would not agree to the swap unless he or she held an opposing point of view.

CITATION

Citation is an affiliate of Merrill Lynch & Co. and is responsible for its "soft dollar" business. In effect, the affiliate solicits commission business but permits that commission to be paid for in "soft dollars"; that is, in the form of research subscriptions, computer services, or portfolio analysis.

CLAIM, A

A legal right to a future distribution.

1. In conjunction with a distribution by an issuer, if the entitled new owner fails to reregister before the company closes its books, the new owner can acquire the distribution only by making a claim against the old owner.
2. The same is true if the new owner fails to reregister and wishes to receive a proxy. To do so, the new owner must make a claim against the old owner.
3. The same is true if the new owner fails to reregister and thus fails to get a cash dividend, interest, or return of principal.

Generally, such a failure to reregister in time is caused by the old owner's late delivery of the certificate. In such a case, the new owner's broker will not accept delivery unless it is accompanied by a "due bill" or "due bill check" for the distribution. This establishes the claim against the old owner.

CLARA BOW

Clara Bow was the "It" girl of the 1920s. IT was also the NYSE ticker symbol of International Telephone and Telegraph Co.

Although the symbol for the company is currently ITT, there is some recurring popularity for the concept because of current media commercials sponsored by International Telephone and Telegraph.

CLASS ACTION
Legal term for a grievance filed on behalf of a group of shareholders or other injured parties. In effect, because all of the persons in the group have an identical complaint, they will be represented in court by a single action under a single attorney (or group of attorneys). This approach also appeals to legal counsel because the awards are generally quite large and represent larger fees for counsel.

"CLAWBACK" PROVISION
Slang for a provision that usually occurs in the underwriting agreement of public property that is being "privatized"; that is, sold to the public. Because such sales often generate a large international demand for the resulting securities, the "clawback" provision permits the selling government to so restrict overseas subscriptions that domestic demand is satisfied first. For example, when British Airways plc and British Gas plc were sold, the British government scaled back American and Canadian orders in favor of domestic U.K. buyers.

CLC/PLC
Acronym: Construction Loan Certificate/Project Loan Certificate. CLC/PLC is a GNMA debt security comprised of two distinct parts: a two-year construction loan that is used to construct the project, and a 40-year project loan that refunds the construction loan and provides longer-term financing for the project. In effect, the lender can bail out after two years, or exchange it for the 40-year project loan. The latter obligation is constructed like a standard GNMA pass-through with all of the government guarantees associated with these securities.

CLEAN PERIOD
Slang term in Japan for the period before a corporate issuer announces a forthcoming offering of equity securities. During the "clean period" the issuer may negotiate with various underwriters, and underwriters may act for themselves and for customers, but they must be very careful not to destabilize the marketplace for similar securities of the same issuer.

CLEARING AGENCY
An intermediary between contra brokers who validate the terms of their transactions and arrange for payments and deliveries. The function of a clearing agency is to reduce the number of physical settlements and to assign allocation responsibilities among trade participants.

CLEARING MEMBER ACCOUNTING AND CONTROL SYSTEM
See C/MACS.

CLOSE OUT
This is the generic term for the procedure taken by either party to a transaction if the contra broker defaults. Thus, if the contra broker fails to deliver, the purchasing broker will "buy in" to complete the contract. A "sell out" occurs if the contra broker fails to pay. Buy-ins and sell-outs are the financial responsibility of the contra brokers and will be charged to them. They, in turn, will debit their customer for the fail.

CLOSING A MARKET
This is jargon used when the traders narrow the difference between bid and offer prices (the spread). They do this by raising the bid, or lowering the offer (asked) price, or by a combination of both.

C/MACS
Acronym: Clearing Member Accounting and Control System. C/MACS is a computer driven communication linkage between some member firms and the Options Clearing Corporation. Through it, members can:
1. Retrieve daily options activities and position reports.
2. Exercise valid long positions.
3. Give OCC instructions for same-day security and cash collateral movements.

CMOP
Initials represent Change of Mode Payment, a service offered by the Depository Trust Co. (DTC) to enable participants to change the frequency by which they receive dividends from selected unit investment trusts and variable preferred stocks. Payments on those issues can be requested on a monthly, quarterly, semiannual, or annual basis, or be changed periodically at the preference of the investor. Changes are arranged between DTC and the transfer agent in a computer-to-computer interface.

COATS
Acronym: Canadian Over-the-Counter Automated Trading System. COATS is an electronic quotation and trade reporting system for Canadian issues not listed on any Canadian stock exchange. It is similar to the NASDAQ system in the United States. At present, COATS is still a pilot project in the province of Ontario.

COATTAIL INVESTING
This term refers to the practice of buying and selling the same securities as do well-known persons or institutions as soon as their activities are publicized. In effect, such participants are using the research of promi-

nent market investors. Because of the built-in time lag this practice is fraught with great risk.

Also called "piggyback investing."

COB
Initials, and commonly used, for "Commission des Operations de Bourse." COB is the French version of the SEC in the United States. Thus, it is a regulatory agency responsible for the proper functioning of financial markets in France.

COCKING A SNOOK AT THE MARKET
This is a quaint English expression used to describe a marketmaker's bid and offer at the same price. This practice is frowned upon in the United Kingdom because it forces the order flow to the marketmaker who has bid and offered at the same price, and it interferes with any competitor's ability to profit on a transaction because there is no spread and, hence, no margin of profit.

From the English expression "to cock a snook"; that is, to thumb one's nose. The origin of the expression is unknown.

COCOANUTS
A light-hearted nickname given to Coastal Caribbean Oil Co. by traders on the Boston and Philadelphia stock exchanges. The nickname is derived from a play on its ticker symbol: CCO.

COCOONING
Used by securities analysts to describe certain practices of the food processing industry whereby food is prepared for microwaving in family kitchens. In effect, it is the industry's application of "fast foods" techniques for home food preparation.

COF
See COST OF FUNDS.

COLA
1. Acronym: Cost of Living Adjustment. For example, in 1988 there was a 4% COLA added to Social Security payments.
2. Acronym: Certificate of Land Appreciation note. This is a debt security created by Merrill Lynch to raise capital for AMFAC/JMB Hawaii, Inc. Among other features, this note, which matures in 2008, entitles its holder to 4% in annual cumulative interest plus an additional 6% in additional payments dependent upon the issuer's cash flow surplus.

COLD CALLING
A popular term in the United States for an unsolicited personal visit or any oral communication with a customer or a potential customer. This, together with referrals, is probably the chief source of new customer accounts.

In England, under the Financial Services Act of 1986, this practice was made a criminal offense except in accordance with certain limited rules and procedures.

Cold calling is also prohibited in some Canadian provinces.

COLLECTION RATIO
An important measurement of the efficient use of corporate assets.

The ratio, in effect, measures how quickly a corporation turns a dollar of "accounts receivable" into cash on the corporate balance sheet. For example, if Corporation A turns an account receivable dollar into cash in 35 days, it is more efficient than Corporation B that takes 60 days to do the same thing.

Ratios vary by industry. In practice, a year-to-year comparison is the best insight of the efficiency of a particular company.

COLLEGE CONSTRUCTION LOAN INSURANCE CORPORATION
See CONNIE LEE.

COLTS
Acronym: Continuously Offered Longer-Term Securities. COLTS are offered by the International Bank for Reconstruction and Development (World Bank) to fund its general operations. As the title implies, COLTS are an open-ended distribution of 3- to 30-year bonds with some zeros. Rates may be fixed or variable as determined by bank management at the time of each offering. Four agent broker/dealers, all internationally prominent, act as underwriters and distributors.

COMING IN
A term used both by equity and bond traders when describing a market situation that is turning from positive to negative. For example, the expression "the market is coming in" means that sellers are materializing and will depress prices from their current levels.

COMISSAO DE VALORE MOBILIARIOS
See CVM.

COMMERZBANK INDEX
This index is the oldest measurement of stock market performance in Germany. It is named after Commerzbank, one of Germany's largest banks.

The index is computed once each day at noon. It is capitalization weighted and represents the accumulated value of 60 widely traded German stocks.

COMMODITY SWAP
An exchange of variable payment liabilities between two parties made on the proviso that the basis on which payments are made will not be a financial instrument benchmark but will be considered a spot price transaction. Thus, the prices will not be part of a futures index.

Commodity swaps may also involve the exchange of different physical commodities in specific amounts on a future date.

COMMON MARKET
See EUROPEAN ECONOMIC COMMUNITY.

"COMP"
Slang term used by traders asked to bid for (or offer) debt instruments to a portfolio manager. The term signifies "in competition" and means that two or more dealers are requested to state a price (or yield) at which a transaction will take place with a customer. The expression could be: "We are asked for a comp bid on the Mohawk 7s of '99."

Using more than one dealer to arrive at a price or yield assures the customer of a fair price level.

COMPANION CMO
An offshoot of a conventional collateralized mortgage obligation (CMO) marketed almost exclusively to retail customers. In exchange for about $1/4$ point more in interest, these bonds serve as a buffer for the conventional CMOs sold as part of the same issue. In effect, if interest rates fall, these bonds will be called first; if rates rise, they will be prepaid last by underlying mortgage holders.

Because they are always disadvantaged vis-à-vis the institutional classes (tranches) of the same issue, companion CMOs are more volatile.

COMPENSATING BALANCE
A banking term used by commercial banks when they make unsecured loans. In exchange for a lower rate of interest on a loan (or even a line of credit), the borrower agrees to leave a specific minimum sum of money in a demand deposit account, bearing nominal or no interest, to "compensate" the bank for its willingness to lend money at a lower rate. Whether or not a compensating balance is worthwhile financially depends on the amount required and the preferential loan rate.

COMPETITIVE BASKET MARKET MAKER
See CBMM.

COMPREHENSIVE CRIME CONTROL ACT OF 1984
This act revised some federal statutes regarding criminal practices in securities-related transactions. Among other prohibited practices, this law prohibits the counterfeiting of municipal and corporate securities, or the forging thereof. The law also extended the scope of federal bank bribery statutes to include other types of financial institutions.

COMPLIANCE
1. The act of being in conformity with the laws, rules, and regulations of the securities industry.
2. The concept of self-policing, whereby SROs set rules and regulations to protect customers and to observe federal securities laws.
3. That department of a member firm that advises management of procedures aimed at obedience with federal, state, and local laws, and with industry standards. Such a department also enforces internal regulations of the firm.
4. As an adjective to qualify certain words, such as compliance manual, compliance standards, compliance officer, and the like.

COMPUTER ASSISTED ORDER ROUTING AND EXECUTION
See CORES.

COMPUTER FRAUD & ABUSE ACT OF 1986
A federal law which, in general, makes it a crime for a broker/dealer to perpetrate a fraud in a securities transaction while using the facilities of a computer. The law becomes operable if more than $1,000 worth of damages is involved.

CONDITIONAL CALL OPTIONS
SEC-registered contracts issued by corporations with high-coupon debt outstanding. These contracts provide purchasers with the right to receive a non-call-for-life bond with the exact terms as the outstanding bond if the outstanding bond is called. The issuer receives tax benefits, both currently and in the future, while the bondholder is assured of high income for the life of the instrument. In effect, these conditional call options are warrants providing call protection insurance to the holders of otherwise callable securities.

CONFERENCE OF SECURITIES ASSOCIATIONS
See CSA.

CONGRATULATORY ORDERS
Term used to designate the myriad of orders, both buy and sell, presented to a new member of the Tokyo Stock Exchange. The principal contributor is usually the "godfather" of the new member. This token of congratulation is intended to help the new member start off business in the right direction.

CONNIE LEE
A nickname for the College Construction Loan Insurance Corporation. Connie Lee is a direct guarantor or insuror of debt issues sold by universities and colleges that have insufficient creditworthiness to market them directly. Authorized by federal legislation, Sallie Mae (Student Loan Marketing Association) is an equity participant in Connie Lee which, in turn, helps rehabilitate and modernize educational facilities without direct access to domestic bond markets.

CONSIDERATION
A consideration is something that makes an informal promise legally binding; usually, it is something of value given in return for the promise.

Although the term is used both in the United States and in the United Kingdom, in the latter it is used more frequently in conjunction with the transfer of securities for value received. For example, the transfer of ABC securities from father to son was completed for a nominal consideration.

CONSOB
A government-appointed regulatory authority in Italy with jurisdiction over that country's stock market practices. The largest stock exchange within its jurisdiction is the Milan Stock Exchange.

CONSOLIDATE
Term frequently used by market technicians to designate that a previous trend (either up or down) has, after a pause, again started.

CONSUMER CREDIT PROTECTION ACT OF 1968
This federal law requires that lenders provide borrowers with current (and future) terms and conditions associated with interest charges and expenses. It is also called the "Truth-in-Lending Act."

SEC Rule 10b-16 requires that such a truth-in-lending statement be sent to customers who open margin accounts. Periodic updates are also required if rates or conditions are changed.

CONSUMER MARKETS

Industry term used to designate the retail part of the securities industry, as opposed to the institutional (or capital markets) part of the industry. Many member firms divide their sales efforts and operations into a "consumer markets" and a "capital markets" side.

CONSUMER PRICE INDEX (CPI)

The CPI is compiled monthly by a government agency of the United States. The CPI, which is based on the comparative prices of a market basket of consumer items—including food, clothes, shelter, transportation, and entertainment—gives users an insight into the relative cost of these items on a month-to-month basis. Thus, CPI also shows inflationary or deflationary trends.

The CPI is also important because it is used as the basis for the assignment of Social Security cost-of-living adjustments (COLAs)

CONTINGENT DEFERRED SALES LOAD (CDSL)

CDSL is a term used in the mutual fund industry to designate a sales charge (load) that is charged not when the customer buys the fund but, on a contingent basis, when the fund is redeemed.

Funds that charge a CDSL are registered under SEC Rule 12b-1 of the Investment Company Act. The deferred sales charge is generally applied on a sliding scale; for example, 5% if redemption is in the 1st year, 4% if redemption is in the 2nd, and so on.

Most funds that have contingent deferred sales load—also called a "back-end load" or "exit fee"—also apply a distribution fee on an annual basis to compensate the fund for advertising costs and to compensate registered representatives (RRs) for the fact that the fund was sold without an initial sales charge.

CONTINGENT IMMUNIZATION

Term used to describe a bond portfolio management strategy. In the beginning, the bond portfolio is so managed and traded to maximize gains and return in excess of that achievable by passive management.

A minimum acceptable yield is set (called the "base yield"). If the return drops to the minimum yield, the portfolio is immunized in the usual manner (using the duration of the bonds) to lock in the minimum yield thereafter.

CONTINUATION

Term used on the International Stock Exchange of the United Kingdom and Republic of Ireland to describe the fact that large institutional investors who bought and sold the same securities on a continuous basis could aggregate their trades and thus be eligible for reduced commissions. In effect, the normal ½% rate could be reduced to ⅛%.

Continuation was based on the fact of fixed commissions and certain rebates. Following the "big bang" on October 27, 1986, all commissions on the ISE are negotiable; thus, the term is no longer in common usage.

CONTINUING COMMISSIONS
In the past, contractual mutual funds were popular with some investors. It was the practice to pay continuing commissions on such plans to retired registered representatives (RRs) or their widows or beneficiaries if this was stipulated in the contracts between the RRs and member firm.

Although NYSE and NASD rules differ slightly on this matter, such continuing commissions are not permitted on new business or new customers introduced to the firm.

CONTINUOUSLY OFFERED LONGER-TERM SECURITIES
See COLTS.

CONTRARIAN
In the financial industry, a contrarian is someone who—as a general rule—takes an opinion that is in opposition to that taken by the majority.

Examples of a contrarian approach to the market are myriad. For example, investors who buy depressed stocks for a turnaround are contrarians. Investors who sell into a rising market (to preserve profits) and buy into a falling market (to buy undervalued securities) are contrarians.

As a general rule, contrarians are intermediate- to longer-term investors who buck current trends for longer-term rewards.

CONTROLLERS DEPARTMENT
A work area in a broker/dealer organization that is responsible for preparing and maintaining the firm and the customer financial reports, plus records and statements as prescribed by law or SEC rules.

Also called the "controller."

CONVERSION BOND
See CONVERTIBLE GILTS

CONVERT AND PARTICIPATE ORDERS
See CAP ORDERS.

CONVERTIBLE GILTS
English Treasury obligations (gilts) with an option attached, whereby the holder may exchange the present holding for a longer-maturity is-

sue under certain circumstances. This conversion privilege is the equivalent of a European option in that it is exercisable only on a certain date.

The longer-maturity bond is called a "conversion bond" and may or may not be in existence at the time the holder exercises the option.

CONVERTIBLE UNIT INVESTMENT TRUST
See CUIT.

CONVEXITY
A term used in conjunction with duration to measure interest-rate risk on intermediate- and longer-term bonds with coupon interest. The terms do not apply to zero-coupon bonds.

Duration is defined as the midpoint (in time) of the present values of the cash flows from a bond. This is a measure of interest-rate risk.

If interest-rate changes cause the midpoint to shorten (the duration is shortened), the bond is said to have "positive" convexity. If interest-rate changes cause the duration to lengthen, the bond is said to have a "negative" convexity. Callable bonds often have negative convexity, and for this reason increase the interest-rate risk if they are selling at a premium.

COORDINATION
A form of eligibility requirement for the public offering of securities under the blue-sky laws of many states. If registration is required in a state, and coordination is the method prescribed, an offering may be made to citizens domiciled within that state concurrent with the effectiveness of the issuer's SEC-filed registration statement.

COP
Acronym: municipal Certificate of Participation. The word is popularly used in the plural as COPS. COPS are similar to corporate collateral trust bonds; that is, a municipality enters into a lease-purchase arrangement for such things as computers or telephone systems, with the equipment used as collateral for the financing. The equipment is usually paid off in 7–11 years from operating budgets of the municipality and thus does not become part of the bonded debt of the municipality.

COPENHAGEN STOCK MARKET
One of four stock markets in Scandinavia, this Danish exchange is better known for bond, rather than stock, trading. For trading purposes, the Copenhagen Stock Market is open on weekdays from 9:30 A.M. until 3:30 P.M. and all trading is done electronically. Contract settlement is due on the third working day after the trade date (except Friday trades, which settle the following Tuesday).

COPPER A TIP
English marketplace expression that means to do the opposite of what touts advise. In effect, it is the same as the United States concept of contrarian investing strategies. Thus, when English investors were given "golden information" by advisors of dubious stature, they turn the gold into a baser metal. From the verb *to copper*; that is, to cover with copper.

CORBEILLE
The French term for a trading pit, corbeille signified the old location of securities trading on the Paris Bourse. Pit trading on the bourse survived for more than 160 years, but it has now been supplanted by electronic methods. In the old pits, bids and offers were shouted aloud in a way that is similar to trading on the US commodities marketplaces.

CORE CAPITAL
The term is used in conjunction with the financial requirements of thrift institutions. Core capital is the bank's common stock, surplus accounts, perpetual preferred stock, and minority interests in consolidated subsidiaries. In effect, core capital is real and reliable money derived from stockholder equity. Under proposals from the Federal Home Loan Bank Board, core capital must equal at least 2% of total assets.

CORES
Acronym: Computer Assisted Order Routing and Execution System. CORES are used for the routing and handling of orders on the Tokyo Stock Exchange. The concept is similar to that of the DOT system on the NYSE, in that orders for designated stocks can be entered, recorded, and executed by pairing the order with comparable contra corders at that trading post.

COST OF FUNDS (COF)
1. In the brokerage industry, COF is used to designate a broker/dealer's expense in borrowing money to finance inventory positions.
2. In the banking industry, it is the expense of obtaining deposits; that is, the interest that must be paid to finance loans to borrowers.
3. In mortgage banking (under the California Plan), it is a three-month blended rate of interest payable by the district savings and loan associations in that Federal Home Loan Bank (Freddie Mac) area.

COUPON PASS
Term used of the daily activities of the Fed's FOMC (Federal Open Market Committee) as it endeavors to fine-tune money and credit in the US economy. Under this concept, the "desk" (FOMC's trading arm) canvasses dealer banks and nonbank dealers to determine their long/short

inventory in Treasuries. Based on this information, the FOMC will arrange to buy/sell certain specific issues (coupons) to either inject or withdraw bank reserves and thus alter available credit.

COUPONS-UNDER-BOOK-ENTRY-SAFEKEEPING
See CUBES.

COVER
1. Term used in investment banking to describe the difference, either in net interest cost or dollars, between the winning and the second-place bid. For example, "The cover was only 0.15% in net interest costs on the Ajax deal."
2. Verb designating a closing transaction on an option, future, or short-sale contract. For example, "I covered my short position at a profit of $3 per share." Also used of short against box when client instructs broker to deliver box securities against short position.
3. Of corporations: the ability to pay fixed charges on debt securities by earned income. Important in ratings of bonds.

COVERED BEAR
U.K. term for someone who sells short versus a long position, and who intends not to cover the short with delivery of the long position but with the purchase of stock at a price lower than the short sale price. The strategy, if completed in the same account period, permits settlement by a single check for the profit or loss.

COVERED STRANGLE
An equity option position in which the writer of a straddle (short call and short put) is also long the underlying stock. Thus, in exchange for two premiums, the writer accepts the risk of being called or put.

The term is also used of a short combination, with the call strike price above the current market price of the underlying, and the put strike price below the current market price of the underlying. While such a strangle has less risk than a straddle write, it also generates less premiums because both options are out-of-the-money.

CP
Common abbreviation for commercial paper.

CP is short-term discounted debt instruments issued by corporations (and some municipalities) to meet current cash requirements. Corporate CP is exempt from registration under the '33 act if it initially has 270 days or less to maturity.

CPI
See CONSUMER PRICE INDEX.

CRAM-DOWN DEAL
Slang expression used by investment bankers if a merger is so arranged that shareholders have no option but to accept the compensation offered. For example, in a merger or LBO, if stockholders are offered only "junk bonds"—with no choice of cash or stock—it would be an example of a "cram-down" deal.

CRASH
Street term for a sharp and sudden plunge in securities prices, usually the prices of common stocks. As a general rule, a crash is accompanied by large trading volume. The October 19, 1987, event in which the DJIA dropped by 508 points (on a base of 2,700) and trading volume jumped to 600 million shares versus an average volume of 200 million, is generally conceded to have been a crash.

The term *spike* is used of similar sudden plunges in the price and rise in the trading volume of individual securities. Spike, on the other hand, is also used of upward price movements.

CREDIT ENHANCEMENT
A term used by credit analysts to identify letters of credit or surety bonds or other forms of insurance that back debt instruments. Usually such backing raises the rating of the bond to AAA.

Such credit enhancement is used both by issuers whose credit rating is low and by issuers who have high credit ratings but who wish to enhance it for investor appeal and thus be in a position to issue debt at lower coupon interest rates.

Although credit enhancement is paid for by the issuer, it is ultimately paid for by the buyer in the form of lowered rates of return.

CREDIT SHELTER TRUST
A trust that provides for the maximum use of the $192,800 tax credit (in effect, exempting $600,000 from estate taxation) upon the death of a US person who is also a spouse. By placing $600,000 in the trust, these assets become after-tax dollars. They can then be used for the benefit of the surviving spouse and other beneficiaries. The remainder of the estate passes tax free to the surviving spouse to be subject to estate tax upon his or her death. Thus, two $192,800 estate tax credits will be obtained.

It is not unusual to place insurance in such a trust and thus take it out of the estate of the decedent.

Professional tax advice and legal counsel is needed.

CREDIT WATCH

The term used by Moody's and Standard & Poor's or other credit-rating services to designate the fact that an issuer's debt securities may be subject to a ratings review (usually a lowering).

Such credit watches are announced by the rating services following some economic event, such as a class action suit, a proposed issuance of junk bonds, a merger, and the like that could lower the creditworthiness of the issuer.

CROSS-CURRENCY INTEREST-RATE SWAP

See CIRCUS.

CROSS TRADING

In the United States, cross trading designates the internalization of commodities orders; that is, executing customer orders against in-house proprietary orders without exposing them to other bids and offers in open outcry in the commodity pits. The practice is illegal.

In Japan, the practice is legal and is known by the name "baikai." Baikai order crossing is permitted for customer orders after the market is closed but only if the futures merchant traded the same number of contracts at the same price during the market day.

CROWN LOAN

The term is taken from the name of Henry Crown, a Chicago industrialist who pioneered the concept. A Crown Loan is a loan from a high-bracketed family member to a lower-bracketed family member. When the lower-bracketed borrower invests the money, it is taxed at his or her lower rate.

A 1984 Supreme Court decision validated the concept, but only if the loan is made at prevailing interest rates.

The practice has little applicability following TRA 86 because the investment income of the borrower (after the first $1,000 of income) is taxed at the parent's tax bracket.

CSA

Acronym: Conference of Securities Associations. CSA is the Japanese counterpart of the Securities Industry Association (SIA) in the United States. Neither organization has governmental status but is used primarily for financial discussions and mutual member interest—although the government may listen to their suggestions.

CSA is composed of:
The Securities Dealers Association of Japan.
The Bond Underwriters Association.
The Investment Trust Association.

The Tokyo Stock Exchange.
The Association of Tokyo Stock Exchange Regular Members.

CSD

Abbreviation for "central school district," a quasi-government entity created by a municipality to provide educational services to its residents on the grade and high school levels. As such, the CSD is authorized to issue bonds for construction and renovation of educational facilities, and such bonds are serviced by *ad valorem* real estate taxes (plus tuition charges in some cases) levied on residential and commercial real estate in the district.

As a general rule, CSD bonds form "overlapping debt" for the municipality that created the school district, and, in the event that revenues are insufficient, the municipality will be obliged to make up for the shortfall.

CSD bonds are always so designated on the bond certificate.

CSFB

An identifier for Credit Suisse First Boston Corporation. CSFB is a partnership to foster the commercial banking and investment banking interest of its two founders, Credit Suisse and First Boston Corporation. Although this Europartnership is independent of either founder, it is influenced significantly by the economic and political maneuvers of its parents.

CSFB is a major player and a significant primary and secondary market participant in European securities markets.

CSI LEVY

CSI (Council for the Securities Industry) is a sort of watchdog and ombudsman for the public interest in the financial community of the United Kingdom. To support its activities, there was a levy of 60p (about $1) on customer transactions of 5,000 pounds or more. Often this levy was absorbed by the brokerage firm.

Although the levy is still charged, the role of the CSI was greatly curtailed with the passage of the 1986 Financial Services Act in Britain.

CUBES

Acronym: Coupons-Under-Book-Entry Safekeeping. CUBES was a U.S. Treasury program in effect from January 5 through April 30, 1987, whereby holders of physical coupons stripped from selected government bonds were able to include them for book-entry ownership at a Federal Reserve Bank. Through CUBES, over 400,000 physical coupons were made automatically payable at maturity by the Fed's electronic system.

CUBES are not included in nor interchangeable with the Federal Reserve's STRIPS program.

CUBS
Acronym: Calls Underwritten by Swanbrook. CUBS are annual options on zero-coupon Treasury securities that result in a guarantee of annual interest rate to holders exercising them at expiration. Swanbrook Limited Partnership is a Nevada-based investment firm and is the issuer of these call options. Swanbrook uses the custodial and processing facilities of Security Pacific National Bank of Los Angeles (SEPACO). The calls are fully covered by the underlying instrument.

See also BEARS.

CUIT
Acronym: Convertible Unit Investment Trust. This was an E. F. Hutton product created to provide a steady income stream and potential capital growth through investment in a diversified portfolio of convertible bonds and convertible preferred stocks.

CUPS
Acronym: Canadian/U.S. Principal Securities. This Bankers Trust product was designed for retail speculators in the currency markets. CUPS are a debt security of a Canadian issuer. The holder has the right to receive payment in either Canadian or U.S. funds but need not decide which currency to request until just before the maturity date.

CURB TRADING
1. Securities industry expression for transactions that take place on the American Stock Exchange. The ASE or AMEX—as it has been known since its move to Trinity Place in New York in 1921—was originally known as the New York Curb Exchange.
2. The practice on some commodities exchanges—often considered improper—of liquidating positions by exchange members after the closing bell signaling the end of trading for the day.

CURRENCY EXCHANGE WARRANT (CEW)
CEWs are a Bear Stearns product designed to appeal to currency speculators who believe that the Japanese yen will lose value in terms of the American dollar during the five-year life of this warrant. The warrant is purchasable in conjunction with a debt security and has a separate premium, which is used to offset the cost of borrowing. If the dollar rises versus the yen in a significant way, holders of the warrant can exercise it anytime during the five-year period.

CUSIP INTERNATIONAL NUMBERING SYSTEM (CINS)

A foreign security identification being developed at the request of the SEC to expedite foreign clearances and settlements. CINS is like CUSIP (Committee on Uniform Security Identification Program) in that it is a 9 alphanumeric symbol that is compatible with U.S. broker/dealer operations. When fully adopted, CINS will unify settlement procedures no matter where executions are effected.

C.V.M.

Acronym: Comissao de Valores Mobiliarios. CVM is the Brazilian name for a governmental agency similar in function to the SEC. CVM's powers, however, are more extensive than those of the SEC.

CYLINDERS

A term used in foreign exchange markets for certain currency futures options. A cylinder combines a long put and a short call based on estimations of the currency's future performance. The premium from the call substantially lowers the cost of the put alone.

Cylinders, also known as "tunnels" or "fences," can set a floor and a ceiling (a collar) around foreign currency exposure. Needless to say, the long put and short call are "on the same side of the market," and the strike prices must be carefully chosen to protect from the upside risk caused by the short call.

D

D

Fourth letter of the English alphabet used:
1. Lowercase in stock transaction tables to designate a new low for the previous 52 weeks. Thus, d 21⅞ designates a new low. The next day the 52-week high/low figures will be changed to reflect this; the previous low figure will be replaced by 21⅞.
2. Temporarily, as the fifth letter in a NASDAQ/NMS security traded over the counter to designate that a reverse split has recently occurred. Thus, for a while, LMNO may be symboled as LMNOD.
3. Alone in uppercase, D is the NYSE tape symbol for Dominion Resources of Virginia, a major utility.

DB-25

Short name for the Deutsche Bank 25, a model portfolio of 25 German blue-chip stocks. This portfolio is designed to track the stock market's performance in that country. This indexed portfolio provides institutions with more liquidity than if they attempted to deal in the underlying issues themselves.

DBA
1. Acronym: Dealer Bank Association. In this sense, DBA is an organization that represents commercial banks that engage in municipal securities trading. As such, these dealer banks are members of and ascribe to the rules of the Municipal Securities Rulemaking Board (MSRB).
2. Abbreviation for "doing business as. . . ." This expression is abbreviated d/b/a. For example, AJAX Partners, d/b/a Phoenix Associates. The term is also used of private individuals who use another name for their business enterprises.

DE
1. Used on order tickets by RRs to designate that the RR used discretion (DE = discretion exercised) in entering that order for the customer's accounts. Such discretion may be used only if the customer has given prior written authorization and the member firm has accepted the discretionary authorization.
2. The tape symbol for Deere & Company, a large manufacturer and distributor of farm equipment whose shares are listed on the NYSE.

DEAD CAT BOUNCE
Colorful slang heard each year in December on the Street. It is a reference to the partial recovery of issues that were depressed by tax selling. If the stocks were substantially oversold, this rally may continue even into the following January, causing a January rally.

DEAL FLOW
Corporate finance department term used to designate the rate at which new investment banking proposals come to the attention of other investment banking associates; in effect, how fast does a deal flow through the investment banking area. Paradoxically, riskier deals tend to flow faster than conservative deals.

DEAL STOCK
Street term for an equity issue that is rumored to be the potential target of a merger, takeover, reorganization, or an LBO. Such issues are "in play" and lure speculators and risk arbitrageurs prior to the formal announcement. Needless to say, if there is no deal, the speculators can lose large amounts of money. If there is a formal announcement, the price rise may be minimal because speculators and arbitrageurs have already pushed up the price with their purchases.

DEBT SERVICE COVERAGE
1. In general, the income flow of a corporation or municipality in terms of the net annual payment of interest and principal. For example, Center City has $25 million in revenues to cover a debt service of only $3 million per year.
2. Specifically, the ratio of available income to annual debt service. Thus, in the example given above, the ratio of revenue to debt is 8⅓ times. As a general rule, municipalities should have a minimum debt service coverage of 4 to 1.

DEAR MONEY
Term used by traders and economists to describe the fact that interest rates are high because money and credit are scarce. In this context, "dear" means excessive or very expensive.

DEATH-BACKED BONDS
These bonds are also known as "policyholder loan bonds." The expression is associated with a private placement originated by Prudential-Bache Securities and Morgan Stanley. The bonds are collateralized by loans to life insurance policyholders and are so named because the loans will be repaid from the insurance policy if the borrower dies.

DEATH PLAY
Macabre expression for this situation: the CEO or principal stockholder of a corporation is dying and it is predicted that the company will be broken up and sold off. The speculation is that the parts of the company are worth much more than the whole, and the death of the strong-willed previous owner will subject the company to dismemberment and a rally.

DEATH VALLEY CURVE
An English corporate finance term. The concept: a newly reorganized company—often following a leveraged buyout—is losing so much of its equity capital so fast that it simply cannot borrow sufficient further funds to maintain its existence.

DEBENTURE
1. In the United States, a longer-term debt security that is unsecured by any collateral and thus is junior to other debt securities of the same issuer. Only the good faith of the issuer backs the issue. If issued for 10 or less years, it is not unusual to have such securities called "notes."
2. In the United Kingdom, it is the highest, not the lowest, ranking debt issue of a corporation. In the United Kingdom, debentures are typically secured by a mortgage on the issuer's property.

DEBT SWAP

A cross-currency swap in which each party actually exchanges the entire underlying debt obligation. There is an immediate exchange of currency so as to provide the contra party with sufficient funds to satisfy the principal responsibility. Each party then assumes the other's obligation to make interest and principal payments on the debt over its lifetime.

DECK, THE

1. The collection of unexecuted orders in the possession of a member. The term is used both in the equity and the futures markets.
2. Nickname derived from the stock symbol DEC for Digital Equipment Corporation, a leader in the electronic computer industry.

DEFERRED AMERICAN OPTION

A put or a call option with this restrictive qualifier: it is not exercisable for a designated period following its creation. Following this period, the option may be exercised anytime up to and including its expiration date.

DEFERRED DIVIDEND SHARES

The expression refers to certain equity issues of Australian companies. They are called "deferred" because they have junior ranking to ordinary common stock and will have their dividends postponed until a specified time in the future. When they are dividend paying, such shares will have equal status with other outstanding common shares.

DEFERRED SHARES

In the United Kingdom, deferred shares are a type of equity share that has greater voting rights or greater residual claims, or both, to extra dividends. In this latter regard they are similar to participating preferred shares in the United States.

In some instances, deferred shares have dividends deferred for a number of years; but when dividends are started, they have a cumulative arrearage that must be paid before dividends are paid to ordinary shareholders.

DEMERGER

Pronounced: dee–merger. An English finance term used:
1. To designate a spin-off by a company of a subsidiary to its shareholders. The spun-off company can then act independently.
2. To designate the sale by a parent company of its ownership in a subsidiary to the management of the subsidiary. The new company can then act independently (and often as a competitor) of the original parent.

DENKS

A tongue-in-cheek acronym for Dual-Employed, No Kids. A type of family unit in which both members are employed but do not have the responsibility of child rearing; thus, they are able to enjoy more luxuries or to invest more. Similar to DINKS (q.v.) but the latter may infer that one of the parties holds down two jobs (double income) and the other none.

DEPOSITORY

An entity that receives and holds securities for subscribers.

The most popular depository is the Depository Trust Co. (DTC). It is a major factor in DVP/RVP (Deliver versus Payment/Receive versus Payment) transactions for banks and brokerage firms because it "immobilizes" certificates and arranges for book-entry transfers between participating members.

DERIVATIVE PRODUCT(S)

Popular term of the 80s and 90s to designate tradeable equity, debt, or futures instruments stemming from specific underlying securities or commodities. Such products may or may not be the responsibility of the issuer.

Popular derivatives are options (equity, debt, currency, and index) that are not the responsibility of the issuer. Other derivatives are asset-backed securities, including mortgage-backed, CMOs (collateralized mortgage obligations), "baskets of securities," TIGRs, CATs, COUGARs, all of which are ultimately the responsibility of the issuer.

DESIGNATED PRIMARY MARKETMAKER

See DPM.

DESIGNATED SECURITY

As defined in SEC Rule 15c2-6, a designated security is a non-NASDAQ equity issue, traded over the counter, whose tangible assets are $2 million or less.

DEUTSCHE TERMINBOERSE GmbH

See DTB.

DEWKS

Tongue-in-cheek acronym: Dual-Employed, with Kids. This is the largest and fastest growing segment of the U.S. population as more and more persons endeavor to put together parenting and business careers. With both the husband and wife working in business, despite the financial drain of children, they have a substantially higher income and standard of living than would be otherwise possible.

DIALING AND SMILING
A euphemism for a salesperson's cold calls to build a roster of customers for business. To attract and motivate unseen strangers, salespersons must not only phone (dialing) but must also exude a personal warmth and concern (smiling) if they are to be successful.

DIE
Acronym: Designated Investment Exchange. DIE is a U.K. term introduced under the Financial Services Act. Under the act, a DIE is any stock exchange located outside the United Kingdom that provides trade visibility and fairness of pricing for its listed issues. If this is determined, the exchange will be "designated" by the Securities Investment Board (SIB) as an acceptable marketplace for U.K. investors.

DIFF
The Euro-Rate Differential (hence the initials) is a futures contract introduced in 1989 on the Chicago Mercantile Exchange (CME). The purpose of the contract is to lock in an interest-rate spread (differential) between the U.S. dollar and either the British pound, the West German deutsche mark, or the Japanese yen. Although the contract is designed primarily for institutions dealing in international markets, it can also be used by currency speculators.

DIFFERENCE CHECK
A single settlement check for the differences between total costs and net proceeds of trades to be satisfied on the same day. Under the Fed's Regulation T this is permitted for same-day substitutions. On the other hand, if the purchases and sales were made on different dates in a corporate security, each trade must be settled individually.

DIGITAL INTERFACE SERVICES
See DIS.

DINKS
Acronym: Double-Income, No Kids. This term is often used by analysts when referring to young married professionals with no children who become financially secure and who were investors in the U.S. economy during the 80s. Previously, the term for such professionals was *Yuppies* (Young Urban Professionals), although that term had no intimation of marriage as does Dinks.

DIP
A small temporary drop in the price of a security, usually a few points but certainly not more than 10% of the current price. In general, dips are

a form of profit taking following a rise in the price of a stock, and astute investors use such dips as an opportunity to buy more shares.

DIRECTIONS UNIT INVESTMENT TRUST
See DUITS.

DIRT BAG
A term used of a person considered to be a sneak and a crook. Although the term is not restricted to investments, it has been introduced as evidence by the government in the prosecution of various violations of securities laws. In effect, a "dirt bag" is someone who is not to be trusted.

Also called a "sleaze bag."

DIRTY STOCK
Securities industry slang for a stock certificate not in proper deliverable form between NASD/NYSE members. It may mean that the certificate is mutilated, counterfeit, or in nontransferable form; for example, in the name of a decedent, alien corporation, or is "legended" (not registered with the SEC).

DIS
Acronym: Digital Interface Services. DIS is an NASD pilot program that enables subscribers to convert transmitted market information into information that can be displayed on the user's own terminals. Thus, the NASD date in digital form can be sent to a firm's dedicated computer and then routed to the actual marketmaker for that broker/dealer.

DISCIPLINARY REPORTING PAGE
See DRP.

DISCLOSURE REPORTING PAGE
See DRP.

DISCOUNTER
The term applied to a broker/dealer that offers all customers a substantial reduction in commission, compared to that charged by full service member firms. Important names in this category are Charles Schwab & Co. and Quick & Reilly Corp.

DISTRESS SALE
The sale of a security under adverse market conditions, such as a margin call or to meet net capital requirements. Such distress sales usually lead to large losses. A popular axiom on Wall Street is: "Sell 'em when you want to, not when you have to."

DISTRIBUTION PLAN
A plan whereby a mutual fund charges certain distribution costs, both advertising and RR fees, against the assets of a fund.
See the 12b-1 PLAN for a fuller explanation.

DIVIDEND CAPTURE
General name for a variety of techniques whereby purchasers of stocks acquire dividend distributions with a minimum amount of market risk. These strategies include: dividend rollovers, auction rate preferred shares, sales of covered calls, and stock portfolios hedged by bond or stock index futures or options.

DIVIDEND ROLLOVER
A tax-advantaged dividend capture technique used by some U.S. corporations. Concept: purchase a high-yield utility stock and/or preferred stock and sell it more than 46 days later after an ex-dividend date. The dividend received is 70% tax free. Under normal and stable interest-rate trends, the market price of the stock should be close to the price at which the stock was purchased.

DIVIDEND STRIPPING
This term describes the other side of a dividend rollover; that is, in response to a customer's request to buy a forthcoming dividend, the broker/dealer sells it short to the customer just before the ex-dividend date and, soon after, buys it back from the customer (remember, it is less the dividend) to cover the short position. Settlement is arranged so that it is after the record date. The net effect is for the broker/dealer to pay the dividend out of its own pocket to the lender of the stock. This strips the dividend from an otherwise riskless transaction.

DNC
An order instruction that means "do not cross." This instruction may be made on stock exchange floor tickets in conjunction with index program executions. Because the same stocks are represented in several stock indexes, and because it may be necessary to sell one basket while buying another basket, orders are marked DNC to avoid a "wash sale" consideration.

DNI
See DO NOT INCREASE.

DOLLAR BEARS
Term used for traders and speculators who believe that the value of the U.S. dollar will decline in the forseeable future. Although there is often

a large amount of volatility in the major world currencies, these speculators consider the U.S. dollar a prime subject for decline because of the
constant U.S. trade deficit.

DOLLAR BILS
Acronym: Bond Index-Linked Security. BILS are a Merrill Lynch product that are a 10-year zero-coupon debt instrument. BILS are priced
initially according to the current performance of the Merrill Lynch Index of 506 high-grade corporate bonds with maturities of 15 years or
more. DOLLAR BILS are designed for small institutions because at
maturity they return the full principal price plus the future value of 25
basis points (4.24%). The bonds are backed by the credit of Merrill
Lynch.

DOLLAR ROLL
A form of questionable financing in the Ginnie Mae securities market. A
dollar roll involves the purchase of a TBA (terms to be announced) Ginnie Mae and a concurrent sale of that security for settlement in a later
month. Because the purchase and sale will be paired off on the same
dealer's books, no money is necessarily deposited and the commitment
represents an uncollateralized forward settlement trade. Depending on
the investor's perception of interest-rate trends, the sale will be made
first and then the TBA contract will be made for a settlement in a future
month.

"DOOMSDAY" VALUE
A popular tax term in England when referring to an investor's cost basis
for calculating capital gains and losses. When the capital gains tax
(CGT) was imposed in England on April 6, 1965, investors were permitted to use that date's closing prices as the basis for future liability—this
gave them a one-time "step-up" in value. Because this was a one-time
event, the name "Doomsday" caught on. This is an obvious reference to
the *Doomsday Book* (correctly, *Domesday Book*) completed in AD 1086
on the direction of William the Conqueror. This book was based on a survey of all lands in Britain and listed the legal owner and the value as
determined at that time.

DO NOT INCREASE
Abbreviation: DNI. An instruction that is placed on good-til-cancelled
buy limit and sell stop orders on the NYSE and ASE. In the event of a
stock split or stock dividend, the customer does not want the quantity of
his or her order increased on the ex-date of the distribution.
   To illustrate, there is to be a stock dividend of 10%. Normally the
stock price would be multiplied by $10/11$ and the order quantity would be

increased by $^{11}/_{10}$. The customer who enters a DNI order does not want these calculations to apply; he or she wants the original order to stand. The customer will do his or her own reentering of the order.

DON'T FIGHT THE TAPE
An expression of analysts and traders to caution against using personal prejudices or feelings in making investment decisions. In fact, it does not make any difference what the fundamentals are if the market is going the other way; right now it is more profitable to join the crowd, rather than go counter to it.

DOUBLE OPTION
An English term for what in the United States is known as a straddle; that is, a long put and long call (or a short put and short call) at the same strike price and with the same expiration date. Everyone is agreed up to this point.

If the strike prices differ, terminology may be confusing. Conventional (otc) options with differing strike prices are often called "spreads"; standardized (listed) option terminology, if there are differing strike prices (or differing expiration dates), tends to center on the word "combination."

DOUBLE-UP, TO
A strategy that reaffirms the original reason for investing—either a purchase or short sale—by doubling the risk of the original investment. For example, if a client buys 1,000 shares of LMN at $50 and, when the stock drops to $45, the client buys another 1,000 shares, he or she is doubling up. Note that the client is reaffirming confidence in the security. Note also that the client needs a 10% rise in the stock from $45 to $50 to break even. Following the double-up, the client needs only a 5% stock price rise from $45 to the doubled-up average price of $47.50 to break even.

Doubling up is a sophisticated strategy and generally should be used only by wealthy investors who can afford to accept the doubled risk.

DOUBLE WITCHING DAY
The Japanese version of the U.S. "triple witching" day. In Japan, both futures on the Nikkei Index and the TOPIX Index expire at the conclusion of the third trading day before the 10th day of March, June, September, and December. The Nikkei Index trades on the Osaka Exchange and the TOPIX Index trades on the Tokyo Exchange. These are weighted indexes and many of the stocks are different in the two indexes—as a result, many arbitrage situations exist.

DOWNSIZING
A euphemism for the reorganization of a company that results in a lowering of the number of employees and its payroll. Downsizing often occurs after a period of rapid expansion, when it is realized—either because of return on capital or a recession—that the company would be better managed if it would stick to its most profitable areas of business.

DPM
Acronym: Designated Primary Market Maker. DPM is a title used by the CBOE to identify the firm (or individual) primarily responsible for maintaining fair and orderly markets in selected nonequity options. This is under the exchange's Modified Trading System (MTS). In effect, the DPM has a function similar to that of the specialists on the major stock exchanges.

Trading in equity options features competitive marketmakers on the CBOE.

DRAFT DELIVERY
A settlement procedure whereby securities are delivered to a buyer with an unsigned check attached as a condition of acceptance.

The buyer must sign the check already drawn for the contract amount payable to the seller. Only when this check is signed and presented to the deliverer is the trade considered as "settled."

DRAWDOWN SCHEDULE
An estimated list of payments to be made to a contractor in the course of the completion of a construction project. The schedule of such payments is usually set forth in the contract of a municipal or a REIT loan.

DRESSING UP A PORTFOLIO
A term used to describe the policy of portfolio managers whose endeavors are subject to periodic scrutiny; for example, a quarterly or semiannual report to investors or pension fund holders.

To make sure that all looks well, the manager makes sure that at the time for the cut-off for the report to fund holders, only "in vogue" stocks are in the portfolio. This is done by selling off high-risk stocks just before the end of the reporting period and substituting more palatable stocks. Except for the transaction costs, such "dressing up" does little for the performance of the portfolio.

Also see WINDOW DRESSING.

DRIP-FEED TECHNIQUE
An English term that is also called "evergreen funding." The concept is simple: installment payments are used to capitalize the start-up of a

newly reorganized company. Thus, as needed, new capital is added to the company in a way that is analogous to the feeding of a plant by the gradual dripping of moisture and plant nutrients.

DROP-DEAD DAY
Used in financial circles to describe the last possible day on which an important event can take place. For example, the debt limit will expire tomorrow and Congress has done nothing to raise the limit: tomorrow is "drop-dead day."

DRP
Acronym: Disciplinary Reporting Page. This is an attachment to the standard Form U-4 employee application for registration with the NASD, NYSE, and other exchanges. This attachment solicits details in a standardized format about the disciplinary history of an applicant. By thus standardizing the information in a brief format, it is possible to temporarily transfer registration until further information is received.

DTB
Acronym: Deutsche Terminboerse Gmbh. This is the official name of the German Options and Financial Futures Exchange. The DTB is designed to function in competition with similar exchanges throughout the world; it must also be in conformity with other German exchanges.

Cash deposits and settlements are linked to the Hessische Landes-Zentral Bank, which acts as the DTB's agent. Securities are deposited with the Frankfurter Kassenverein, which is similar to the DTC in the United States. Only major German banks are shareholders in DTB; no foreign institutions are eligible.

DUAL BANKING SYSTEM
General term for the U.S. form of commercial banking. Under the Federal Reserve Banking Act of 1913, a commercial bank may elect to register and to be regulated by either the Federal Reserve or by an individual state banking commission. Both subject their members to continuous scrutiny and high operating standards.

Of about 14,000 commercial banks in this country, 40% are members of the Federal Reserve banking system and they control about 75% of all deposits in the United States.

DUAL CAPACITY
This term is used equally in the United States and the United Kingdom following the "big bang" in 1986.

The term refers to the fact that a securities firm may act either as a broker (agent) or dealer (principal) in executing different transactions in the same security, or even for the same customer in the execution of different transactions. It is prohibited to act as both broker and dealer on the same transaction.

DUAL CURRENCY CONVERTIBLE
This is a debt instrument of an overseas subsidiary domiciled in England. It is convertible into stock of the parent company but at a ratio of currency exchange determined at the time of issuance. For example, if the U.K. subsidiary of a U.S. company issued a dual currency convertible, it could be issued and traded in pounds sterling, but it could also be convertible into 50 shares of the U.S. parent's common stock traded in U.S. dollars. All things being equal, the convertible's value would be a function of the ratio of pounds to dollars.

DUAL TRADING
1. The simultaneous trading of a stock or a bond on two stock exchanges or marketplaces. In this regard, it is a form of arbitrage.
2. The ability of a commodity exchange member to transact both for a client's account and for a personal account in the same commodity on the same day. This potential conflict of interest is permitted in the commodities exchanges, but it is forbidden on the NYSE, without specific consent from the customer.

DUBLIN STOCK EXCHANGE
This stock exchange is officially part of the International Stock Exchange of the United Kingdom and the Republic of Ireland (the old London Stock Exchange).

This affiliate employs a call market each business day at 9:30 A.M. and again at 2:15 P.M., although after-hour activity is allowed until 5:30 P.M. Settlement, as in England, is scheduled at the end of each two-week account period.

DUE-DUE BILLS
Tongue-in-cheek name for short-term floating rate instruments collateralized by poor-quality automobile receivables. Due-due is a sound-alike name for "doo-doo"—a vulgar description of the low quality of the pledged collateral. Banks and finance companies are often the securitizers of such poor obligations.

DUIT
Acronym: Directions Unit Investment Trust. DUITs were invented by E. F. Hutton to achieve capital appreciation through investment in a diversified portfolio of securities. This "in-house" investment company is

comprised of a fixed portfolio of 30 undervalued stocks selected by Hutton's computer research capabilities.

DURATION
An important term in bond portfolio management. Although there are many definitions, two are more prevalent:
1. The point in time at which the paper loss of principal equals the increased return from the reinvestment of cash flow from coupons if interest rates rise.
2. The midpoint of the present value of all cash flows to be received from a bond held to maturity, provided all cash flows are reinvested (Macaulay's definition, 1938).

Both definitions are an approach to bond portfolio management and a method of moderating interest-rate risk. Duration changes as a bond approaches maturity and as interest rates change. The speed of such changes is called the "convexity" of a bond.

DWARFS
Slang for Federal National Mortgage Association (Fannie Mae) securities with 15-year original maturities and presumed 7-year average lives, as opposed to regular conventional pools with 30-year original maturities and presumed 12-year average lives.

Both regular and dwarf pools are assembled in minimum pools of $1 million.

DYNAMITER
Industry slang for high-pressure salespersons.

The term is pejorative and is used of salespersons employed by "penny stock" firms that convince customers to part with their money in get-rich-quick schemes.

E

E
Fifth letter of the English alphabet used:
1. Lowercase next to the dividend in stock transaction tables to designate that some method of computation is used, other than the product of the last quarterly dividend multiplied by 4. Often accompanies the dividend; that is, the distribution of closed-end funds.
2. As the fifth letter in a NASDAQ/NMS symbol to designate that the company is late in filing its required documents with the SEC. As such, the company may be subject to federal penalties and delisting from NASDAQ.

3. Uppercase on the NYSE tape, this letter stands for Transco Energy Company, a major supplier and transporter of natural gas systems in the eastern part of the United States.

EAC
See EQUITY APPRECIATION CERTIFICATES.

EAFE
Acronym: Europe, Australia, and Far East stock index. EAFE is a portfolio of 900 different stocks selected by Morgan Stanley as the basis of futures contracts and listed option contracts overlying them. These 900 stocks represent more than 60% of the aggregate market value of the stocks traded on exchanges in 16 different countries.

EARLY BARGAIN (EB)
English marketplace term for transactions executed after 3:30P.M., London time. Such trades are submitted for comparison on the morning following trade date, just as though they had occurred the following day.

Although EB trades carry the same settlement date (by account period) as trades completed earlier on the same day, they will be DKd if they are submitted on the same day as the transaction.

EASY QUALIFIER LOANS
See EQUAL LOANS.

EATING SOMEONE'S LUNCH
Slang expression used to indicate the aggressiveness of a competitor. The analogy: the aggressive company is taking food from another person's mouth by aggressive pricing and promotion. Some years ago, for example, Kodak was accused of "eating Polaroid's lunch" as it began to sell instant film. Court judgment in favor of Polaroid appears to have borne this out.

EATING STOCK
1. Used of a block positioner or marketmaker who is obliged to buy stock in a falling market.
2. Used of an investment banker who has purchased a security from an issuer for resale but who is unable to sell it at the present time.

Both terms imply the inability to sell the stock immediately at a profit, as would generally be the case of a dealer or underwriter.

EB
See EARLY BARGAIN.

EC
See EUROPEAN ECONOMIC COMMUNITY.

ECP
Commonly used initials for Euro-commercial paper.

Euro-commercial paper is used by companies outside the United States to borrow short-term funds for ordinary operations, short-term inventory needs, and the like. Euro-commercial paper is similar to commercial paper in the United States but does not have the usual regulatory restraints.

EEC
See EUROPEAN ECONOMIC COMMUNITY.

EIP
Acronym: Equity Index Participations. EIPs are the American Stock Exchange's counterpart to the PHLX's Cash Index Participations (CIPs). The EIP, on the other hand, is an option based upon the performance of the Major Market Index (MMI) or the Institutional Index (II) traded on the AMEX. Like the CIP, holders do receive a proportionate share of the dividends paid to holders of the underlying stocks. There is no specific expiration date on EIPs. It is the subject of a court-issued injunction because of its similarity to a futures contract.

EL BIG BANG ESPANOL
A lighthearted term for some recent reforms in the Spanish stock markets. The reforms have embraced two concepts: an SEC-like body in Spain to monitor and supervise a revised code of market trading rules, and a computer linkage of the regional exchanges in Barcelona, Bilbao, and Valencia with the principal exchange in Madrid.

ELECTION STOCK
Also known as "political" stock, the term is used in Japan to describe an equity that is about to be manipulated upward and thus should be appealing to persons running for political office. The concept is this: a candidate can buy the stock now and in a few months sell it at a good profit to pay off campaign expenses.

ELEPHANTS
A somewhat derogatory term for large institutional investors. The term signifies that, because of their huge assets, these customers are capable of moving markets with their buy/sell programs. The concept is that these elephantine organizations have no qualms about trampling small retail investors in their eagerness to buy or sell portfolio securities.

ELEVATOR BONDS
A slang term that is used in the underwriting market for Eurobonds. If an issue is priced too high for an easy and immediate sale, the underwriters have no other choice than to hold the bonds in inventory. To describe this event, they say: "Send them down in the elevator"; that is, from the trading floor down to the bank vault.

EMBARGO
A government-imposed restriction on the export of goods from its country to another country. This action may have political, military, or economic motivation. From the Spanish embargar, to prohibit.

EMERGING MARKETS FREE INDEX
See EMF.

EMF
Acronym: Emerging Markets Free index. EMF was innovated by Morgan Stanley Capital International (MSCI) to monitor stock market price movements in Mexico, Malaysia, Chile, Jordan, Thailand, the Philippines, and Argentina. These countries were chosen because they offer immediate and direct access to foreign investors.

EMPTY HEAD AND PURE HEART TEST
A tongue-in-cheek description of SEC Rule 14e-3, sub-paragraph (b). The rule prohibits any person, other than the bidder in a tender offer, from trading in that security while in possession of material, nonpublic information about the deal. Sub-paragraph (b) provides an exemption for financial institutions—but only if:
1. The trader did not know the information.
2. The financial institution had created, surveilled, and enforced reasonable policies and procedures to avoid violations of the rule; for example, prepared a restricted list.

EOE DUTCH STOCK INDEX OPTION
The European Options Exchange in Amsterdam offers a European-style index option based on the performance of 20 Dutch companies whose stock is traded on the Amsterdam Exchange. Although other options on the EOE can be traded American-style, this option can be exercised only on its day of expiration.

EOM
Abbreviation for end of month. Brokerage compensation for security salespersons is based on the settlement date, not the trade date. Thus, for those salespersons who are compensated solely on commission pro-

duction, it is important that their sales efforts be geared to the settlement of transactions.

EQUAL LOANS
EQUAL is an acronym for Easy Qualifier Loans. The concept was originated by the Federal Home Loan Mortgage Corp. (Freddie Mac) to help more home buyers to obtain fixed rate mortgages. As an alternative to Graduated Payment Mortgages (GPM) or Adjustable Rate Mortgages (ARM), EQUAL requires that all payments in the early years be for an equal amount, but at a rate that is about 1/4% higher than typical home loans at the time of origination.

EQUITY APPRECIATION CERTIFICATES (EAC)
One of three forms of securities created when common shares are tendered in response to a management proposal for reorganization. The concept was developed by Shearson Lehman Hutton and functions like an Americus trust. Thus, in exchange for their shares, common stockholders receive a 30-year bond, a preferred share, and an EAC. The EAC entitles its holder to any stock appreciation above the par value of the bond component. In effect, they are no longer voting owners, but they have some of the rights of ownership.

EQUITY INDEX PARTICIPANTS
See EIP.

ERM
Acronym: Exchange Rate Mechanism. ERM is the term for an agreement among participating member countries to intervene in the financial marketplace, whenever necessary, to hold the value of their own currency within a narrow trading range of about 2 1/2%.

ESCHEAT
Pronounced: ess–cheet.
  See ABANDONMENT.

ESP
See EXCHANGE STOCK PORTFOLIO.

EUROMARCHÉ
In anticipation of the dropping of trade barriers in the Common Market in 1992, this is an English proposal to trade a "common European list" of major stocks on the ISE. It reflects discussions with major continental stock exchanges to provide market exposure to interested investors via the ISE's SEAQ system of trading.

EUROMONEY/FIRST BOSTON STOCK INDEX
An ongoing statistical survey of price performance of about 1,300 stocks in 17 world markets. The index is sponsored and compiled by First Boston Company and published each month in Euromoney magazine.

EUROPEAN COMMUNITY
See EUROPEAN ECONOMIC COMMUNITY.

EUROPEAN ECONOMIC COMMUNITY
Also known as EEC, EC, the European Community, and the Common Market. EEC is an economic alliance comprised of most countries in Western (non-Soviet) Europe. It functions like a multigovernment cartel by removing trade barriers between members and imposing import duties on nonmembers who import into the community. EEC was founded in 1957 and in 1992 will take on special importance as more trade barriers are lowered between the members.

EUROPEAN-STYLE EXERCISE
A contract qualifier for most listed options traded in Europe and some listed options traded in the United States (example: the S&P 500 Index Option). The holder of a European-style option can exercise the option only on the last day (or perhaps also the day before) it expires.

EUROPE, AUSTRALIA, & FAR EAST STOCK INDEX
See EAFE.

EURO-RATE DIFFERENTIAL
See DIFF.

EVENT RISK
A term coined by industry analysts to refer to unpredictable corporate actions that could have a dramatic impact on the value of a company's stocks or bonds. Generally, the "events" are such that management has considerable control over them, and they would include restructurings, asset write-downs, spin-offs, and leveraged buyouts.

EVERGREEN FUNDING
A picturesque English finance term used in association with the recapitalization of new or newly reorganized companies. The concept refers to a steady stream of capital into these companies by means of installment payments, rather than by lump-sum payments.

EXCEPTION REPORT
A computerized document prepared for compliance and audit personnel. This report extracts information from the daily activities of the broker/dealer that exceed pre-established parameters. For example, an exception report based on a universe of 10,000 daily transactions shows that only 100 exceeded $50,000 in value, or exceeded 5,000 shares in volume, or represented more than 5% of a client's assets. In making such "exceptions," the report points compliance and audit personnel in the direction of transaction that prima facie could represent compliance problems or audit problems.

EXCHANGEABLE DEBENTURE
Similar to convertible securities, except that the holder can exchange the debenture for shares of a company in which the issuer has an equity interest. For example, CIGNA Corporation, an insurance company, has an 8% exchangeable debenture due in 2007. Holders may exchange it for 23.36 shares of Paine Webber Group common stock.

EXCHANGE CONTROLS
This term is used of governmental regulations relating to the buying and selling of foreign currencies.

EXCHANGE STOCK PORTFOLIO (ESP)
ESP is a NYSE-listed product designed to reflect market movements in the S&P 500 Index. ESP is a basket of securities in one ownership package. The package is composed of 462 NYSE issues and 38 other stocks. ESP is primarily designed for institutional investors who can buy a "market basket" and also avoid some of the volatility associated with programmed trading activity.

EXECUTIVE SHARES
A U.K. term used to describe shares purchased on the installment plan over a 1–3 year period. In such a financing, issuers may permit buyers to pay for their shares in predetermined installments on specific dates. The buyer turns in the previously received certificate plus a check for the next installment and receives the next certificate. When the final payment is received, the buyer receives an "executive share" certificate. This last certificate is equal to all other outstanding shares and is fully listed on the exchange.

EXEMPT ACCOUNT
A NYSE interpretation of its margin rules on the purchase of U.S. government securities and certain mortgage-backed securities. Under this interpretation, individuals with net tangible assets of at least $16 mil-

lion, and broker/dealers subject to regulation by the United States, to any of its agencies, or to state and municipal regulation, are exempt from the minimum margin requirements.

EXHAUST LEVEL
Jargon for the price level at which a customer's margin account must be liquidated. In general, it is the firm's or the exchange's minimum equity level at which either more margin must be deposited or the account will be terminated. This will be done by selling off long positions or covering short positions.

F

F
Sixth letter of the English alphabet used:
1. Uppercase to mean foreign in corporate sales and earnings reports.
2. To signify "fast" in commodities markets; that is, rapid price fluctuation and large volume. A fast market may excuse a broker who misses the market.
3. To designate "flat"; that is, a bond that trades without accrued interest.
4. As the fifth symbol in the ticker (tape) symbol of a NASDAQ/NMS stock of Canadian origin. Challenger Intl., for example, is CSTIF.
5. Uppercase to signify the common stock of Ford, a major automotive manufacturer.

F
F is the official logo of the French franc and is often so depicted on the country's currency and postage stamps. This depiction is used to have the symbol compete with the logo for the Japanese yen (¥) or the British pound (£).

FACILITATION ACCOUNT
A Federal Reserve term adopted by the New York Stock Exchange to identify a broker/dealer whose transactions are executed by another broker/dealer. If the original firm initiates proprietary transactions through a second broker/dealer, the executing firm must treat that firm as it would any customer and obtain appropriate margin (or a cash deposit) in a timely fashion.

FACTOR
1. Technical name for an extender of credit that is used to purchase, carry, or trade corporate securities. Thus, brokers and banks are factors in their role of carrying margin account transactions for clients.

2. A firm that buys receivables from other organizations at a discount from the face value of the receivables.
3. That proportion of the unpaid principal amount of a mortgage when related to the original principal (face value) amount. For example, Ginnie Mae Pool #25792 was originally issued with a mortgage amount of $3,257,980. Its factor is now 0.57543; that is, $1,874,739.40 remains unpaid. Holders of pass-throughs receive a monthly statement of the factor of their investment that remains to be paid.

FADING
Term used on stock exchanges when a marketmaker takes the other side of the trade on public customer orders. Rather than see the business transferred to another exchange, some brokers on regional exchanges will act as the contra side of customer orders and offset the position elsewhere.

The word is taken from an expression in dice: to fade is to bet against the thrower. For example, "I'll fade you."

FAIRNESS OPINION
A comment by an expert in mergers, acquisitions, or leveraged buyouts that the tender price is reasonable and in the best interest of the shareholders. It is often provided (for a fee) by an independent investment banker to the potential acquirer to forestall litigation about the terms of the deal.

"FALLEN ANGEL"
English term for a debt security of high quality that has been downgraded by a rating agency into what is now referred to as a "junk" bond. The deterioration of the issuer's business prospects and its ability to pay its bond debt service is the usual cause for such a decline.

"FANCY"
Slang for FNCI (q.v.), an acronym for the Financial News Composite Index.

FARMER MAC
Nickname for the Federal Agricultural Mortgage Corporation, a government agency sponsored by the Federal Farm Credit System. Farmer Mac securitizes farm real estate loans by pooling the loans . . . and selling them as a security. Because its interest and principal are ultimately guaranteed by the U.S. Treasury, Farmer Mac joins Fannie Mae, Ginnie Mae, and Freddie Mac in secondary market transactions in mortgage–backed securities.

FAR MONTH
A term used both in the options and futures business to designate the trading month farthest in the future. For options this may be as many as five months, for futures a year or more.

Antonym: near month or spot month.

FAST
Acronym: Fast Automatic Stock Transfer. Fast is a service provided by the Depository Trust Co. (DTC) through the maintenance of jumbo-sized certificates with principal transfer agents in major financial centers. Through FAST, DTC members can authorize withdrawals of stock in appropriate denominations, cause it to be re-registered into customer name, and deliver it to the beneficial owner within 24 hours following the instruction to do so.

FAST AUTOMATIC STOCK TRANSFER
See FAST.

FASTBACS
Acronym: First Automotive Short-Term Bonds & Certificates. FAST-BACS were a Drexel Burnham Lambert product modeled after Salomon Brothers' CARS. In effect, these securities are asset-backed securities collateralized by receivables on auto loans held by commercial banks.

FAT CAT
A slang expression used to designate:
1. Any very wealthy person.
2. A person who receives preferential treatment, either financially or politically.
3. An investor who has profited beyond expectation in a deal.
4. A person who is so successful that he or she has become lazy.

FAT LADY
Jocular expression for the First Atlanta Corporation, a large bank holding company, based on a play on its NASDAQ symbol, FATL.

FAZ INDEX
FAZ is an abbreviation for the Frankfurter Allgemeine Zeitung. The FAZ Index is based on the price movements of 100 high-quality stocks traded in the West German marketplace.

Some Eurobonds have their redemption value linked to this index.

FCP

Acronym: Fonds Communs de Placement. FCPs are a form of mutual fund recognized in France. There are no restrictions on their investments, and portfolio managers may be quite aggressive in both long and short-term markets. FCPs are organized as joint ownerships within unit trusts.

FEDERAL AGRICULTURAL MORTGAGE CORPORATION

See FARMER MAC.

FEDERATION INTERNATIONALE DES BOURSES DE VALEURS

See FIBV.

FED PASS, A

A Federal Open Market Committee (FOMC) term for an action that will increase reserves, and thereby credit, in the banking system. The FOMC constantly monitors the money supply and the inventory of the primary dealers. To make a Fed Pass, the FOMC could buy securities or arrange certain reverse repurchase agreements that will increase the money supply and thereby fine-tune the economy.

FENCES

See CYLINDERS.

FIBV

Known in the United States as the International Federation of Stock Exchanges, its official title is Federation Internationale des Bourses de Valeurs. This is an organization of 33 stock exchanges in 28 countries and its purpose is to promote closer collaboration and to contribute to the development of securities markets.

FICO

Acronym: the Financing Corporation. FICO was created by the US Treasury Department and the Federal Home Loan Bank Board to finance and recapitalize FSLIC (Federal Savings and Loan Insurance Corporation).

Because FSLIC is insolvent, FICO was authorized by Congress to interpose itself between the 12 Federal Home Loan Banks and the capital markets. Although FICO is not guaranteed by the U.S. government, it carries the moral obligation of the U.S. government.

FICO STRIPS
Obligations of the Financing Corporation for which interest and principal payments are marketed separately in a manner similar to Treasury STRIPS.

See FICO for further details.

FIDDLING WITH THE BOOKS
An English expression used to describe fraudulent corporate record-keeping, which lures investors with fictitious earnings or assets.

Also called "creative accounting" or (in the United States) "cooking the books."

FILOS
Acronym: Fixed Interest Limit Order Service. FILOS is an International Stock Exchange of the United Kingdom and the Republic of Ireland computer service to complement its SEAQ Fixed Interest Market Maker Service. FILOS is designed to permit subscribers to display orders and contingent prices for second-line fixed income securities and thereby attract interested contra parties.

FIMBRA
Acronym: Financial Intermediaries Managers & Brokers Regulatory Association. FIMBRA is the result of the merger of NASDIM and LUTIRO. These two trade associations were merged to give a single jurisdiction over smaller OTC firms, life assurance brokers, and unit trusts in Great Britain. FIMBRA is registered with the SIB under England's Financial Services Bill.

FINANCE ISSUE
Japanese identification for an upcoming public offering of an equity security (stock, convertibles, bonds with warrants attached). Under Minister of Finance (MOF) regulations, each phase of the underwriting from preliminary discussions to public sale and actual payment date requires specific market "postures" by underwriters and nonunderwriters to prevent price manipulation.

FINANCIAL INSTITUTION NUMBER
See FINS

FINANCIAL INSTITUTIONS REFORM, RECOVERY, AND ENFORCEMENT ACT OF 1989.
See FIRREA.

FINANCIAL INTERMEDIARIES MANAGERS & BROKERS REGULATORY ASSOCIATION
See FIMBRA.

FINANCIAL PLANNER
1. An individual or an organization that helps others to plan for educational needs, retirement planning, or estate planning.
2. A registered representative (RR) who specializes in retirement planning.
3. A person licensed by a state or registered with the SEC as an investment advisor.
4. A person who has graduated from the College of Financial Planning in Denver, Colorado.
5. A person chartered by the American College (Bryn Mawr, Pennsylvania) as a chartered financial planner (ChFP).
6. A member of the International Association of Financial Planners (IAFP).

Numbers 2 and 3 have regulatory standing; 4, 5, and 6, although nonaccredited academic institutions, have professional standing.

FINANCIAL SECURITY ASSURANCE, INC.
FSA is similar in purpose to municipal insurance companies in that they insure, for a fee, the principal and interest for subscribing corporate issuers. The debt must be backed by mortgages or other select receivables to qualify for this insurance.

The fee for such insurance is paid by the issuer; but because issues that qualify have AAA rating, the fee for insurance can be quickly repaid by the lowered cost of borrowing.

FINANCING CORPORATION, THE
See FICO.

FINS
Acronym: Financial Institution Number. An identifying number assigned to a banking participant in the Depository Trust Company's (DTC) Institutional Delivery (ID) System. Through FINS, a broker/dealer executing a customer order either "cash on delivery" (COD) or "receive versus payment" (RVP) can do so electronically. After details of the transaction are confirmed by the broker/dealer, the system will:
1. Automatically transfer the security to the agent's bank on settlement date by means of DTC's book entry system.
2. Automatically debit the purchaser's account and credit the seller's account with the trade proceeds on the records of DTC.

FIREWALL
A colorful metaphor to describe the legal barrier that must be erected by a bank holding company if it owns or controls a broker/dealer. If the Glass-Steagall Act is repealed, it will also apply to broker/dealers doing a banking business. In essence, a barrier must be established to prevent banking and brokerage activities from spreading into the other area. For example, the bank could not lend to its securities affiliate or finance underwriting activities. The broker/dealer affiliate must register with the SEC and be subject to its regulations.

FIRREA
Acronym: Financial Institutions Reform, Recover, and Enforcement Act of 1989. This legislation was initiated to resolve the crisis of failing thrift (savings and loan) institutions in the United States.

FIRST AUTOMOTIVE SHORT-TERM BONDS & CERTIFICATES
See FASTBACS.

FIRST BOSTON GLOBAL INDEX
See EUROMONEY/FIRST BOSTON GLOBAL STOCK INDEX.

FIRST DEALINGS
English stock exchange term for the earliest time that transactions are allowed for settlement at the end of the next account period (usually a fortnight). First dealings can be as early as 9 A.M. Greenwich time two business days before the start of that account period; but normally it is on Monday morning at the beginning of that period.

FIRST MONEY
Picturesque term used in the operations area of broker/dealers. It represents the quantity times the contract price; for example, 100 shares at $50 represents "first money" of $5,000, and it does not include commissions and other charges that will be added to (on purchases) or subtracted from (on sales) that amount.

FIRSTS
Acronym: Floating Interest Rate Short Tranche Securities. The term is associated with a Shearson Lehman collateralized mortgage obligation (CMO) security. In effect, one tranche (class) of the debt is short term (the FIRSTS) and has a floating interest rate pegged to LIBOR (London Interbank Offered Rate). The long-term portion of the issue carries a traditional fixed interest rate.

FIXED/ADJUSTABLE CUMULATIVE PREFERRED STOCK
An innovative issue of preferred stock created by Bankers Trust New York with a variety of characteristics. For the first five years, it carries a fixed dividend. Subsequently, the rate is adjusted quarterly, pegged 25 basis points above the higher of the three-month T-bill, 10-year T-note, or 30-year T-bond. During this period there is a 15% cap and an 8% collar. And, after the first five years, holders are entitled to an additional dividend if the common stock's cumulative dividend in the previous quarter is in excess of 93 cents per share.

FIXED PAYMENT MORTGAGE
See FPM.

FIXED PRICE OFFERING
SEC-registered underwritten offerings are usually fixed price offerings. In effect, the underwriters purchase the issue from the issuer at a fixed price and then sell the registered offering to the public at a price that is stated in the prospectus.

Only when the offering is completed, or the contract among the underwriters is terminated, may the participants in the syndicate and selling group sell the security at a price different from their preset and advertised price.

FIXED RATE AUCTION PREFERRED STOCK
See FRAPS.

FIXED TERM REVERSE MORTGAGE
The concept is similar to an IRMA. In effect, a homeowner is permitted monthly borrowings against the equity in a home but only for a limited time. For example, the borrowings are permitted only for a period of, let's say, 12 years. At the end of that period, the loan plus accrued interest must be repaid.

FLAT
1. A bond that trades without accrued interest. This may arise because the bond is in default; an income bond before semiannual interest is declared; or any bond that trades so settlement date is coupon payment date.
2. With reference to yield curve measurements, any class of bonds whose intermediate and long-term returns are similar. If short-, intermediate-, and long-term rates are similar, the expression "flat yield curve" is used.

3. In financial analysis, a quarter in which earnings are neither above nor below the earnings of the previous quarter. For example, "Earnings for ABC have been flat during the past three quarters."
4. It identifies a marketmaker's or trader's position when it has neither a long or short position in a particular security.
5. It is used to describe an underwriter's position when it has completely sold its commitment to customers.

FLEX-DARTS
The service mark of a Salomon Brothers product meaning Flexible Dutch Auction Rate Transferable Securities. This corporate equity issue is designed to reduce the number of Dutch auctions during the year yet permit a new dividend rate to be set for the next 49 days. The "flexibility" feature of this instrument permits the issuer to extend its dividend rate for up to one year but, in reality, the dividend auction is held quarterly.

FLIGHT TO QUALITY
Description of a market in which investors are selling weaker issues and buying higher-rated issues—either stocks or bonds. For example, "Although there was a general drop in stock prices today, the blue chips rose somewhat as investors made a flight to quality."

FLIP-FLOP BONDS
Colorful term for a World Bank perpetual bond that can be exchanged for a three-month note, back into the bond, or put back to the issuer at par value. In effect, the investor can change back and forth or redeem depending on the level of interest rates.

FLIP OVER PROVISION
Nickname for an issuer's "poison pill" defense tactic whereby, if an unfriendly suitor merged with that issuer and became the surviving entity, the minority or surviving shareholders of the original company are given an immediate right to buy equity in the surviving company, generally at one half the current market price.

Possible analogy: certain turtles and crustaceans will die if they are turned on their backs; to survive they must flip over.

FLIPPED TRADES
An expression originating with the Midwest Securities Trust Co. (MSTC), an authorized clearing agency registered with the SEC. Flipped trades are transactions compared by MSTC members through its facilities but ultimately destined for settlement at another clearing

agency; for example, the DTC. The second clearing agency has its clearance and settlement facilities electronically linked with MSTC.

FLIPPER
Jargon with two meanings in the securities industry:
1. A customer who buys a new issue and immediately sells it in the aftermarket. Although this is not condoned, it is done by trading clients who buy a "hot issue" and immediately take the aftermarket profit.
2. Nickname for the FPL Group (formerly Florida Power & Light) based on its NYSE tape symbol, FPL.

FLOATING INTEREST RATE SHORT TRANCHE SECURITIES
See FIRSTS.

FLOATING SWAP
See BASIS SWAP.

FLOOR
1. Often used interchangeably with the term *collar* to refer to the lowest price or lowest interest rate acceptable to the issuer/purchaser of a security. Thus, it is an absolute minimum number required to arrange a transaction.
2. Also used in a relative sense to designate the relationship between two rates. Thus, the Fed raised the discount rate last week, thereby raising the floor at which banks will lend money.
3. Used to designate the trading area of an exchange, a commodity market, or the over-the-counter trading area within the premises of a broker/dealer. For example, "You will find Jim on the bond trading floor upstairs."

FOB
1. On corporate and municipal calendars, FOB (First of Boston) is used to designate the First Boston Corporation, a major broker/dealer and investment banking firm.
2. In commerce, FOB means "free on board." In effect, it means that the seller of merchandise will ship to a buyer's single destination point at a price that includes both the merchandise and the cost of transportation. The buyer, in turn, is required to transport the merchandise from the ship to the warehouse or shop.

FONDS COMMUNS DE PLACEMENT
See FCP.

FOREX FILTER
A service mark of Salomon Brothers for a foreign currency contract intended to eliminate foreign exchange risk associated with investments in the US stock market. It is a currency agreement, with Salomon Brothers as the contra party, in which a foreign investor insures against gains or losses in a US stock portfolio that arise solely from differences between the exchange rate and the spot rate at the maturity of the FILTER contract.

Because it is designed to offset such currency differences, the FILTER contract is a variable hedge agreement for the foreign investor.

FORM RE-3
A NYSE advisory document used by member firms to report rule infractions and other misdeeds by an employee of the firm. The Enforcement Department of the NYSE then decides whether to proceed with further action against the offender.

FOR VALUATION ONLY
Term (and abbreviation FVO) used on the periodic pricings of securities prepared at the request of a customer. Such pricings are not for trading purposes; instead, they are to give an estimate of current or historical prices for the use of the customer. Such FVO valuations may be for estate purposes, to determine the fair market value of a gift, for the equitable distribution of property, and so on.

FORWARD BARGAIN
Typical settlement terms for share transactions executed on the International Stock Exchange of the United Kingdom and the Republic of Ireland (ISE). Regardless of trade date, ISE requires the closing of the account period every second Friday, with full payment due on all outstanding positions on the following Monday. (Instead of the usual fortnight, some account periods are scheduled to run for three weeks because of holidays on settlement date.)

FOUR PILLARS, THE
Canadian term for the four major participants in its institutional markets: principal banks, trust companies, life insurance companies, and broker/dealers in securities. Because of the "little bang" on July 1, 1987, and the corresponding increase of foreign competition, it is expected that the lines of demarcation between the "four pillars" will gradually be eliminated.

FPM

Acronym: Fixed Payment Mortgage—as opposed to a Graduated Payment Mortgage (GPM). In this type of mortgage, the monthly dollar payments remain the same over the life of the mortgage; with GPMs, monthly payments may be lower in earlier years and higher in later years.

FRANKED INVESTMENT INCOME

A term used of investment trusts (mutual funds) in England. The term refers to investment income received by the trust from companies that have already paid corporate taxes on such distributions. Under U.K. law, such dividends when distributed are not again subject to corporate taxation.

FRANKFURT RUNNING INDEX

This index is a minute-by-minute measurement of the performance of 30 blue-chip stocks traded on the Frankfurt Stock Exchange. Using share prices as of December 31, 1987, as a benchmark, this index measures the same stocks as those found in the Boersenzeitung Index but measures them continuously, rather than only once a day.

Formerly known as the KISS Index.

FRAPS

Acronym: Fixed Rate Auction Preferred Stock. A Salomon Brothers product, FRAPS are a preferred stock whose dividend rate is subject to change every 49 days by means of an auction among prospective buyers. The shares are maintained in book entry format and are redeemable at a premium during the early years following issuance.

FREE ON BOARD

See FOB 2.

FREE-RIDER BANKS

A British expression for small banks that originally made loans to less developed countries (LDCs) at a rate of interest that *no longer reflects* the adjusted interest rate evidenced in the new loan agreements with these countries. In effect, these banks are "free-riding" the new loan agreement.

FREE STOCK

1. Stock fully paid for and free of any encumbrances; for example, a margin loan that may be sold by the customer or delivered out in registered format.

2. Stock that is held by an issuer following a private placement but that will be delivered out free of any restrictive legend. In this case, the stock is free and may be sold without further restriction.

FREIT
Acronym: Finite Life Real Estate Investment Trust. As with a typical REIT, real estate is the underlying investment of the corporation. Unlike the typical REIT that has unlimited life, a FREIT has a fixed life of 10–12 years. At this time the underlying assets will be sold and the assets distributed to the holders.

FRICTIONAL COST
Term often associated with portfolios that replicate a specific index in terms of issues, dollar value, number of shares, and so on. By definition, the frictional costs (commissions, portfolio management fees, and the like) will cause the assembled portfolio to underperform the benchmark index unless certain adjustments are made to overcome the frictional cost.

FRIED EGGS
Part of the insider trading jargon of Wall Street, "fried eggs" is used to identify the fraction five-eighths. For example (in a shout across the floor), "It's selling at 55 and fried eggs (55⅝)." It is both quaint and a way of clarifying the quote.

FORM T
An NASD form on which members report equity transactions that are executed outside normal market hours. Certain transactions are exempted from this reporting requirement, but—in general—most equity transactions completed outside trading hours must be reported.

FORM 13D
A form that must be filed with the SEC and which is named after the SEC's Rule 13D. Under Rule 13D, anyone who acquires 5% or more of a registered company's outstanding stock must file a report with the SEC within 10 days of attaining that threshold amount.

FORM 13G
A form that must be filed with the SEC and which is named after the SEC's Rule 13G. Under Rule 13G, broker/dealers, insurance companies, banks, or investment companies must file notice with the SEC if they acquire 5% or more of the equity of a registered company in the ordinary course of their business. This form must be filed within 45 days after the end of the calendar year if the above-named position is still in inventory at that time.

FRANKFURT STOCK EXCHANGE

The Frankfurt Stock Exchange is the largest of the exchanges in the Federal Republic of Germany and it accounts for approximately 70% of all stock and bond trades in that country. Although the floor is open officially only from 11:30 A.M. until 1:30 P.M., the floor's trading technologies have promoted this bourse's popularity. In addition, there is an active and permitted OTC activity after trading hours to handle the interests in German companies traded in London and New York. Contract settlements are set for the second business day after trade date.

FRAUD

Fraud is a legal term for a purposeful deception that results in financial loss to another. Generally, fraud results from misrepresentation, concealment, or omission of material facts, or from the employment of artificial devices or contrivances intended to deceive. Fraud is prohibited by federal and state law and is subject to prosecution, fine, or imprisonment under securities laws.

FRONT OFFICE

Brokerage term used to identify sales and trading personnel. As a general rule, the term is used to include revenue producers in a member firm, including sales management; and the term is used in opposition to "back office"—that is, operations and other support personnel.

FSA

See FINANCIAL SECURITY ASSURANCE, INC.

FT—ACTUARIES WORLD INDEX

This is a statistical monitor of the price performance of 2,400 securities traded in 23 countries throughout the world. As such, the index represents over 70 percent of those countries' market values. This index appears daily in the *Financial Times* (of London), and is a joint production of FT, Goldman Sachs, Wood Mackenzie, and two U.K. actuarial organizations.

FULLY PAID AND NON-ASSESSABLE

This terminology appears on virtually all stock certificates issued in the United States. In practice, it means that, in the event of bankruptcy and dissolution of the company, the owner of the certificate can lose no more than the amount paid to acquire the security.

Earlier in United States history and before the passage of certain protective state laws, if a corporation sold securities below their par value, the subscriber could—if the company became bankrupt—be forced to pay the difference between the subscription price and the par value.

FUTURE VALUE OF A DOLLAR

The amount of money a dollar will become during a specified time period at a specified rate of compound interest. The formula is:

$$(1+R)^n$$

where: 1 is the original dollar,
        R is the compound rate of return,
        n is the number of time periods.

Thus, $1 invested at 8% for 10 years compounded semiannually would be computed by:

$$(1+0.04)^{20}$$

Note: Because of semiannual compounding, the rate was divided by 2 and the number of periods increased to 20. The answer is:

$$\$2.1911$$

FUTURE VALUE OF AN ANNUITY

The number of dollars that will be achieved if a person invests a fixed number of dollars, at a fixed rate of compound interest, for a fixed number of years. The formula is:

$$\frac{(1+R)^n-1}{R}$$

where R is the rate of return,
       n is the number of compounding periods.

Thus, a client who puts $2,000 per year into an IRA for the next 25 years at 11% compounded return will have:

$$\$228,826.52$$

The formula presumes that the annual contribution into the annuity is made at the *beginning* of each year.

FVO

See FOR VALUATION ONLY.

G

G

This is the seventh letter of the alphabet used:
1. Lowercase in stock transaction tables to denote that the dividend is paid in Canadian funds, although the prices are in U.S. dollars.

2. Uppercase in the NASDAQ/NMS symbol as the fifth letter if an OTC bond is convertible; for example, FCBNG is the symbol for Fluorocarbon Co. convertible 8% debentures due January 15, 2011.
3. Uppercase alone to represent Greyhound Financial Corporation, a large conglomerate involved in business systems, food services, and equipment leasing.

GAAS
Acronym: Generally Accepted Auditing Standards. GAAS is a system of audit quality controls set forth and overseen by the Financial Accounting Standards Board (FASB). The SEC has also adopted these standards and permits their use in the filing of the mandatory financial statements with the commission.

GAIJIN
Japanese word for foreigner. Although all non-Japanese people can be so labeled, the term is used particularly of those non-Japanese broker/dealers who are established in Japan and thus compete directly with the "Big Four" Japanese brokers: Nomura, Daiwa, Nikko, and Yamaichi. The gaijins are usually the most prestigious of the brokerage firms in the United Kingdom or the United States.

GAIMUIN
Japanese term for a salesperson of a registered broker/dealer who is authorized (qualified) to do sales and sales promotion work *outside* of the employer's physical offices. Such persons must register with the Minister of Finance (MOF). This is normally done through the Japanese Association of Securities Dealers (JASD). Qualification is contingent upon passage of a special examination or equivalent supervisory experience.

GAIMU KOUI
Japanese term for the actual sales and sales promotion activity done outside the offices of a registered broker/dealer in that country.
    See GAIMUIN for further details about the registration and qualification of the personnel who do such activities.

GAN
See GRANT ANTICIPATION NOTE.

GAP OPENING
Street term used to identify an opening transaction that is significantly higher/lower than the previous market day's closing price. Generally, if there is to be a gap opening, the specialist will give indication notice on

the tape to attract contra brokers. Although there is no legal definition of a gap, a good rule of thumb is 1 point for stocks selling below $20, 2 points for stocks selling between $20 and $100, and 5 points for stocks selling above $100.

GAS 100
Acronym: Global Analysis Systems 100 International Equity Index. It is a two-tiered index, which uses all 100 international issues in its computation and a second tier that uses only the 58 non-Japanese components in its measurement. Merrill Lynch is the sponsor of GAS 100.

GARDEN LEAVE
A U.K. term for a meritorious employment practice in England as well as in the United States. It provides that, if an employee resigns to compete with that firm (either personally or on behalf of someone else), its employee must immediately retire from that business for up to 90 days. This practice is designed to prevent that person from stealing customers, business, or trade secrets from the former employer. It is assumed that, in the interim period, the former employer (i.e., broker/dealer) will attempt to retain the customer base and prospective business relationships. In the meantime, it is assumed that firm will continue to pay benefits to the "beached" former employee.

GATORS
Acronym: Government and Agency Term Obligation Receipts. GATORS were originated by Moseley, Hallgarten, Estabrook, and Weeden to compete with CATS and TIGRs and are substantially the same as these and similar zero-coupon treasuries.

GD
1. NYSE symbol for General Dynamics, a large U.S. defense contractor and a major participant in the aerospace industry.
2. An order qualifier on purchase or sale instructions on the London options marketplace. GD signifies "good for the day only" and means that the order—if not executed—expires at the end of the trading day.

GEARING
Slang for the percentage of debt in terms of total capital in an investment. For example, if the total capital of an investment is 10 million, debt of 4 million would indicate a 40 percent gearing and a 60 percent shareholder equity.

GEMM

Acronym: Gilt Edged Market Maker. GEMM is used of any of the recognized dealers in U.K. government securities. These firms are members of the International Stock Exchange of the United Kingdom and the Republic of Ireland and make continuous two-sided markets in GILTS. They are the principal means whereby the Bank of England fine-tunes the U.K. money supply.

GENERIC SECURITY

An expression used to designate a newly issued publicly owned security that as yet has no track record; that is, any history of how the security will react to different market scenarios.

The term is often used of new real estate backed issues because it is not known how fast the mortgagees will "pay down" the principal amount of their loans; thus, it is not known how long will be the average life of the investment nor the yield to maturity on the original investment.

GES

Acronym: Guaranteed Execution System. GES is a nonautomated small order execution system on the Boston Stock Exchange, analogous in purpose to DOT (NYSE), SOES (NASDAQ), PACE, and the like.

GES handles orders for 1,299 shares or less, based upon prevailing prices in the Consolidated Quotation System (CQS).

GETTING HEAVY

A term used in conjunction with a decline in prevailing prices for a security, or for the market in general. Generally, the term is used to designate that sellers are trading in volume and thereby depressing prices. For example, "ABC is down 2 points and trading is getting heavy."

G-5

A political term used to designate the "Group of Five"; that is, the finance ministers of the United States, Britain, Japan, West Germany, and France. The original purpose of the group's meeting in 1985 was to lower the value of the US dollar in terms of other world currencies.

Also used as G-7 if the finance ministers of Italy and Canada are included.

In nonpolitical contexts, G-7, G-8, and G-10 are used to designate significant groups of management-type persons.

GHOSTING
Term used of a form of collusive manipulation of stock prices by two or more securities firms.

It is called "ghosting" because one firm dictates price levels and the other firm follows its lead. The investing public, on the other hand, is led to believe that the price level is determined by the opinions of several "independent" marketmakers.

GHOST SHORTING
This colloquial term describes a marketmaker's improper act of selling a security not owned and not even bothering to borrow it in order to make delivery to the purchaser.

Also called "naked shorting." See GHOST STOCK.

GHOST STOCK
Slang for stock sold short by a firm or customer and neither borrowed nor delivered to the purchaser. It is also called a "naked short," and the initiating seller hopes that the price declines before the buyer initiates buy-in procedures.

GIC
See GUARANTEED INVESTMENT CONTRACT.

GILT EDGED MARKET MAKER
See GEMM.

GLOBAL ANALYSIS SYSTEMS 100 INTERNATIONAL EQUITY INDEX
See GAS 100.

GLOBAL FUND
An investment company or managed pool of investments whose portfolio is comprised of foreign securities, both those denominated in U.S. dollars as well as those in other currencies.

GNOMES
1. Jargon made popular by the television program "Wall Street Week" for the 10 widely followed technical analysts whose composite opinion is used by the program to indicate the short-term direction of the market. For example, "This week our gnomes are 3 up, 3 neutral, 4 down, for a net of minus 1." From the Greek *gnome* (gnomay), an opinion; then introduced into Germanic folklore to signify a shriveled person who delivers this opinion: the gnomes of Zurich.
2. Slang for Freddie Mac mortgage pools with 15-year, rather than 30-year, maturities, and also a shortened average life.

GODFATHER
On the Tokyo Stock Exchange, a member who sponsors and assists a new member in preparing for admission and eventual prosperity on that exchange. It is not unusual for a new member of the Tokyo Stock Exchange to ask one of the "Big Four" (Nomura, Daiwa, Nikko, or Yamaichi) to act as "godfather."

GOFFEX
Originally the acronymic name of the German Options and Financial Futures Exchange modeled after the similarly named Swiss entity SOFFEX. As the organization proceeded to incorporate, it changed its name to DTB (Deutsche Terminboerse Gmbh.)

GOLDEN BOOT
Term used to designate the layoffs of older employees with maximum incentives and financial benefits. Such layoffs may be disguised as "voluntary" but are often coerced under the veiled threat of termination without any financial benefits. As such, these layoffs may violate EEOC guidelines against discrimination because of age and the like.

GOLDEN CROSS
In Japan, a market technician's powerful indicator of a forthcoming rise in prices. This bullish sign occurs when the 80-day moving average of stock prices crosses from below the 200-day moving average of stocks on the Tokyo Stock Exchange.

GOLDEN HANDSHAKE
Euphemistic term to describe an incentive plan geared to entice employees into early retirement. Such a plan may include salary continuation programs, continued health and insurance benefits, a lump-sum pension payment, and so on. Such plans are aimed at creating openings for younger employees or to lower (ultimately) payroll or benefit costs, or both.

GOLDEN HELLO
Slang in the English securities marketplace to signify a large start-up bonus paid to new employees to induce them to join a particular securities organization.

GOLDEN SHARE
In the United Kingdom, a situation where the seller retains voting privileges to elect the issuer's board of directors. This occurred in the privatization of Britoil, plc, where the British government sold its interest in

that company but the buyers were not in a position to elect the board of directors.

GOLD FIX
In London, the twice-daily setting of the price per ounce of bullion gold. This price becomes the worldwide standard for the price of gold and of gold bullion futures. The fixing is picturesque: three dealers sit at a table and, as the price is changed (up or down), they are at liberty to hold the flag in front of them up until the price reaches a level that they feel will satisfy their orders, both received and anticipated. When all three flags are lowered, the price is fixed.

"GONE FOR A BURTON"
Quaint local English slang for a sharp market decline. The term originated when an RAF pilot in World War II was shot down and killed. In explanation, it was said that "he had gone for an ale in Burton-on-Trent." That was quickly shortened and used to signify financial destruction in a falling market.

GOODBYE KISS
Tongue-in-cheek expression for the payoff of an unwanted suitor by a company threatened by a takeover. The pirate's stock is purchased at higher than market prices; hence, the expression "goodbye kiss."
    Similar in concept to "greenmail."

GORIKA
An electronic order and trade routing system under development by the Tokyo Stock Exchange. It is similar to the NYSE "order book" and it will disclose market depth at all prices for interested prospective broker participants ("Saitori" q.v.).

GRAVEYARD MARKET
Colorful term used to describe a bear market in which many investors have substantial paper losses and thus are not able to sell without realizing the losses and substantial amounts of capital. The other side of the coin is this: those who did not suffer paper losses and who, instead, have either substantial cash or large gains, feel that it is too early to jump back into the market. They feel that the market has not yet bottomed.

GRAY KNIGHT
Colorful term used in mergers and acquisitions for a second bidder for a takeover target.
    The second bidder is not a "White Knight" because it is not coming to

the rescue of the target. Nor, is it a total enemy of the target, a "Black Knight." That only leaves one color, a mixture of white and black: gray!

GREENFIELD VENTURE
Quaint British term for a venture capital deal by a group without a previous track record. Thus, neither the new company nor the capital suppliers has a record for the other to gauge prospective success because both are "start-up" operations.

GREENIE
Picturesque term used on the floor of the New York Stock Exchange for a memorandum on green paper given by the specialist to indicate the opening price of a stock. If such a memorandum is given to a broker whose stock was used to determine the opening price, the broker must compare the price with that of the contra broker for the execution price to be valid.

GRIT
Acronym: Grantor Retained Income Trust. GRIT is an estate-tax saving device that is predicated on the grantor's survival of the trust termination date. GRIT is an irrevocable trust with at least a 15-year life. It allows the grantor to transfer assets but retain the income of the trust for the life of the trust. Upon termination, the remainderman (who owns the property) now also gets the income. The grantor now pays a gift tax based on the original value of the gifted property. The gift tax could be at a rate that is fully covered by the unified gift and estate tax credit permitted by law. Upon the grantor's death, such a gift is added back to the estate of the grantor at the value as of the day of the gift, not its current value. Therein lies the principal estate tax saving.

GRIZZLY
Verbal acronym for a Growth Retirement Investment Zero-Coupon Treasury Certificate. GRIZZLYs were originated by Swanbrook Limited Partnership. Issued by Security Pacific National Bank of Los Angeles as custodian for Swanbrook's underlying government securities that collateralize the issue. The GRIZZLY represents ownership of a specific amount of a bond underlying Swanbrook's CUBS and BEARS (q.v.).

GROSS LEASE
A short-term commercial loan in which the landlord pays all expenses incidental to ownership. The tenant is responsible only for the lease payments and for maintenance and operating expenses.

Antonym: NET LEASE, in which the landlord pays only taxes and all other operating, maintenance, and insurance expenses—plus the payment of a net sum—are the obligation of the tenant.

GROSS MARGINING
Term used on the Chicago Mercantile Exchange (CME) regarding the carrying of positions in futures contracts. Under gross margining, the "Merc" requires each member to deposit margin daily not for its net position but for all of its open positions. For example, if a member has 100 open long positions and 50 open short positions in the same commodity, it must deposit margin on all 150 open positions, not on the net position of 50 contracts.

GROUP OF FIVE
See G-5

GROUP UNIVERSAL LIFE POLICY
See GULP.

GSBD
Acronym: Government Securities Brokers and Dealers. A form of SEC registration for government securities dealers after July 25, 1987. Under federal law, those firms not registered as general securities brokers under the 1934 act with the SEC must register as GSBDs if they wish to act as brokers or dealers in government securities. This requirement applies also to dealer banks (or separate trading units within banking institutions) with this exception: the registration of banks must be with their own regulators, rather than with the SEC.

GSCC
See GOVERNMENT SECURITIES CLEARING CORPORATION.

GSOP
Acronym: Government Security Option Permits. GSOPs are three-year privileges offered by the CBOE that enables holders to deal as market-makers in these specialty instruments. These permits do not require that the permit holder be a member, nor do they carry a right to purchase a membership in the exchange.

GOVERNMENT & AGENCY TERM OBLIGATION RECEIPTS
See GATORS.

GOVERNMENT BROKER
1. In the United States, the term identifies a securities firm that acts as an intermediary between two government securities dealers who

prefer to trade anonymously. In this regard, the term is similar to the term *broker's broker* in the municipal securities markets.

2. In the United Kingdom, the term applies to a firm called Mullens & Company. Mullens acts for the Bank of England on behalf of the English government. At the direction of the Bank of England this firm buys and sells gilts through various marketmakers.

GOVERNMENT SECURITIES ACT OF 1986, THE
Federal law that regulates broker/dealers in U.S. government securities and agency securities. Banks and securities firms that transact in those securities must register with the SEC *and* with their own regulators (e.g., securities firms with the NASD; banks with their regulators). Exempt are organizations that:

1. Handle U.S. savings bonds exclusively.
2. Execute less than 500 trades a year.
3. Act only as fiduciaries
4. Engage only in REPO (Reverse REPO) transactions.
5. Are registered with the Commodities Futures Trading Commission (CFTC) and whose government trades are incidental to such business in futures.
6. Are a branch or agency of a foreign bank whose customers are non-U.S. citizens.

GOVERNMENT SECURITIES BROKERS ASSOCIATION
A trade group of government securities brokers organized to lobby in Washington to present the industry's ideas and viewpoints to Congress. These firms act as intermediaries for government dealers trading anonymously and formed their organization in 1986 to promote mutual economic interests.

GOVERNMENT SECURITIES CLEARING CORPORATION
Initials GSCC. This is an offshoot of the National Securities Clearing Corporation (NSCC), which was founded originally to settle OTC transactions. GSCC was founded in 1986 to compare and make net settlements in government securities for participating dealers.

GOVERNMENT TRUST CERTIFICATES
See GTC.

GRADUATED CALL WRITING
A program of selling call options against an underlying stock position at increasing strike prices and increasing premiums as the stock price rises. If the strategy is successful, the result is the sale of the entire stock position at the call prices at an average price (including premiums and

dividends) that is higher than the original prices of the options. Also known as "incremental return writing strategy."

Should the options not be exercised, the premium income will cushion downside stock fluctuations. In effect, a client with 1,500 shares sells 5 calls at 50, then 5 calls at 55, then 5 calls at 60. If called, the client will garner the increased strike prices, the increased profit on the underlying, and the increased premiums. If not called, the premiums will cushion downside risk.

GRANT ANTICIPATION NOTE
GAN are municipal securities issued in expectation of federal government monies to be received for a specific project. The notes are a form of bridge financing to begin work on a highway, water facility, and the like. The federal government statutes will spell out the ways in which the monies are to be used.

GRANTOR RETAINED INCOME TRUST
See GRIT.

GRANTOR TRUST
Legal term for the conduit used to entitle ownership interests in a pass-through security. In effect, the grantor trust provides equity units of participation in an instrument holding title to an issue of debt securities collateralized by mortgages, credit card receivables, automobile loans, or other asset-backed instruments.

"GRAVESTONE" SALES
A derogatory term used in Japan to describe high-pressure securities sales tactics much like the concept of "boiler room" sales in the United States. The term is derived from an unsavory practice in Japan of selling family gravestones in a culture that is dedicated to ancestor honor, with an overtone that the sellers either fail to deliver on their promises or what they deliver is lacking in real value.

GROUP ROTATION
Technical and market analysis term that centers on the fact that the stocks of a particular industry go in and out of fashion. Thus, when Industry A goes into fashion, portfolio managers jump in to make it too "pricey," and then they jump to Industry B because it is now underpriced. The term does not infer that there is conscious manipulation of the prices of one industry over the other; rather, it is an inference that there is an element of "follow the leader" in portfolio management as there is in any industry.

GTC
Initials that are used to signify:
1. On an order to buy or sell, that the order is valid until it is cancelled by the customer. Industry or member firm practice is to require periodic revalidation of such orders; for example, at the end of 31 days, or every six months.
2. Government Trust Certificates. These are US government guaranteed (90%) refinancings of loans to foreign countries enabling them to buy American military equipment. GTCs were created in 1988, and such loans enabled these countries to pay less interest for their loans originally negotiated in the early 1980s. GTCs have no provisions for prepayments, calls, or sinking funds.

GUARANTEED EXECUTION SYSTEM
See GES.

GUARANTEED INVESTMENT CONTRACT
GICs are investment contracts sold by insurance companies to pension and profit-sharing plans, usually for a period of 3 to 10 years. The pension or profit-sharing plan makes a large capital investment; in return, the insurance company guarantees a specific rate of return on the invested capital. The insurance company assumes all market, interest-rate, and credit risks on the securities that are held in trust to collateralize the obligation. The pension or profit-sharing plan assumes all inflationary risk.

GULP
Acronym: Group Universal Life Policy. GULP is a form of employee benefit plan made available by many financial services firms. GULP centers on a form of term life insurance but adds savings features and residual value not found in most whole life policies. As a group policy, GULP features economies not found in personal universal life policies. GULP policies are "interest-rate sensitive" and returns may vary. Often GULP policies are offered not only to the employee but also to other immediate family members.

GUNNING
A slang term for market manipulation. In this case, the manipulation occurs when a person or a group of persons purchases a security at increasing prices. The goal is to lure greedy investors, who will end up holding securities with inflated values.

Manipulation is outlawed by the Securities and Exchange Act of 1934 and by state securities laws.

"GUNSLINGER"

A 1960s term for an aggressive portfolio manager who purchased highly speculative stocks, or who used leverage to increase returns. Subsequent bear markets and economic downturns helped to remove most of these speculators.

H

HAMMERED

An English term for a stock exchange member who became insolvent.

The term originated when the London Stock Exchange hammered a bell during trading hours and announced to the other members that this or that member firm was now insolvent.

HAMMERING THE MARKET

Picturesque metaphor used by traders to reflect the downward pressure on the market caused by heavy selling. In effect, speculators and investors have become pessimistic and their selling, either constant or in waves, is causing the market to drop rapidly.

Used both actively and passively; for example, "The programmed trading is hammering the market . . ." or, "The market is being hammered by aggressive selling."

"HANDS-OFF" INVESTOR

Expression used to describe a capital contributor to a corporation who is willing to accept a passive role in its day-to-day operations.

"HANDS-ON" INVESTOR

An investor who makes a major capital contribution to a business enterprise and who expects to play an active role in its day-to-day management. "Active" may mean in an advisory role, or through a seat on the board of directors, or as a manager or officer.

HAPPINESS LETTER

A letter signed by an officer or branch manager to a customer—either new or continuing—to ensure that the relationship between the customer and the broker/firm is satisfactory.

Such "happiness letters," as they are picturesquely called, are usually required by the broker/dealer's legal department whenever a customer account:
1. Is introduced to the firm or transferred thereto,
2. or is subjected to unusual activity,
3. or changes investment objectives,

4. or buys something of questionable suitability.

The purpose of the letter is to forestall customer complaints or future litigation.

"HARD BULLET" ASSET-BACKED SECURITIES
A debt obligation collateralized by credit card receivables, but with a "maturity guarantee" by a bank issuer in case principal collections are insufficient to meet principal requirements at maturity.

HARD DOLLARS
This picturesque term is used to mean payment for goods or services in actual dollars. Payment for research services, computer services, or brokerage commissions are generally paid in "hard dollars."

Antonym: "soft dollars." This term is used when payment is made in kind; for example, commissions in exchange for research services or other statistical services, or if payment is made by a third party.

HEAF
Acronym: Higher Education Assistance Foundation. HEAF is a private guarantor of student educational loans and, as such, is a significant participant in the U.S. government's student loan program. HEAF specializes in guaranteeing loans to finance technical school training, junior colleges, and two-year degree programs.

In general, HEAF, if a student defaults, insures the loan repayment and is, in turn, partially reimbursed by the government. If not, it will honor the loan out of its reserve fund.

HEALTH INDUSTRY BOND INSURANCE COMPANY
Abbreviation: HIBI. A bond insurance program backed by Crum and Forster and American Health Capital Management to assure payment of interest and principal to holders of debt securities in qualifying health care institutions. HIBI does not limit its insurance to nontaxable debt. Generally, HIBI-insured issues carry AAA ratings.

"HEAVEN AND HELL BONDS"
Slang for a unique product of Mitsui & Co. (USA).

Heaven and hell bonds are parts of a Eurobond issue linked to the performance of a specific U.S. Treasury issue. The holder of a "heaven" bond receives par plus a premium if the U.S. Treasury bond *outperforms* the Eurobond issue. The holder of a "hell" bond receives par plus a premium if the U.S. Treasury bond *underperforms* the Eurobond issue. Interest on both bonds is nominal: 3–4% annually; their value is in the premium paid under differing circumstances.

These bonds are similar in concept to bull and bear bonds (q.v.) but differ in their benchmark index and type of underlying security.

HEDGE RATIO
A ratio of the number of option contracts needed to hedge a position in the underlying equity based on the beta of the underlying.

For example, a client is long 100,000 shares of LMN, which has a beta of 1.15. To hedge this position, the client could buy 1150 long puts, or sell 1150 covered calls. Reasoning: the underlying will tend to perform as though it had a dollar value equal to 115,000 shares of stock; thus, it should be hedged as such. Remember: the word *hedge* means to take an offsetting position; that is, on the opposite side of the market from the underlying. Long puts and short calls are on the other side of the market from the long position because they partially protect on the downside.

HEDGE WRAPPER
An expression used to designate this strategy: a customer who is long the underlying stock buys a put and sells a call. No matter which way the underlying moves, the customer stands to benefit—although losses are possible. If the underlying does not move, the customer benefits from the difference between the income in (from the call) and premium paid (on the put). If the stock moves up, the customer will be called at a profit; if the stock moves down, the customer is hedged (hence, the name) by the put. The strategy is also used with index options but requires that the customer have a diversified portfolio of stocks similar to the overlying index.

HELSINKI STOCK EXCHANGE
Located in the capital of Finland, this exchange is one of the smallest in Europe because foreign ownership of Finnish companies is severely restricted. Trading hours are from 9:30 A.M. until noon, but afternoon trading is permitted for another two hours. Settlement takes place on the fifth banking day after trade date.

HELSINKI STOCK EXCHANGE AUTOMATIC TRADING & INFORMATION SYSTEM
Popularly known by its acronym HETI, this is a computerized program to support securities trading on the Helsinki Stock Exchange. The system coordinates both exchange trading and trading done in the offices of Finnish brokerage firms.

HETI
See HELSINKI STOCK EXCHANGE AUTOMATIC TRADING & INFORMATION SYSTEM.

HIBI
See HEALTH INDUSTRY BOND INSURANCE COMPANY.

HIBOR
Acronym: Hong Kong Interbank Offered Rate. HIBOR, an obvious analog of LIBOR, is similar to the prime rate in the United States and forms a pricing standard for interest costs in the Far East. HIBOR is an "inside market" for interest rates made available only to prestigious banking and financial institution members in southeast Asia.

HIGH FLYER
An expression that is aptly used of stocks with extreme price volatility. "High flyers" are stocks "in vogue" that are marked by extremely high price earnings ratios and characterized by rapid price movements in reaction to business news about the company. In the latter part of the 1980s, computer issues and high-technology companies tended to be in the category of high flyers.

"HIGHJACKING"
This is a literal translation of the Japanese word *nottori.*

The word is used in Japan to identify a takeover situation. It (highjacking) is also used in the United States of merger and acquisition activities.

HIGHLY CONFIDENT LETTER
A letter, pioneered by Drexel Burnham Lambert in conjunction with certain issues of "junk bonds," stating that they were highly confident (but without official commitment) and that they would be able to successfully market an offering of a particular type of security. Such a letter often arose in connection with a tender offer, or a leveraged buyout, where significant amounts of money would be needed from an issue to have the funds to purchase control of a company.

HIGHLY LEVERAGED TRANSACTION
See HLT.

HIGH STEPPER
Conventional industry term for a growth stock that combines high technology, high price volatility, and an "in vogue" status with investors and portfolio managers. Thus, the stock had all the ingredients to attract large cash flows in a competitive high-volume marketplace.

HIGH-YIELD BONDS
Industry term for "junk bonds"; that is, bonds with ratings of BB (Moody's Ba) or lower. Bonds with no rating are often placed in the same category.

Such bonds often have yields of 400 plus basis points above Treasuries of comparable maturities because of the default risk inherent in the bond. Unfortunately, both terms are deficient: high yield because it is euphemistic; junk bond because it is pejorative. In fact, only about 600 companies in the United States (out of 5,000 publicly traded) merit an investment grade rating; thus, "junk bonds" are the only access some companies have to the credit markets.

A HIT
As a noun the term is used to designate:
1. A large monetary loss—either realized or on paper. Thus, an investor who had a rapid 10% loss would be said to have had a "hit."
2. A large monetary gain—either realized or on paper. Here the analogy is with the term used in baseball, *to make a hit.*
As a verb the term is used to designate:
1. The borrowing of money; for example, "The company hit its stockholders for another large bond issue."
2. The appearance of news or rumors; for example, "It didn't take that rumor long to hit the Street."

HLT
1. Acronym for a Highly Leveraged Transaction, a euphemism for a bank loan to a company with a disproportionate amount of debt. What constitutes disproportionate will often vary by industry and traditional debt structures. Thus, in the United States, debt to equity ratios tend to be smaller for industrial and service companies than for utilities and banks. And, in Japan, debt to equity ratios tend to be much larger than in the United States.
2. NYSE ticker symbol for Hilton Hotels Corporation, one of the world's largest hotel chains.

HOEKMAN
Title of those members of the Amsterdam Stock Exchange (ASE) who have a function similar to that of the specialists on U.S. exchanges. The hoekman indicates quotes, takes and matches orders from other members, and also buys and sells as principal. It is also the hoekman's duty to report prices of actual transactions for the exchange's records and computer screens. As with U.S. specialists, they have assigned stocks and are expected to maintain "fair and orderly" markets.

HOME RUN
This analogy from baseball is used to designate anyone who combines two concepts: a large profit in a short time. For example, "His purchase and resale of AJAX Corporation for a $40 million profit was a home run in anyone's league."

HOMES
In England, the designator of National Home Loans: the originator of a debt instrument representing the pooled mortgages of British home-owners. Similar in concept to Ginnie Mae pass-throughs in the United States, HOMES are backed by private insurors—although they have tacit approval of the Bank of England and the Inland Revenue Service.

HONG KONG STOCK EXCHANGE
This exchange marketplace is second only to Tokyo in terms of volume and trading activity in Asia. Trading is held each business day from 10:00 A.M. until 12:30 P.M. and from 2:30 P.M. until 3:30 P.M. No after-hour trading is permitted. Settlement the regular way is the next business day.

Its Hang Seng Index of market performance is followed worldwide.

HOSHO-KIKIN SYSTEM
This system augments the guaranty of the Japanese commodity exchange community by settling client equity liabilities in the event that a commodity futures merchant becomes insolvent. It was established in 1975 as a nonprofit foundation and is recognized by several ministries with industry jurisdictions.

Also known as: Association of Compensation Fund for Consigned Liabilities in Commodity Futures, Inc.

HOUSE
1. A large broker/dealer organization with many offices and employees interconnected by internal wire systems; for example, Shearson Lehman Hutton is a large house.
2. A bank or broker/dealer dominated by a well-known person; for example, the House of Morgan.
3. Designation of a securities or commodities clearing agency set up to compare, confirm, and settle transactions; for example, the house says that we owe 1,000 shares of ABC.
4. Collective name for the contra bettor in a gambling casino; for example, the vigorish favors the house.

HOUSE ACCOUNT
A customer account held by a broker/dealer that is active but not assigned to a specific salesperson. Such house accounts often arise from a traditional relationship between the firm and the customer; for example, a pension and profit-sharing account that has always been at a particular firm. House accounts continue to generate commission business, but the allocation of production credits is generally lower than the ordinary allocation; for example, 10% rather than 25%, or it is used by the branch manager in return for favors.

HOUSE CALL
Wall Street euphemism for a margin maintenance call; that is, a request for additional funds in a margin account to meet either the firm's or the industry's maintenance requirements.

Antonym: T-Call; that is, a request for funds to meet an initial margin requirement on a purchase or short sale as required by Regulation T of the Federal Reserve Board.

HUMPTY DUMPTY BOUNCE
Taken from the nursery rhyme, this is a lighthearted allusion to corporate management's ability to write-down (write-off) large losses and expenses in one accounting period—thereby virtually assuring the next quarter's earnings will look very positive. For example, an automotive company closed a plant and stopped research on a particular vehicle and took a $500 million loss this quarter.

Such write-offs are not illegal and make a lot of financial sense, but they do make it difficult to compare corporate quarterly figures.

"HUNKERING DOWN"
Street jargon used by traders to signify an ongoing endeavor to lower one's risk in a position. For example, a trader, to accommodate a customer, took a large position in a stock; now he or she is trying to gradually sell off the position to lower risk exposure.

From "hunkers"; that is, one's haunches. To hunker is to squat on one's heels—and by analogy, to protect oneself by lowering one's profile.

HYBRID INVESTMENT
A trading vehicle whose investment value depends on more than one type of convention or supply/demand coalescence. For example, a futures or option contract whose value is related to supply/demand vectors and forces in its marketplace but whose ultimate value is dependent upon an equity, debt, or index fluctuation in another marketplace. Thus, a divergence in market prices may create arbitrage situations (profit) or increase risk exposure.

I

IDB
See INDUSTRIAL DEVELOPMENT BOND.
See INTER-DEALER BROKER.

IDBI
See INDUSTRIAL DEVELOPMENT BOND INSURANCE COMPANY.

IDD
Acronym: Index Disclosure Document. IDD is a special explanation of the features that surround Index Participations (IP). This document supplements "Characteristics & Risks of Standardized Options." This is the document that must be presented to a prospective options customer prior to approval by a registered options principal and the transaction of option trades in the account.

IDIOT
Tongue-in-cheek acronym: Institutional Detection of Inside-Information Offices and Techniques. The term, which represents a hypothetical governmental office, was coined by counsel representing investment banking firms and is an attempt to spoof regulatory criticism of the financial industry in the light of trading scandals. Congressional calls for more compliance and greater surveillance to detect improper use of nonpublic information prompted this suggestion for a formalized governmental group to oversee the investment banking activities of broker/dealers.

IIEDS
See INDIVIDUAL INVESTOR EXPRESS DELIVERY SERVICE.

IMA
See INTERNATIONAL MARKET AGREEMENT.

IMBALANCE OF ORDERS
This term is used to describe a premarket opening situation on an exchange. There is an overabundance of either buy or sell orders for a security and the amount is such that it overwhelms the specialist's ability to establish a balance between supply and demand. In this circumstance, the specialist will announce on the tape that contra orders are needed to set a fair opening price. The tape announcement could appear:

LMN   OPENING DELAYED INFLUX OF BUY ORDERS

This will tell interested sellers that they may be able to sell at a substantial profit on the market opening.

IMMEDIATE REPORTING ON QUOTE
See IRQ.

IMMUNIZATION
Term used in bond portfolio management when interest-rate risk has effectively been removed from the portfolio. The strategy takes place when the portfolio manager so adjusts the duration of portfolio bonds that it conforms to the time when the manager will need the funds in the account. In this way, any principal loss caused by a rise in interest rates will be offset by increased return from the reinvestment of the cash flow (coupon interest) at higher than anticipated rates. Immunization is not easy to attain because bond duration can vary with the maturity time of bonds, their coupon rate of interest, and prevailing competitive interest rates.

IMRO
Acronym: Investment Management Regulatory Organisation. This is an SRO in the United Kingdom under the Financial Services Bill. IMRO has supervisory authority over investment managers, advisors, trustees of collective investment plans, and pension fund administrators who join the industry trade group.

INADVERTENT RESTRICTED STOCK
Expression used when an insider buys stocks of a publicly traded company and uses stock of the insider's company to pay for the stock. If the seller accepts this form of payment—in effect a swap in kind—the stock thus acquired continues to be restricted. Such stock may be sold only after it has been held at least two years.

"IN AND OUT" COVERAGE
An International Stock Exchange of the United Kingdom and the Republic of Ireland term for the insurance coverage required for its members. In effect, this coverage is a fidelity bond protecting customers of members against improper activities by officers and employees of the members. Minimum coverage of any member is 100,000 pounds sterling.

INCREDIBLE JANUARY EFFECT, THE
Title of a book written by Robert Haugen and Josef Lakonishok in which they expound this theory: investor returns in January of any year are greater than the combined returns of the other 11 months of that year. The authors contend that this is not a US phenomenon but is worldwide—even in countries without a capital gains tax.

INCREMENTAL RETURN WRITING STRATEGY
See GRADUATED CALL WRITING

INDEMNIFICATION
In a contractual relationship, indemnification is the assurance by one party that it will make whole the other party under certain circumstances. In the securities industry, the term is used primarily of underwriting agreements in which the issuer guarantees to indemnify the members of the syndicate if suit is brought that questions the legality of the offering.

See LETTER OF INDEMNIFICATION.

INDEX ARBITRAGE
General term used to describe a trading tactic whereby "baskets of stocks" and stock futures contracts are bought or sold, or both, according to their deviation from a recognized stock index. Generally stocks are bought and futures are sold—or vice versa—so one position hedges the other. The tactic is called an "arbitrage" because there is a locked-in profit that can be made.

INDEXATION
The act of forming an equity portfolio in such a way that it will track a pre-established index used as a benchmark. The act of indexing need not mirror the components of the index—just its performance.

In general, indexation is often called "passive portfolio management," as opposed to active portfolio management whereby the portfolio manager endeavors to outperform a pre-established index.

Portfolio charges, management fees, and other overhead costs will often make it impossible to mirror the results of the index. See FRICTIONAL COST for a further explanation of this concept.

INDEXED BOND
A debt security whose principal amount at maturity (no matter whether it be zero-coupon, fixed coupon, or variable coupon) is linked at the time of maturity to value of a specific commodity. This commodity could be gold, silver, crude oil, and so on.

For example, Goldman Sachs underwrote a bond for Standard Oil (Ohio) that is pegged at maturity to the value of West Texas Intermediate crude oil.

INDEX FRONTRUNNING
Frontrunning can be a form of price manipulation. It occurs if someone with prior knowledge of what another is going to do acts before that person in order to profit. Thus, if a broker/dealer knows that a client is

about to enter an order for an index option and aggressively buys the underlying stocks or buys the option first so the client pays more, the broker/dealer would be frontrunning.

This term is also used of index futures and the underlying basket of stocks (depending on the valuation of the stocks in terms of the index futures) and their subsequent purchase or sale based on a knowledge of client intentions. It is not frontrunning to anticipate the activities of others through proper market analysis.

INDEX PARTICIPATION (IP)
A generic term for a broad-based option encompassing a basket of common stocks. Most index participations are based on stocks found in the S&P 500 or the Dow averages.

For example, the Philadelphia Stock Exchange calls its version Cash Index Participation (CIP); the American Stock Exchange calls its version Equity Index Participations (EIP); the CBOE calls its version Value of Index Participations (VIP); and the NYSE calls its version Exchange Stock Participations (ESP). This latter index participation is comprised of 462 Big Board issues and 38 non-Big Board issues. They are all subject to a court-issued injunction because of their similarity to futures contracts.

INDIVIDUAL INVESTOR EXPRESS DELIVERY SERVICE
Also known as IIEDS, this is the official title for the NYSE's Rule 80 A. This rule is also known as the "side car" rule.

In effect, the rule says that, if the S&P Index or the Dow Jones Industrial Average rises or declines by a predetermined amount on the same day, institutional program orders entered via the DOT system will be rerouted for five minutes to give ordinary customers execution priority.

INDIVIDUAL REVERSE MORTGAGE ACCOUNT
See IRMA.

INDUSTRIAL DEVELOPMENT BOND INSURANCE COMPANY
Abbreviation: IDBI. A bond insurance program sponsored by Corroon and Black, with policies written by Continental Insurance Company.

IDBI assures payment of both interest and principal for qualifying industrial and commercial development projects. Once so insured by IDBI, the bonds have the highest rating.

INFRASTRUCTURE
Generic term for the fundamental facilities provided by a municipality for its citizens. Included are roads, communications, sewers, schools—in other words, facilities provided by the capital, rather than the operating

budget, of the municipality. In times of budgetary crises, it is often easier for politicians to neglect the infrastructure, rather than tighten the belt in operating expenses. This often leads to neglect of the infrastructure.

The term is often used in an Official Statement of a municipal bond issue to discuss a municipality's growth, the use of funds from the issue, or in anticipation of later problems and the need for more funds to repair the infrastructure.

INITIAL PUBLIC OFFERING
IPO is used to describe an issuer's first public offering of a security of any class, although the term tends to be limited to common stock. The term is also used to designate an offering of previously authorized but unissued securities.

IN-PLAY
Term used by arbitrageurs and finance associates to describe a company that is a prime target for a takeover, either hostile or friendly.

Thus, to make a takeover attempt attractive to current shareholders, an offer is made substantially above the current market. This will draw others in to buy the "cheap" shares, or to make a counter proposal at a higher price. In this way, the company is "in-play."

INS
Acronym: Institutional Net Settlement. INS is an extension of the Talisman service on the International Stock Exchange of the United Kingdom and the Republic of Ireland for institutional investors. INS is similar in function to DTC in the United States: it permits institutional investors to settle trades at the end of the account period by a single difference check, despite the fact that they may have made many trades through many brokers during that period.

INSEAD
Acronym: Institut Europeen d'Administration des Affaires. INSEAD is a leading business school located outside Paris and is renowned for its on-campus business executive programs.

INSTITUT EUROPEEN D'ADMINISTRATION DES AFFAIRES
See INSEAD.

INSTITUTIONAL HOLDINGS CMOS
See PLANNED AMORTIZATION CLASS BONDS.

INSTITUTIONAL CD
Generic name for any certificate of deposit in denominations in excess of $100,000—the upper limit of federal deposit guarantees. Sophisticated institutional buyers of such instruments are usually more sensitive to the credit rating of the issuing institution than are typical public banking customers.

INSTITUTIONAL INVESTOR
Although individual brokerage firms may use different dollar parameters for this classification, the most typical designations include:
1. A bank, savings and loan, insurance company, or registered investment company with assets of $100 million or more.
2. A registered investment advisor with more than $100 million under management.
3. A person, either natural or legal, with total assets of at least $100 million.

The definition, therefore, is sufficiently broad to include individuals, partnerships, corporations, or trusts with substantial investible funds. If a brokerage firm handles both retail and institutional business, there is usually a different sales and support service for institutional clients.

INSTITUTIONAL NET SETTLEMENT
See INS.

INSIDER TRADING
This expression implies the use of material nonpublic information to make a securities transaction (either a buy or a sell) thereby working to the detriment of the contra party who does not have this information. Such use of inside information can be construed as a violation of the Securities and Exchange Act of 1934. To violate the law, the user of inside information need not be an affiliate of the company or a member of his or her family. Tippees and others who have received and used the inside information in a clandestine manner have also been judged to have violated the law.

INSIDER TRADING SANCTIONS ACT OF 1984
An amendment to the Securities and Exchange Act of 1934. Under this amendment, the SEC may seek civil or criminal penalties, or both, against:
1. Anyone who purchases or sells securities while in possession of material nonpublic information.
2. Anyone who communicates material nonpublic information to someone who buys or sells securities.

3. Anyone who aids and abets someone in the purchase or sale of securities while possessing material nonpublic information.

Fines may be levied up to three times the amount of the illegal profit gained (or losses avoided). the law is also applicable to derivative products.

INSTANTANEOUS INDEX
This is a gauge of price movements of 50 issues traded on the Paris Bourse. From 10 A.M. until 5 P.M., this index reflects price movements on a real time basis; hence, its name. It was originally conceived as an improvement on the CAC Index, but in practice the CAC 40 remains more popular than the innovation.

INTEGRATED SECURITIES COMPANY
A designation used by the Japanese Minister of Finance to identify those securities firms licensed to engage in all four categories of securities business, which are:
1. Dealing; that is, to act as a principal in the trading of securities,
2. Brokerage; that is, to act as an agent in the execution of customer transactions,
3. Underwriting; that is, to engage in financings and refinancing through public offerings,
4. Selling; that is, to make retail offerings of publicly traded securities.

INTER-DEALER BROKERS (IDB)
A British term used to designate intermediaries who effect transactions between primary dealers in English government securities. They are similar in functions to "brokers' brokers" in the United States in that they are used to maintain anonymity between transactors and receive a fee for their services.

INTEREST
1. Money paid for the use of money. In general, debt instruments and other loans have a predetermined rate of interest that is to be paid for the use of borrowed money. The rate may be fixed, variable, or zero depending on the indenture. Debts whose interest is not paid in a timely fashion are said to be in default.
2. Used to describe an equity participation in a partnership; for example, a partnership interest.
3. Used synonymously for an intent to buy (or sell); for example, the registered representative canvassed his or her clients for indications of interest in a new public offering.
4. Used to describe a benefit that may accrue from some action or activity; for example, "Jim could not become engaged in the sale because of a conflict of interest."

INTEREST EQUALIZATION TAX (IET)
A special excise tax on the purchase by US citizens of foreign securities from foreign owners. The law was designed to curb the outflow of capital from the United States. The law was repealed in 1974.

INTERMARKET FRONTRUNNING
The term refers to transactions in index futures that are initiated when one hears of an impending index program execution in the stock market; in effect, the index future action is taken in anticipation of the effect that will be caused by the stock transactions.

Such activities may be in violation of NYSE rules, which are validated by the SEC. It is anticipated that the CFTC will also make the action unethical.

INTERMARKET SURVEILLANCE INFORMATION SYSTEM
See ISIS.

INTERNATIONAL FEDERATION OF STOCK EXCHANGES
See FIBV.

INTERNATIONAL FUND
An investment company or managed pool of investments whose portfolio is comprised of securities denominated in other currencies than U.S. dollars.

INTERNATIONAL MARKET AGREEMENT (IMA)
A contract between the Options Clearing Corporation (OCC), the American Stock Exchange (AMEX), and the European Options Exchange (EOE). Under IMA the terms are set forth under which the EOE will trade the AMEX's Major Market Index (XMI) and such trades will be cleared by the OCC. In this way, XMI became the first international option traded by a link between an American and a foreign securities exchange.

INTERNATIONAL MARKET INDEX
Originated by the American Stock Exchange, this product gauges the market performance of 50 stocks representing 10 foreign nations traded in the United States. In effect, the index is an option with cash settlement traded on the AMEX. It is also called the "ADR Index Option," in that it enables investors to subscribe to foreign issues with their currency fluctuations without the inconvenience of foreign currency conversions.

INTERNATIONAL SECURITIES CLEARING CORPORATION
See ISCC.

INTERNATIONAL SECURITIES REGULATORY ORGANISATION
See ISRO

INTERNATIONAL STOCK EXCHANGE OF THE U.K. AND THE REPUBLIC OF IRELAND
This is the successor organization to the London Stock Exchange. The formal name (popularly abbreviated ISE) was officially adopted following the merger of the LSE with ISRO. The reorganization involved two separate functional responsibilities: as a Registered Investment Exchange (RIE) and as a Self-Regulatory Organisation (SRO).

INTERNATIONAL TIER TRADING
See INTIER.

"IN THE YELLOW"
A United Kingdom term to designate the best bid and offer for a security traded on the SEAQ system (q.v.)

In the SEAQ system, these prices are culled from the other prices offered and displayed against a yellow background to gain the viewer's attention.

INTIER
Abbreviation for International Tier Trading, a NYSE prototype of a trading system designed to facilitate international trading on the exchange.

INTIER is a computerized screen that links marketmakers in international issues and makes it possible for members to deal directly with them from the floor of the NYSE.

INVESTMENT MANAGEMENT REGULATORY ORGANISATION
See IMRO.

INVESTOR
An investor is a general term for anyone who puts money to use in the hope of producing income, interest, or an increase in value.

In practice, the term may be distinguished from a saver; that is, a person who uses money to produce current income without any risk of capital loss. The term is also used in distinction to a speculator; that is, a person who uses money in the pursuit of short-term investment profits.

Unless otherwise stated, it is to be presumed that an investor is not concerned with short-term price fluctuations but has a time horizon of one year or more for the investment.

INVISIBLE CALENDAR
A general term used to describe prospective distributions of securities. The concept includes both issues that have been announced (the visible calendar) and those shelf registrations and other issues that are dependent on changes in the interest rate (the invisible calendar). Municipal securities, in particular, do not need to be registered with the SEC, and their issuance is often dependent on interest-rate changes and the resulting "window of economic opportunity" that presents itself. Such offerings are made quickly and with little prior notification to the financial community.

IOA
Acronym: International Operations Association, a division of the U.S.-based Securities Industry Association (SIA). IOA has a membership of approximately 700 broker/dealers, banks, and institutional investors, and its goal is to help standardize the settlement terms for foreign securities transactions in the United States.

IO/PO
Acronym: Interest Only/Principal Only. IO/PO is a term associated with certain mortgage-backed securities (either MBSs or CMOs) in which interest payments and principal payments are traded separately and independently of one another; in effect, the interest payments are "stripped" from the principal repayment. Such IO/POs have all of the interest-rate risk features characteristic of zero-coupon bonds.

IP
1. See INDEX PARTICIPATIONS.
2. NYSE stock ticker symbol for International Paper, a large manufacturer of paper and paper products found in the Dow Jones Industrial Average.

IPO
See INITIAL PUBLIC OFFERING.

IRMA
Acronym: Individual Reverse Mortgage Account.
IRMAs, originated in England, permit elderly homeowners to borrow up to $1,000 per month against their equity in their home, as long as the borrowers live in the home and are alive. The loan comes due when the

owners decide to sell the house or they die. In this way, elderly persons who are otherwise poor may use part of their equity as collateral while they live. Generally, when the owner dies the beneficiaries have the option of paying off the loan or selling the house (with the IRMA debited against the proceeds) as the estate is settled.

IRMAs are true reverse mortgages; thus, interest accrues against the outstanding loan. Just as monthly mortgage payments cause a mortgage to be paid down, so IRMA monthly payments cause the outstanding loan to go up.

IRQ
Acronym: Immediate Reporting on Quote. IRQ is an electronic linkage of some member firm order departments to selected specialist market-making books on the floor of the NYSE.

Firms and specialists that subscribe to this service can direct orders up to 1,000 shares directly into the system for execution. Buy orders are executed against the offer, and sell orders are executed against the bid—just as they would if sent through the DOT system. The report is simply faster.

In eighth-of-a-point markets, IRQ provides the same price that would be provided were the order sent through a floor broker or the DOT system.

IRREDEEMABLES
In the United Kingdom, these are debt securities with no dated date nor maturity date. In general, such securities are redeemable at the issuer's request or option, or upon special events, such as a takeover.

Such securities are rare in the United States and when extant are called "perpetuals."

ISCC
Acronym: International Securities Clearing Corporation. ISCC was founded in 1985 as a subsidiary of the National Securities Clearing Corporation (NSCC) to support the ever increasing volume of international clearances and settlements.

ISE
See INTERNATIONAL STOCK EXCHANGE. . . .

ISE/NIKKEI 50
An index of 50 Japanese common stocks based on their prices.

The ISE/NIKKEI 50 is picked up each day in Tokyo by Nihon Keizai Shimbum (NIKKEI), follows these stocks as they are traded on the Tokyo Stock Exchange. When the Tokyo Stock Exchange closes, the index value is picked up by the ISE (International Stock Exchange of the United Kingdom and the Republic of Ireland), where trading in these same stocks continues through SEAQ International.

In effect, ISE/NISSEI is a global index monitored for more than 12 hours on each market day.

ISIS
Acronym: Intermarket Surveillance Information System. ISIS is a data base of trading information maintained by the surveillance departments of the various stock exchanges in the United States. In effect, each exchange can match trade information—including contra parties—and thereby analyze such information for possible trading violations by market participants.

ISRO
Acronym: International Securities Regulatory Organisation. ISRO is a professional trade association of U.K. brokers and dealers who participate in nondomestic debt and equity and options transactions. ISRO has applied with SIB as an SRO under England's Financial Services Bill of 1986.

ISTANBUL STOCK EXCHANGE
This bourse is intended to deepen Turkey's capital markets. Trading is from 9:30 A.M. until 12:30 P.M. each business day, with after-hour activity permitted. Settlement is scheduled for the third business day following the trade date.

This market was reopened in 1985. It is relatively inactive because it is dominated by banking interests.

ITAAWASE TRADING
This is a proposed method of trading commodity future contracts in Japan. It is similar to the auction markets in the United States in that it publicizes contract prices and quantities. Then, when contra offers are received, they are transacted and the trade completed. In effect, the Itaawase trading method provides a continuous market.

See ITAYOSE TRADING.

ITAYOSE TRADING
In this method of trading—which is used both on the commodities exchange in Japan and in the afternoon (1–3 pm) session of the Japanese exchanges—orders to buy and sell are accumulated until a single price can be set that will satisfy both supply and demand. This results in a single trade price for that issue or contract on that day.

J

J

The tenth letter of the alphabet used:

1. Uppercase as the NYSE symbol for Jackpot Enterprises, a large manufacturer of slot machines.
2. As the fifth letter in the symbol of certain NASDAQ/NMS equity securities to designate that the stock is issued by a quasi-governmental entity. For example, SLMAJ is the publicly owned common stock of Student Loan Marketing Association, an agency founded to fund, promote, and guarantee loans for college educations.

JACUZZI LOAN

Tongue-in-cheek term for an uncollateralized loan that is both weak and easily subject to default. The analogy: the lender's money could easily flow "down the drain" just as the water in a Jacuzzi.

JANUARY EFFECT

See INCREDIBLE JANUARY EFFECT.

JAPANESE DIVIDEND ROLLOVER

Also called a "dividend capture." In effect, the technique is based on one of the vagaries of Japanese tax law, which permits dividend payouts but not capital gains payouts under certain circumstances.

Under the rollover (capture), a Japanese insurance company buys a high-yielding American stock before ex-dividend date (thus, it gets a dividend) and sells the stock almost immediately for seller's option delivery after the record date. The negotiated price of the sale is such that there is a capital loss approximately equal to the dividend gained. The dividend is converted to yen and distributed to the policyholders of the insurance company.

JAPAN INDEX

This is an AMEX option product. The underlying for the option is the closing price of 200 stocks traded on the Tokyo Exchange. Calculated in yen and translated into dollars, the index then becomes the basis for the strike price and premium. This contract is traded on the floor of the AMEX.

JAPAN SECURITIES CLEARING CORPORATION (JSCC)

JSCC is the Japanese counterpart of SIAC and DTC in New York. Membership in JSCC is limited to members of the Tokyo Stock Exchange.

JSCC serves as a clearing and settlement facility for all securities (including bonds, warrants, foreign issues, and the like) traded on the Tokyo Exchange.

JASD
Acronym: Securities Dealers Association of Japan. Although that is its technical name, the association is almost universally referred to as JASD. It is similar in function to the NASD. Although membership is optional, the JASD was authorized in the Japanese Securities and Exchange Act of 1973 and all trade practices in Japan are regulated by the JASD.

JASDEC
Short name for the Japanese Securities Depository Center.

JASDEC is an adjunct of the Tokyo Stock Exchange and was founded in 1984. Its purpose is to compare and settle members' transactions. It is similar in function and scope to the DTC in the United States.

"JEEP"
Slang based on the first two phonemes of GPM, an acronym for graduated payment mortgage. Under a graduated payment mortgage, payments in the early years are lower than in the intermediate and later years.

GPMs are also known as "GYP-UMs."

JEWISH DENTIST DEFENSE
An antitakeover defense developed by Joseph Flom, a partner in the law firm of Skadden Arps Slate Meagher and Flom.

When Sterndent, a dental supply company, was threatened by a takeover by Magus, a Kuwaiti concern, Flom had customers and suppliers complain that they did not want to be owned by an Arab firm. Magus then reconsidered its proposal and backed away from its intended takeover—hence the name.

JGB
Acronym: Japanese Government Bonds. These yen-denominated debt securities are issued by the Imperial Japanese Government to finance its budgetary programs. JGBs are similar in stature in Japan as U.S. government bonds are in the United States.

JITTERS
See MARKET JITTERS.

JOHANNESBURG STOCK EXCHANGE
The JSE is open for trading from 9:30 A.M. until 1:00 P.M., and again from 2:00 to 4:00 P.M. After-hour trading in gold shares is permitted for overseas orders. Regular way settlement is on the seventh business day following the trade date.

The JSE is noted for illiquidity because of USA (Union of South Africa) rules governing the flight of capital from the country. In practice, the greatest number of stocks traded represent gold mining shares. Many USA gold mining shares are available in ADRs and are actively traded OTC in this country.

JSCC
See JAPAN SECURITIES CLEARING CORPORATION.

JUBILEE
See YEAR OF THE JUBILEE.

JUMBO CERTIFICATE
1. The form of security custodial service whereby the DTC holds in the nominee name of CEDE large deposits of securities made by members of the Depository Trust. These certificates may be of varying sizes. Nothing prevents, for example, securities owned by the customers of Merrill Lynch from being comingled with those owned by customers of Salomon Brothers. Having thus formed a jumbo certificate, DTC on its own books lists the amount attributable to the individual member firms.
2. The certificate that is evidence of time deposits in denominations of $100,000 or more. Such certificates generally have a coupon rate of interest, a fixed maturity, and are readily negotiable.

JUNIOR SECURITY
From the Latin, *juvenis*, meaning younger.
1. Used absolutely of common stock, the security that has the last claim on corporate assets in the case of dissolution of the company.
2. Used relatively of any security that is subordinate to another in its claim on corporate assets. Thus, debentures are junior to secured bonds, preferred stock is junior to any debt security, and so on.

K

K
Eleventh letter of the alphabet used:
1. Lower or uppercase to signify 1,000. From the Greek, *kilion*, a thousand. Used with an Arabic number, it multiplies that number by 1,000; for example, 24K = 24,000.
2. Uppercase in computer language to designate a kilobyte.

3. As the fifth letter in a NASDAQ/NMS symbol to designate a nonvoting common stock; for example, PHELK designates Petroleum Helicopters' nonvoting common.
4. Alone uppercase as the stock symbol for Kellogg, Inc., a major manufacturer of breakfast products in the Unites States and the United Kingdom.

KABUTO-CHO
Name for the financial district of Tokyo and used in practice as Wall Street is used in the United States to signify the place where financial dealings are conducted.

KAFFIRS
Wall Street slang for South African mining shares as a general class of securities. The word stems from the tribe of native black workers who work in the mines and make them function profitably.

The word was originally used only of the Xhosa tribe in South Africa but eventually came to be used of all black workers. From the Arabic *kafir* (pronounced kay–fear), meaning an infidel or nonbeliever.

KAISHIME GROUPS
Japanese name for groups of stock manipulators who "corner" a specific issue for the purpose of extracting "greenmail" from the management of these companies. In effect, they monopolize the stock and then sell it back to management at a significant profit.

KANGAROOS
Slang term used in a general way to describe Australian common stocks ("ordinaries"). The obvious reference is to the marsupial most closely connected with that continent.

KB BELGIAN INDEX FUND
A mutual fund sponsored by the Kreditbank (KB) of Belgium. The fund is indexed to the market performance of the Brussels Stock Exchange and contains stocks of 22 companies that constitute 75 percent of that market's total capitalization.

KEOGH PLAN
Revised from *Words of Wall Street* because of tax law changes:

Self-employed persons are permitted to make tax-deductible contributions to a retirement plan. The plan may be a defined contribution, a defined benefit, or a profit-sharing plan; this is determined by the owner of the plan and is incorporated into the plan documents.

Defined benefit and profit-sharing plans need legal advice.

Defined contribution plans permit the self-employed person to contribute 20% of gross self-employed income (or $30,000 whichever is less) into a tax-sheltered plan. As with IRA plans, withdrawals before age 59½ are subject to a 10% penalty. Withdrawals based on actuarial expectations must begin the year the owner becomes 70½.

Tax advice is needed by those who are the beneficiaries of another person's Keogh plan.

See also VOCON.

KEYNESIAN ECONOMIST

This financial philosophy is named for its founder, John Maynard Keynes (rhymes with "canes"), a British economist who flourished in the 1930s and 40s. This school of economic thought advocates governmental control of the economy in times of recession by spending and tax adjustments. In effect, Keynesian economic thought makes the government the "employer of last resort" in poor economic times. This school of economy greatly influenced the "New Deal" and the "pump priming" that marked the early days of the presidency of Franklin Delano Roosevelt.

KEY REVERSAL

An expression used by technicians to describe the chart pattern of a stock that *rehit* a record high or low in the stock. A key reversal does not forecast a changing trend; instead, it usually means that there is simply a pause before the stock penetrates the old level high or low.

KICKBACK

1. An illegal rebating scheme.
2. Any systematic program to rebate or reduce commissions charged by a broker to a customer.

In general, a kickback made to influence a decision is considered unethical or illegal. If given because of the volume of business, it may not be unethical.

"KIDDIE" TAX

Jocular term used in conjunction with a feature of the Tax Reform Act of 1986. Under this feature, investment income received by a minor under 14 years of age is taxed as follows:

$1 to $500	untaxed
$501 to $1,000	15% tax
$1,001 or more	taxed at the parents' bracket

The "kiddie tax" does not apply to earned income nor to gift taxes that are paid by the donor.

After the age of 14, the minor (and subsequent major) would pay taxes at his or her bracket on taxable income, although the bracket may be applied somewhat differently if the minor is a deduction on the parents' return.

KISS INDEX
Acronym: Kurs–Information–Service–System.

This long-name title for the index was abandoned some years ago.

See FRANKFURT RUNNING INDEX for more information about the index and its contents.

KLSE
See KUALA LUMPUR STOCK EXCHANGE.

KONDRATIEFF CYCLE
Named after Nikolai Kondratieff, a Soviet economist. In his view, Western capitalist economies are subject to major cycles of 50 to 60 years in duration. Since Kondratieff claims to have predicted the 1929/30 depression and market collapse, it would seem that we are to expect another financial downturn soon.

KOP
The initials designate the three largest rival banks to the Union Bank of Finland. These banks are the Kansallis, the Osake, and the Panki. KOP helped organize the Optionsmaklare, the major equity options exchange in Finland.

KRUGERRAND
Legal tender in the Republic of South Africa, the Krugerrand has a value of RSA 25 rand. The coin contains one troy ounce of "feingeld" (puregold) and thus its value fluctuates as the value of gold bullion fluctuates. In recent years, as a protest against South African apartheid policy, many U.S. dealers will no longer buy (but will sell) this South African coin.

KUALA LUMPUR STOCK EXCHANGE
This exchange was originally affiliated with the Singapore Stock Exchange but is now independent and is the largest securities exchange in Malaysia. The exchange uses an "open outcry" system. There are two trading sessions daily, Monday through Friday. Settlements are scheduled on a weekly basis.

L

L

Twelfth letter of the alphabet used:

1. Uppercase in typewritten manuscript (often with a serif, such as £) to designate pound sterling.
2. Uppercase in typewritten manuscript to designate Italian lira (more common, Lit).
3. As the fifth letter in NASDAQ/NMS symbols to represent nonvoting stock of a government-founded company; for example, SLMAL represents nonvoting stock of the Student Loan Marketing Association.
4. Uppercase as the ticker symbol of Loblaw Companies, Ltd., a major food wholesaler in Canada.
5. Uppercase to represent 50 in Roman numerals, although this is not used to designate securities quantities.

LAFFER CURVE
The graphic expression of an economic theory founded by Professor Arthur Laffer, a government advisor and economist, which holds that there will be a growth in economic output if tax rates—particularly on businesses—are cut. This theory was the foundation of President Reagan's dramatic tax cuts of 1981 and following, and the beginning of "supply side" economics. Unfortunately, neither the president nor Congress was willing to undertake the other side of the theory: the dramatic cut of governmental spending.

LARGE ORDER EXECUTION
See LOX.

LAST DEALINGS
A British expression frequently used on the International Stock Exchange of the United Kingdom and the Republic of Ireland (ISE) to designate trades that occur on the last day of the account period. The account period is usually a fortnight in length and all trades made during that period must be settled at the end of the period.

A LAUGH
Quaint term used by order clerks and stock exchange floor members to signify a fractional price of ½. For example, a price of 22½ could be expressed as "twenty-two and a laugh."

Although the expression was originally intended to be used jocularly, the expression quickly caught on and is now used extensively.

LAUNDER

To "clean up" money obtained illegally through the drug trade or from organized crime. Generally, the laundering is done by so funneling the money through other legitimate businesses that the "paper trail" is very difficult to follow.

The U.S. Treasury requires that all transactions of $10,000 or more in cash be identified on a prescribed form. Nevertheless, it is difficult to trace such laundering.

LAUNDRY BUSINESS

Tongue-in-cheek expression for "wash selling," a market manipulation practice outlawed in the Securities and Exchange Act of 1934. In this context, wash selling describes the practice of creating artificial transactions—usually by buying and selling for your own account in quantity—so unsuspecting investors are brought to believe that an accumulation is taking place prior to a takeover bid. This may push up the price of the security and at that time the wash seller will unload previous holdings at a profit.

LAUTRO

Acronym: Life Assurance and Unit Trust Regulatory Organisation. LAUTRO is a trade association in the United Kingdom that regulates life insurance companies unit trust managers and their trustees. In Britain, a unit trust is similar in form and function to a mutual fund in the United States.

LBO STUBS

These are the publicly owned equity securities of a company after a leveraged buyout (LBO) has been completed and the issuer is now a "private" concern. It is difficult to determine the true value of such minority interests in the absence of a public market for the remaining securities (the "stubs").

LDC

See LESS DEVELOPED COUNTRIES.

LEAD MARKETMAKER

This is a category of marketmaker on the Chicago Board Options Exchange (CBOE) who is authorized to assist the order book official (OBO) in expediting the opening rotation in the OEX (S&P 100 Index) option.

The lead marketmaker is appointed on a month-to-month basis by the CBOE's Market Performance Committee and is obliged to quote firm two-sided quotes and to facilitate customer order imbalances in all OEX index option series that are being traded within a given area of strike prices.

Once the opening rotation is completed, other marketmakers join in the competition for trades.

LEAD REGULATOR
1. In the United States, because of the wide diversity of business done by broker/dealers and the large number of regulators (SROs), it often happens that one regulator investigates and then reports to other SROs. For example, it is not uncommon for the NYSE to investigate an action and then report to other SROs. In this role, the NYSE is the "lead regulator."
2. In the United Kingdom, under the Financial Services Act, each bank, broker/dealer, investment trust, or insurance company has a "lead regulator" appointed to investigate its activities in terms of capital adequacy and good business conduct. Every endeavor is made to avoid a duplication of regulatory oversight by other organizations that may have jurisdiction.

LEAKY LETTER OF CREDIT
Conventional letters of credit (LOC) are often issued by banks in conjunction with the issuance of a security either as collateral or as a guarantee of performance. If the issuing bank is itself a credit problem or has had its credit rating recently downgraded, the LOC is said to be "leaky."

LEASE
A legal contract whereby an owner grants use of its assets for a fixed (time) period for a fixed fee (rent) to a lessor. Such leases may include any asset that is usable. In recent years, there has been an increased use of leases to permit exchange memberships to be used by others for an annual fee. The most common use of leases is in the rental of real estate, and this may include not only the use but also mining rights for oil, natural gas, or other minerals.

"LEG BREAKER"
See SHERIFF.

LEGGING
Jargon for an ultimate two-sided position of which only one side has currently been established. For example, "I'm legging a spread but I only have the long call in place."

The expression may be used of any risk arbitrage (it is presumed that a bona fide arbitrage has both legs in place), an option spread, or a straddle or combination. However, since such two-sided positions are basically "hedged" there is great risk if the legging is delayed.

Antonym: to "take off a leg"; this is the reverse of legging.

LEMON
Quaint expression used to designate any investment or product that gives poor performance or results. The expression can be used of things, whether tangible or intangible; for example "That is certainly one lemon of an automobile," or "My investment in ABC stock turned into a lemon."

LE PETIT BANG
A facetious term used of the French government's attempt to deregulate that country's financial industry. Using methods similar to the British deregulation of 1986, the French government permitted foreign banks and brokerage firms to purchase equity interests in French financial institutions and thus become members of the Paris Bourse.

LESOP
Acronym: Leveraged Employee Stock Ownership Plan. LESOP is a program by which employee pension and profit sharing plans can easily convert or exchange assets for shares in the underlying issuer-employer. This places a large block of ownership in friendly hands and thereby discourages corporate predators.

The leverage arises when the company lends money to the pension plan, or issues convertibles to it with payment made on the installment basis. If convertibles are used, the company purchases a block of common stock in the marketplace and puts them in reserve against a subsequent conversion. Generally, conversion takes place only if a prospective raider comes on the scene to threaten the existing management.

LESS DEVELOPED COUNTRIES
Acronym: LDC.

LDC is a "buzz word" in the financial industry for countries considered economically primitive; that is, with low per capita income, a great deal of inflation, and extensive negative balance of payments and borrowings.

LDCs as a group are often referred to as belonging to the "Third World"; that is, the Industrialized World, the Communist World, and the Third World.

LETTER OF CREDIT
Popular acronym: LOC. A LOC is a document issued by a commercial bank that enables the subscriber to draw monies as needed at the issu-

ing bank. The subscriber pays an annual percentage fee to the issuing bank even if the credit is not used.

LOCs have extensive world usage in commerce, in international business, and are also used extensively by broker/dealers to establish credit with clearing associations. For example, a broker/dealer could provide a letter of credit to the OCC to take care of the varying margin obligations of its positions with the OCC.

LETTER STOCK (LETTER BOND)
Popular term used to designate stocks/bonds that have been purchased privately from an issuer and thus have not undergone the process of SEC registration. As such, both letter stock and letter bonds may be difficult to transfer because the transfer agent knows their restricted status.

Also known as "stock (bond) with an inscription" or "stock with a restriction" because the certificate may be inscribed to designate the fact that they were purchased privately.

The term *letter stock* is so denominated because the issuer will ordinarily require of the private purchaser a letter designating the fact that the securities were purchased as an investment and not for resale.

LEVEL PLAYING FIELD
Expression used to denote equality among competitors in a specific marketplace or under particular market conditions. For example, in a given market environment, all participants should be subject to the same trading rules, the same tax requirements, the same capital requirements, and the same disciplinary risks.

It would violate the concept of a "level playing field" were one nation to have restrictive import quotas while another did not, or for one nation to permit collusion in the fixing of prices while the other does not, or—particularly—to permit "dumping"; that is, sales below cost to gain market share at a disadvantage to the other nation.

LEVERAGED RECAP
Abbreviation for leveraged recapitalization plan. In effect, this is a corporate finance strategy to discourage corporate raiders. Under the plan, a company substitutes as much debt as possible for equity by borrowing and then distributing as much as possible of the company's assets to the shareholders in the form of cash. As a result, the company is now highly leveraged and is no longer as attractive as it originally was to the raider.

LIBERTARIANISM
Although the term is used primarily of those who propose freedom of conduct in any circumstance, or who propose that freedom of will is supe-

rior to any other restraint, the term is also used as an ultimate form of "laissez-faire" capitalism in which all citizens should be permitted to control their own business and social destinies.

LIFE AND UNIT TRUST INTERMEDIARIES REGULATORY ORGANISATION
See LUTIRO.

LIFE ASSURANCE AND UNIT TRUST REGULATORY ORGANISATION
See LAUTRO.

LIFEBOAT FUND
Term used to describe the $20 million financing set up in 1985 to rescue some members of the Kuala Lumpur Stock Exchange who sustained large forward contract losses due to a crisis involving Pan-Electric Corporation. The financing was dropped in 1987 when the involved members were able to unwind their positions.

LIFEBOAT ISSUE
Term used in the United Kingdom for an issue of stock or bonds whose proceeds will be used to save a company that is otherwise sinking into bankruptcy.

In the United States, we use other terms. If bonds, we may call such debt "junk bonds." If stock, it may be referred to as a "bridge financing."

A LIFT
Term used to designate an upward movement in the price of a security because of buying pressure.

In the United States, the term is neutral and descriptive; for example, heavy buying by mutual funds gave a lift to the market.

In the United Kingdom, the term often suggests a form of manipulation in that the buyers are aggressive and are doing so without regard to the fundamentals of the company; for example, speculators are giving a lift to XYZ Company.

LIMITED
1. In the United States, the term is used in conjunction with a partnership interest in an enterprise where the limited owners have no voting privileges and liabilities are limited to the money contributed to the enterprise.
2. In the United Kingdom, an official suffix (abbreviated Ltd.) of a corporation. The concept: owners are limited in their obligations to the

debt of the company. In recent years, the suffix (public liability company) has become common.

3. The name of a large retail ready-to-wear chain store with the NYSE symbol LTD. Official name: The Limited.

LIMIT ORDER SYSTEM
The Limit Order System is an integral part of the Designated Order Turnaround (DOT) system on the NYSE. Under the Limit Order System (LMT), limit orders in quantities up to 2,099 shares are stored and automatically executed if a contra order is available. Upon execution, the system generates a report back to the firm that entered the order.

LINE-OF-CREDIT REVERSE MORTGAGE
A real estate loan that uses the borrower's home as collateral. They are unlike IRMAs, however, in that there is generally no monthly payout; instead, under the line-of-credit reverse mortgage, money may be borrowed as needed for larger expenses. Under such a reverse mortgage, principal and interest are generally deferred until the death of the client or the sale of the residence.

LINKED TRANSACTIONS
See ADJUSTED TRADING.

LISBON STOCK EXCHANGE
One of the smallest and least active of European exchanges, this exchange is located in Lisbon, the capital of Portugal. Trading is from 9:30 A.M. until 1:00 P.M., Tuesdays through Fridays, with after-hour trading permitted. Settlement is scheduled for the third business day following the trade date.

LITTLE BANG
Expression used to describe the legislation in the province of Ontario (Canada) whereby foreign securities dealers were permitted, starting on July 1, 1987, to register in Ontario and to begin to compete for business there. The term is modeled after the so-called "big bang," which originated in England in October, 1986, and which deregulated securities brokers there.

LITTLE DRAGONS
Term used of four Asian nations (Singapore, Hong Kong, South Korea, and Taiwan) who, because of low labor costs, competitive production, and aggressive sales, are a threat to the "big dragon," Japan, on the western rim of the Pacific.

LIVING DEAD
An oxymoron used in two ways:
1. To describe a company on the brink of insolvency; that is, one that is barely operating on a day-to-day basis.
2. To describe a stock price that is not moving as expected. In effect, it is used by RRs as an alibi for a stock they recommended but that is moving sideways, or somewhat down, but not up.

LMN
See LEAD MARKETMAKER.

LMT
See LIMIT ORDER SYSTEM.

LOAFS
A British tongue-in-cheek expression standing for "large open area floor spaces." In effect, the term is pejorative for the large spaces used by securities salesmen and traders in a typical brokerage office.

In the United States, with no pejorative meaning, the term used is *boardroom.*

LOAN CONSENT
The specific approval given by a customer to a broker/dealer whereby the broker/dealer may lend securities to itself or to customers to complete short sales. The loan consent is usually part of the margin agreement form but a separate customer signature is required.

Also called the "stock loan agreement" or the "loan consent agreement."

LOAN STOCKS
In the United Kingdom, where corporate equity is called "shares" and debt is often called "stock," this term is the equivalent of what we in the United States call "debentures." (See DEBENTURES for the British meaning of that term.)

In effect, loan stock is an asset secured only by the general credit of a corporation. In the event of a corporate liquidation, holders of loan stock will be paid off only after all secured creditors are paid, although loan stock owners take precedence over equity claimants.

LOB
Partial acronym for an unsecured *lease obligation bond;* this is a modern term for a debenture whose proceeds are used to build and lease an operating plant for a public utility. If the lessee defaults on payments, the bondholders become general creditors (debenture holders) of that util-

ity. They do not have a specific claim on the asset built with the proceeds of the loan.

LOC
See LETTER OF CREDIT.

A LOCAL
Term associated with a futures exchange member who trades primarily for his own account and risk. The term has longstanding usage on the Chicago Board of Trade (CBT) and the Chicago Mercantile Exchange (Merc). A local, in effect, designates initiation of an "on-floor" transaction for the member, as opposed to "off-floor" transactions sent to the trading pits for execution from a member firm's offices.

LOCH
Acronym: London Option Clearing House. LOCH compares and settles option transactions made by members (or their customers) in the United Kingdom. It is similar in function to the OCC in that it grants and guarantees option contracts and collects margin to assure their validity.

"LOCKED IN" TRADE
Term used of a transaction in a marketplace's automated system. The term is used both of exchange and NASDAQ trades in that both contra parties are automatically "captured," compared, and submitted for settlement.

In such a system, the number of fails and mistaken trades approaches zero because there can be no comparison without both parties to the trade in the system.

"LOLLIPOP"
Street slang for a sucker; that is, a customer who is willing to buy anything offered if it comes with a persuasive story. Needless to say, such persons are frequently duped and lose large amounts of investment funds.

LONDONCLEAR
Written LondonClear, this is an automated clearing facility for CDs traded in the secondary market in London. LondonClear does not charge for the clearing service but does charge a custodial fee. LondonClear is affiliated with Euroclear, a service offered primarily for Euro-issues traded outside the United States.

LONDON FOX
Short name for the London Futures and Options Exchange. London Fox was established to complement activity on the London International Financial Futures Exchange (LIFFE) and specializes in the automated trading of coffee, cocoa, and raw sugar futures. Orders are entered directly into the computer and matched with contra orders; there is no trading pit nor open outcry.

LONDON STOCK EXCHANGE
See INTERNATIONAL STOCK EXCHANGE of the United Kingdom and the Republic of Ireland.

"LOOK THROUGH" RULE
Popular name for SEC Rule 11al-2, which restricts proprietary trading by members and member organizations. In effect, if an associated person of a member firm enters an order, the accepting broker must consider it; that is, "look through" the order, as though it had come from the member firm itself and part of the orders under restriction according to the rule.

LOR PRODUCT
Designation for Leland, O'Brien, Rubinstein, Inc., the creators of Portfolio Insurance and—most recently—SuperShares. Portfolio Insurance and SuperShares are investment techniques designed to appeal to portfolio managers and to enable them to participate in market trends. In practice, Portfolio Insurance causes great market volatility, while SuperShares do not.
See: PORTFOLIO INSURANCE and SUPERSHARES.

LOSS LEADER
Universally applied term that designates merchandise offered at a known loss to entice a buyer into a store in the hope that, while there, the buyer will also purchase other items on which there is a profit.
The use of "loss leaders" is not common in the financial community; but such "lures" are used in terms of "free checking" in exchange for relatively large constant bank deposits, or for lowered securities commissions in exchange for subscriptions to other products and services.

LOX
Acronym: Large Order Execution. A Chicago Mercantile Exchange proposed rule that would permit the off-floor assembly of purchase and sale orders in offsetting quantities. Thus, it would be possible to "cross" such orders on the floor. The cross would be by public outcry, thus brokers with orders could participate in the transaction. Basically, the proce-

dure will be initiated to forestall manipulation and to permit institutional block-size crosses of hedging positions.

LTD
See LIMITED.

LUMP SUM
1. A form of mutual fund investing whereby the initial investment is the only investment (except for dividend reinvestments) made into the fund.
   Antonym: periodic investments, or dollar cost averaging.
2. The payment of a single premium to fund a life insurance policy or a fixed or variable annuity in perpetuity. Subsequent growth is based on the internal return of the policy or annuity.
3. A single payment made from a qualified pension and profit-sharing plan to a retiree or upon separation from the company or termination of the plan. If the recipient is not yet 70½ years old, such lump-sum distributions may be invested in a rollover IRA to continue the tax shelter.

LUFTHANSA SYNDICATION
Tongue-in-cheek term for investment bankers, acting as a team, who flew into Frankfurt, Germany, to launch a deutsche mark debt offering and immediately flew back to Britain. The concept: their efforts in Germany were temporary, but their base of operations (and profits) were elsewhere.

"LULLING LETTER"
Street term for a brokerage firm's letter to a customer on the occasion of a recent investment that lost money. The letter from the firm's management tells the customer not to worry; the next product to come along will probably act better.

The purpose is to placate the customer, to give the customer confidence, and—indirectly—to persuade the customer not to initiate litigation.

LUTIRO
Acronym: Life and Unit Trust Intermediaries Regulatory Organisation. LUTIRO is a trade organization in the United Kingdom that regulates insurance and unit trust (mutual fund) intermediaries in connection with their day-to-day activities in these products. LUTIRO competes with LAUTRO (q.v.) for the same constituency, although their oversight differs somewhat.

M

M
Thirteenth letter of the alphabet used:
1. As a single uppercase letter, M, to designate one thousand as a bond denomination quantity; for example, 50M stands for $50,000 face value of bonds.
2. As a doubled uppercase, MM, to stand for one million. More commonly abbreviated MYN.
3. As a triple uppercase, MMM, to stand for Minnesota Mining, a large manufacturer of adhesives, building products, and so on. MMM is one of the 30 stocks that comprises the Dow Jones Industrial Average.

"MA BELL"
Used by investors and traders alike to designate American Telephone & Telegraph, the world's largest communication network.

The term is endearing and designates the long-term image of the company in its advertising of maternalism and concern for others in the use of the telephone to "reach out and touch someone."

MACARONI DEFENSE
A jocular term for a corporate defense strategy designed to thwart a hostile takeover. It calls for a threatened company to issue bonds that expand to a mandatory higher redemption value when a takeover is proposed by a raider. The expanding redemption value—much like the expansion of cooking macaroni—should discourage an unfriendly merger proposal.

MACROECONOMIST
Academic term for someone who studies, measures, and predicts the flows of funds, goods, and services on a world or national scale. In this sense, a macroeconomist endeavors to measure the economic events that influence financial, political, and social decisions and to quantify growth, recession, surplus, and trends in the big economic picture.

Antonym: microeconomics (also called "fundamental analysis"), which endeavors to measure financial trends in individual corporations.

MACRS
Acronym: Modified Accelerated Cost Recovery System. MACRS (which followed ACRS) was initiated by the Economic Recovery Tax Act of 1981 (ERTA) and modified by the Tax Reform Act of 1986 (TRA).

These acts divide assets into two categories: real and personal. Real assets must use straight-line depreciation. Personal assets are divided

148

into classes (3-, 5-, 7-, 10-, 15-, and 20-year property) and may use accelerated depreciation.

Form 4562 is used for the filing of income tax reports on the depreciation of such properties. Tax advice is needed.

"MAD BOMBERS"
So-called nickname given to foreign firms in Japan engaged in program trading there. The term originated in February 1990 when firms engaged in index arbitrage between the futures and stock markets in Japan sold baskets of stocks on the Tokyo Stock Exchange, precipitating substantial declines in the Nikkei stock average.

MAGIC-T THEORY
This is a market timing technique and philosophy originated by a technical analyst named Terry Laundry.

Simplistically, this theory holds that the market moves up and down for the same time period—only the amount of the upward or downward movement differs. Moreover, the theory holds that there are two highs and lows for each issue each day. Thus, the way to profit is to buy when the volume for the low declines and to sell when the volume for the high declines.

MAJOR LEAGUE BUYER/SELLER
A picturesque term used to describe a buyer or seller of large amounts of publicly traded stock. For example, a person who normally buys blocks in the 6-7 digit quantity is a major league buyer. The same concept applies to large sellers.

"MAKE-UPS"
English slang for a "third-party" settlement. "Make-ups" are frequently used in the tradings of gilts in the United Kingdom if the trade occurs in the same account period. For example, a dealer buys gilts from another dealer and, within the same settlement period, sells them to a third dealer. The buying dealer requests that the gilts be delivered to the third dealer who, in turn, either remits or collects the cost differential from the original buyer.

MANAGEMENT BUY-IN
See MBI

MANAGEMENT BUY-OUT
See MBO.

MANAGEMENT GROUP
Official title for the organization that serves as investment advisor of an investment company. The management group may, in addition to its advisory service, provide the investment company with legal, clerical, public relations, and portfolio execution services.

Often, the management group may advise many funds with differing investment objectives. In this case, such funds may be in the "same family of funds" and may be exchangeable for one another without an additional sales charge.

MANILA STOCK EXCHANGE
The largest of the stock exchanges in the Philippines. Activity is relatively inactive which, in turn, is a manifestation of the political unrest there.

The exchange is open on weekdays from 9:30 A.M. until 12:10 P.M. Settlement is scheduled for cash within five business days.

MANUAL EXEMPTION
This is a privilege that enables broker/dealers to offer unlisted securities to persons domiciled in a state without the obligation of an annual re-registration of those securities. This exemption is permitted because registration is expensive, the paperwork is extensive, and there is no evidence that such constant registration will prevent "penny stock" scams in any event.

This is not an exemption from original registration; just from the onus of re-registration.

MARGIN STOCK
As used in Federal Reserve regulations, this term applies to those issues for which the Federal Reserve allows banks, broker/dealers, and other registered lenders to extend a specified percentage of credit to purchase, carry, or trade in them.

MARKET BREAK
1. Any major decline in an index of selected common stocks. For example, "Bad inflationary figures and persistent high interest rates caused a severe market break today."
2. In the parlance of the SEC, the term is almost exclusively used of the October 19, 1987, 508-point drop in the Dow Jones Industrial Average—the largest drop to date in the history of the NYSE.

MARKET DISRUPTION
A euphemism used by the SEC to describe stock market events of October 13, 1989. When UAL pilots were unable to assemble financing for a

proposed buyout, the DJIA dropped 191 points. It was, at that time, the second worst decline in NYSE history. Because the DJIA quickly made up for the decline, the phenomenon is called a "disruption," rather than a "break."

MARKET EYE
A new financial information service sponsored by the International Stock Exchange (of London) that is designed to augment the SEAQ service but at a lower cost. Market Eye is transmitted by BBC and is received through a special desk top system. Market Eye provides current market information plus statistical data on U.K. equities, gilts, and international issues traded in London.

MARKET INDEX OPTION ESCROW RECEIPT
See MIOER.

MARKETING OF INVESTMENTS BOARD
See MIB.

MARKET JITTERS
A term used by analysts to describe a period of selling that is the result of investor reaction to economic news. This news may be bad, or not as good as expected. During this period, market prices will tend to trend downward. Typically, as investors become fearful—hence the term *jitters*—they will tend to sell until the news becomes better. The term does not endeavor to judge the news itself, but rather the resulting state of general fear that affects market participants.

MARKET PERFORMANCE COMMITTEE
Acronym: MPC. This is a NYSE group of members and allied members who continuously monitor the marketmaking activities of specialists. The group evaluates each specialist unit in terms of trading, price differentials, and liquidity of the market for each stock. MPC has authority to allocate newly listed stocks (or reallocate already listed issues) among the specialist units as they consider this or that unit capable of doing a better job in the public interest.

MARKET SWEEP
A mergers and acquisitions term used in this context: when a tender offer is terminated, the buyer usually has a relatively large portion of the company. At this time, it makes a second offer to institutions at a price that is slightly above the tender price. This moves the institutions to give up their shares and, before the market can react to the end of the tender, the buyer has effective control of the company.

A MARKING NAME
U.K. term for a certificate registered in the name of a bank, broker/dealer, or a nominee other than the beneficial owner.

In the United States, the similar form of registration is called "nominee name" or "Street name" registration.

The term is not used of "book entry" registration.

MARRIAGE PENALTY
The term is used of a quirk in the U.S. tax code whereby married persons who file jointly actually pay more in taxes than they would if they were unmarried and were to file as individuals.

There is no marriage penalty on gift and estate taxes, only on income taxes in certain circumstances.

MARUYU
Term used to describe the Japanese system to encourage savings. Under this system, 80% of the interest paid on deposits is exempt from taxation.

The system began over 100 years ago and centered on accounts with the Japanese Post Office Savings Bank. This central account, in terms of deposits, is about three times as large as the next largest commercial bank in the world. Deposits in other savings banks are also subject to the tax exemption.

MARXISM
A form of economic theory that advocates the collective; that is, public ownership of the means of production. It is similar to Communism, although Communism embraces both the concept of public ownership of the means of production and adds the public planning of production changes and a centralized government (praesidium) to oversee these changes.

The events of late 1989 in Eastern Europe have shown that Marxism is no longer viable in these countries. Whether or not the centralization of political and planning power will also change remains to be seen.

MAS
Acronym: Monetary Authority of Singapore. MAS is a governmental agency that is responsible for the supervision and regulation of the financial industry in Singapore. Originally centered on the regulation of banking, MAS in 1986 also took over the regulation of the securities industry.

MASTER LIMITED PARTNERSHIP
See MLP.

MASTER OF BUSINESS ADMINISTRATION

Common abbreviation: MBA. An intermediate academic recognition between that of BBA (bachelor of business administration) and DBA (doctor of business administration). Generally, MBA candidates must choose between an emphasis in finance, management, or marketing.

In the mid-70s through the 80s, either an MBA or a JD degree was considered a prerequisite to a finance position with most broker/dealers.

In many schools, candidates may also choose to work on a MPA (master of public administration) if they wish to follow a finance career in city or state government.

MATIF

Acronym: Marche a Terme d'Instruments Financieres. MATIF is a futures exchange in Paris where contracts for 7–10 year French government bonds with a nominal 10% coupon are traded. Trades are made in French francs. In the late 1980s, as part of deregulation, foreign investors were permitted to trade these contracts for hedging, speculation, or arbitrage.

MATIF is a competitor in the area of government securities futures with LIFFE (London International Financial Futures Exchange).

MAXIMUM SLIPPAGE

A term used of a corporation that is having great difficulty in preserving its capital. The term, therefore, is an extension of the expression *slippage*—which may occur to any corporation.

Despite the inclusion of the expression *maximum,* maximum slippage does not yet mean that no one will lend it further capital; in effect, the company is not moribund.

MAY DAY

1. Internationally used distress call.
2. Used in the United States to describe May 1, 1975, the day the SEC required that all securities commissions become unregulated and subject to negotiation.

In practice, such negotiation is used extensively in institutional trading and with very large retail accounts. Most retail trades are subject to a prestated "statement of charges" that apply equally to almost all retail trades.

May Day—or its equivalent—has slowly spread to almost all countries with active securities trading.

MBA

1. Initials used to designate the academic achievement of master of business administration (q.v.).
2. Acronym: Merchant Banking Acquisition.

MBEARS

A trademarked acronym originated by Morgan Stanley & Co. for: Municipal Bond Exempt Accrual Receipts. MbearS are similar to Salomon Brothers' M-CATS in that they represent investment interest in municipal securities stripped of their interest payments. MbearS are collateralized by pre-refunded municipals. The stripped interest coupons are then offered in registered format. Buyers get tax-free interest on an annual basis.

MBI

Acronym: Management Buy-In. MBI is the English equivalent of a venture capital investment.

Under an MBI, a group representing capital contributors purchases stock (or even control) in a relatively new enterprise and expresses confidence in present management by retaining it to run the business. The purchase may be of newly issued stock (or even a repurchase from dissatisfied stockholders).

As a general rule, venture capital contributors buy a combination of a marketable idea *and* management; thus, it is uncommon to replace management in these circumstances.

MBO

Acronym: Management Buyout. The term describes the purchase of a company from existing stockholders by current management. The buyout, if it involves extensive borrowing, is also called a "leveraged buyout" (LBO). LBO is more popularly used in the United States, with MBO used more frequently in Europe.

Do not confuse with the infusion of new capital from a venture capital firm; this is called a "buy-in," not a buyout.

MBS

Acronym: Mortgage-Backed Security. The concept of an MBS centers on the pooling of mortgages and their resale in the form of a single security to new owners. Generally, the mortgage originator retains an agency relationship to the pool and processes the mortgage payments but has no principal risk. Principal risk is assumed by the purchaser of the pass-through securities. In many cases, principal repayment and the prompt payment of interest may be guaranteed by a third party. (See GINNIE MAE MODIFIED PASS-THROUGH).

MBS differ from CMO (collateralized mortgage obligations) in that the mortgage originator in a CMO retains ownership but uses them as collateral for additional debt securities.

M-CATS
Salomon Brothers acronym for: Municipal Certificates of Accrual on Tax-exempt Securities. M-CATS represent an investment interest in the tax-exempt coupons stripped from prerefunded municipal bonds. M-CATS are sold in two kinds: coupon M-CATS that provide tax-exempt income; and principal M-CATS that provide capital gains on the discounted principal amounts.

MCS
See MuniComparison System.

"MEATBALL"
Colorful nickname used by traders and salespersons to identify the common stock of Wilson & Co., a meatpacker and a distributor of meat specialties. The nickname is derived from the slang term used to describe one of its products.

MELLO-ROOS FINANCING
Mello and Roos were two California politicians. They sponsored 1982 legislation to foster the development of real estate based on the promise of tax revenues. Although the original bill was intended to foster rural development, nothing in the bill prevents its use to foster urban development, also.

MEMORANDUM OF UNDERSTANDING (MOU)
The term is used to designate an agreement between the SEC and the securities regulators of a foreign country regarding mutual regulatory interests.

At present, only two such MOUs are in effect:
1. With the United Kingdom's SIB that enables U.S. broker/dealers to work in the United Kingdom without regard to that country's unique net capital rules.
2. With Brazil's CVM pledging cooperation in cases involving insider trading, regulatory disclosure, financial qualifications, and some cases of manipulation and securities fraud.

MEMPHIS BOND DADDIES
See BOND DADDIES.

MERC
Popular jargon identifier of the Chicago Mercantile Exchange.

MERCATO RISTRETTO

This is the Italian name for the Unlisted Securities Market, and a common identifier of small companies whose shares are traded (alongside the larger companies traded) on the Rome, Milan, Turin, Genoa, Florence, and Naples stock exchanges. Thus, these shares are not technically *unlisted*; but they have requirements that are substantially below those for full listing, are more speculative, and have greater financial risk.

From the Italian: restricted market.

MERCHANT BANKING ACQUISITION (MBA)

A corporate finance term originated by the First Boston Corporation.

The term embraces a "bridge loan" by an investment bank to a client that enables that client to acquire another company. Later, the loan will be repaid with interest when the client corporation does a long-term financing.

The MBA can be highly profitable for the merchant bank; it achieves an advisory fee, interest on the bridge loan, and usually a profit on the underwriting of the permanent financing.

MEXICAN STOCK EXCHANGE

The name by which this exchange is known throughout the Latin-American world is Bolsa Mexicana de Valores.

Because 10 of its top stocks constitute over half of its market value and are closely tied to the petroleum industry, this exchange is the most volatile of all stock exchanges; although the Austrian Stock Exchange with its 102% change in 1989 runs a close second.

The exchange is open daily from 10:30 A.M. until 1:30 P.M. with no after-hour market activity. Settlement is on the second business day after trade date and is subject to price modifications based on changes in the Mexican peso.

MIB

Acronym: Marketing of Investments Board.

The MIB is a quasi-governmental body established by means of the Financial Services Act (1986) to oversee and regulate prepackaged investments, such as life insurance and unit trusts (mutual funds), in the United Kingdom.

To provide for economies and for efficiency, the MIB was merged into the SIB to function collectively with the Securities and Investments Board (SIB).

MIBOC
Acronym: Marketing of Investments Board Organising Committee. In the United Kingdom, this was the forerunner of the MIB which—in turn—was merged into the SIB (q.v.).

MICROECONOMIST
Academic term for a person who studies, measures, and predicts the fortunes of individual companies. In this sense, the term is used synonymously with *fundamental analyst*.

The term is also used of the study, measurement, and prediction of the financial activities of households (both collectively and as an average). Thus, this study has great impact on marketing projections, changes in market share, spending habits, inventory needs, and so on, of manufacturers and providers of services.

See also MACROECONOMIST.

MIG
Acronym: Moody's Investment Grade.
MIG ratings are given by Moody's to relatively short-term municipal debt issues. The four ratings that are given are:

MIG 1 — Best quality
MIG 2 — High quality
MIG 3 — Favorable quality
MIG 4 — Adequate quality

As with all debt ratings, the ratings are the opinion of the rating service and are subject to review.

MILAN STOCK EXCHANGE
Although it is the largest of Italy's stock exchanges, it has serious problems. Because no law forbids it, insider trading is rampant and much of this occurs outside of regular trading hours (10 A.M. until 2 P.M.). In addition, contract settlements are notoriously slow—often taking six or more weeks to complete (see MONTE TITOLI). Paper flow control is the heart of the problem and no solution is currently in sight.

TO MILK
To exploit. An analogy drawn from the term meaning to extract the nutritional fluid from an udder or breast.

Used in the securities industry in several senses:
1. To extract all of the "good things" from an account or a customer; for example, to milk an account dry.

2. To achieve all of the profit from an investment situation; for example, "He really milked that investment and when he sold there was nothing left for the buyer."
3. To drain all of the information from a source; for example, "They milked that information for all it was worth."

MINI-MAX
A Salomon Brothers procedure that enables investors to benefit from foreign currency fluctuations without exposure to significant risk. This is a currency-linked money market strategy that permits subscribers to choose a minimum return on investment and still have upside potential in the upper end of a specified range. In effect, the investor can choose either the minimum (mini) or the maximum (max) return while Salomon Brothers provides the other side of the range. The strategy combines (1) a foreign currency spot trade, (2) a repurchase agreement of a short-term nondollar instrument in that currency, and (3) a "range forward" currency contract versus the US dollar.

MINI-MAX OFFERING
A variation of a best efforts—all or none—underwriting. In a mini-max, there is a minimum number of shares required for the offering to be effective, but a maximum number of shares that may be sold in the offering. As in a "best efforts" underwriting, the underwriter has an agency relationship with the issuer.

MIOER
An SEC acronym: Market Index Option Escrow Receipt. This is a written representation (escrow receipt) by a qualified bank stating that the writer of an index option has on deposit cash, cash equivalents, and marginable equity securities (or any combination thereof) *equal* to the margin required for the uncovered sale of that index option.

MIRROR SUBSIDIARY
Merger and acquisition term. The term describes the action of an acquiring firm when it places unwanted assets of its target into the shell of a subsidiary corporation at its prevailing book value. The shell subsidiary is then sold and the proceeds used to reduce the debt incurred by the acquisition.

In effect, the acquiring company and the acquired are looked at in a mirror. Those that duplicate activities of the acquirer are packaged and sold.

MISERY INDEX
A graphic representation of consumer discomfort as interpreted by an economist at Prudential-Bache Securities.

It graphs two components together: the unemployment rate (using federal statistics) and consumer expectations of inflation (using University of Michigan statistics). If these two measurements trend downward (i.e., misery is diminished), it is expected that optimism will increase—and so will stock prices.

MITI
Used in Japan to stand for the Ministry of International Trade and Industry.

MITI shares regulatory oversight and jurisdiction of the commodity futures industry in Japan with the Minister of Finance (MOF).

At present, MITI is starting to exercise control of the developing currency futures business in Japan. That business is not yet recognized, but it is rapidly gaining in popularity as giant Japanese trading houses and US FCMs begin to participate in that market.

MLP
Acronym: Master Limited Partnership. An MLP is a legal entity that provides subscribers (owners) with the income flow-through of an ordinary limited partnership plus the marketability feature that accompanies listed stock on an exchange.

The Tax Reform Act of 1986 caused all new MLPs to be taxed as corporations and thus substantially reduced their appeal as a tax shelter.

Unlike regular C-Corporations, MLPs have a limited life span and will, at a point in time, be liquidated.

MOB SPREAD
This is also known as the "munis-over-bonds spread."

In effect, the MOB spread is based on the decimal quotient found when the typical yield on munis of a certain rating and maturity is divided by the yield of Treasuries of similar maturity. At the time of writing, for example, the MOB spread is 0.875; thus, for each $1 of return on a 20-year Treasury, an investor in 20-year AA-rated munis will receive 87.5 cents.

Because the safety of a muni will never reach that of a Treasury, the spread becomes an important factor in investment decisions, tax considerations, and in the purchase or sale (or spreading) of financial futures contracts.

MODIFIED
The term is generally associated with the expression "pass-through," as in Ginnie Mae Modified Pass-Through.

In this context, *modified* means guaranteed; that is, a packager of mortgages originally backed by the Veterans Administration or the

Federal Housing Authority takes the mortgage pool to the Government National Mortgage Association (GNMA). It, in turn, guarantees performance on the mortgages about the prompt payment of interest and the repayment of principal. It does this by guaranteeing that the original backers (VA or FHA) will repurchase the mortgages if there is a default.

Once "modified" by GNMA, the pool and its participations are readily saleable by government securities dealers to their customers. Because this guarantee is not a *direct* obligation of the United States, interest is subject to federal, state, and local taxation.

MODIFIED ACCELERATED COST RECOVERY SYSTEM
See MACRS.

MODIFIED TRADING SYSTEM
See MTS.

MOFTAN
Japanese slang for the individual at a domestic bank, securities firm, or insurance company who has personal responsibility for dealings with the Japanese Minister of Finance (the MOF part of moftan).

The person so designated as *moftan* is expected to keep current with changing events at this governmental agency *and* to be able to influence favorable consideration for his employer. Because of the almost omnipotent power of the MOF, this position is very important.

MONETARIST
A follower of the financial belief that governmental control of the economy should be limited to the control of the supply of money. In effect, a monetarist believes that an annual expansion of—let's say—2.5% in the money supply is desirable. Minor variations are permissible but major incursions either by the Fed or by Congress will adversely affect the economy.

Nobel Laureate Milton Friedman is the name most commonly associated with the monetarist theory of economics.

Also called "monetarist economist."

MONETARY AUTHORITY OF SINGAPORE
See MAS.

MONEY LAUNDERING CONTROL ACT OF 1986
A federal law that criminalizes the knowing participation in certain illegal activities in the transfer of money. The purpose of the law is to deny anyone the right to conceal ownership of unlawfully derived funds or to avoid federal or state reporting requirements.

"MONORY" SICAVs
The term is named after the proponent of a 1979 French law affecting some mutual funds. Under this law, many French mutual funds must have at least 30% of their assets invested in French-issued bonds and 60% in French-issued stocks. This leaves little for foreign investing.

As a result of this dedication to French industry, such mutual funds are a popular investment vehicle for French insurance companies.

MONTE TITOLI
Name given to the Italian system for securities settlement.

The expression, which arises from the Milan Stock Exchange, is an antiquated manual system of trade comparisons and physical deliveries. Although the exchange does have access to both Euroclear and CEDEL settlement systems, any trade processed through Monte Titoli may take months to complete.

MOOCH
1. Noun: any person who invests before he or she investigates because of a desire to profit. For example, "His book is full of mooches looking for a fast buck in penny stocks."
2. Verb transitive or intransitive: to borrow or beg small amounts without the intention of repaying; to steal. For example, "As a broker, she is always mooching from her customers."

MOODY'S INVESTMENT GRADE
See MIG.

MOON BONDS
Bonds that are "far out"; that is, have maturities that are 20 or more years in the future.

MORGAN STANLEY WORLD INDEX
See CAPITAL INTERNATIONAL WORLD INDEX.

MORTALITY RISK
The financial risk assumed by life insurance companies when they write a policy for a fixed premium and a fixed face value on a given individual with his or her actuarial life expectancy. A similar mortality risk is involved when an insuror writes a fixed annuity and guarantees payments for the life of the annuitant, or the annuitant and a survivor. The writer of a variable annuity policy also assumes mortality risk if the annuitant elects to receive payments for life. In the latter case, however, the mortality risk is somewhat lessened because of the variable payouts.

MORTGAGE-BACKED SECURITY
See MBS.

MORTGAGE ENFORCEMENT
Term associated with the pooling of mortgages having similar terms and interest rates for submission to a government agency for approval and guarantee. Once approved and guaranteed, such mortgages are said to be "enforced."

MOU
See MEMORANDUM OF UNDERSTANDING.

MPC
See MARKET PERFORMANCE COMMITTEE.

MSCI
See CAPITAL INTERNATIONAL WORLD INDEX or see MORGAN STANLEY WORLD INDEX.

MTN
Initials used to designate Medium-term Notes. Such MTNs are used to complement an issuer's commercial paper to finance short- to intermediate-term operations. By adding MTNs to its financial debt securities, an issuer can offer debt at anytime, anywhere, and in any currency with maturities ranging from five months to 10–15 years.

Such MTNs are not underwritten; instead, the corporation posts its intended rate, and investment bankers then compete for the right to publicly distribute the paper.

MTS
Acronym: Modified Trading System. MTS is used by the Chicago Board Options Exchange (CBOE) for selected nonequity options.

For most of its options, the CBOE uses order book officials (OBOs) as agents to record and execute options, and it uses market makers (MMs) who act as principals to provide continuous markets and the necessary liquidity.

For certain nonequity options, the CBOE uses a system of designated primary marketmakers (q.v.) to provide a combination of the same functions.

MUD
Acronym: Municipal Utility District. MUDs are political subdivisions set up by municipalities to provide certain utility-related services: wa-

ter, sewers, electric power, fire protection, and so on. As such, MUDs may issue tax-exempted municipal bonds. Bond debt service is provided by a special property tax on the residents of the district.

MULLET
Mullets are thoughtless fish who, apparently, will follow any bait. Thus, this term is used by salespersons for naive, thoughtless investors who will buy anything that is popular with the crowd.

Needless to say, such investors are easy prey for unscrupulous salespersons who are anxious to create unnecessary activity in an account.

MULTI-PART ORDER
A Philadelphia Stock Exchange/Board of Trade creation that permits the simultaneous entry of an order to buy or sell, or both, a stated number of foreign currency option contracts, *and* a stated number of foreign currency futures contracts. Execution of one part based upon a predetermined spread between prices of these contracts is contingent upon execution of the other part of the transaction. Thus, the spreader or hedger avoids a "one leg" execution; in effect, the entire position is put on at once if the conditions are met.

MUNICIPAL ARBITRAGE
This form of arbitrage entailed the issuance of tax-exempted debt at a fixed rate of interest with the proceeds of the offering invested in U.S. government securities at a higher rate of interest. In practice, the two issues would have similar maturities. Because of the difference in rates, and the fact that the municipality did not pay federal taxes, there was a profit for the municipality.

The TRA of 1986 sharply curtailed this practice.

MUNICIPAL BOND EXEMPT ACCRUAL RECEIPTS
See MBEARS.

MUNICIPAL CERTIFICATES OF ACCRUAL ON TAX-EXEMPTED SECURITIES
See M-CATS.

MUNI-COMPARISON SYSTEM
Written as MuniComparison, MCS is a division within Depository Trust Co. (DTC). MCS provides for a broad range of automated validation and settlement procedures between members in a broad range of municipal transactions. This section of Public Securities Depository Trust Co. (PSDTC) provides for book-entry settlements between participating

members; the ability to compare and settle "when issued" bonds; extended settlements, if requested, for regular way and when issued trades.

MUNIFACTS
A subscription service provided by *The Daily Bond Buyer* that disseminates information about municipal securities. Munifacts is similar in format to Dow Jones and Reuters in their respective fields of news.

"MUNI MAC"
Unofficial name for a government-sponsored agency authorized by Congress and modeled after the Federal Home Loan Mortgage Corporation (Freddie Mac).

The purpose of Muni Mac is to purchase and repackage municipal securities, with each "pool" having securities with similar terms. The pools are then securitized and the resulting debt is sold to investment bankers for resale to the public. The proceeds of the sale repays the original purchase price to Muni Mac.

Guarantees, if any, are made by the underlying municipal issuers and not by the federal government. Interest payments retain their tax-exempt nature.

MUNIS-OVER-BONDS SPREAD
See MOB SPREAD.

"MUSICAL CHAIRS" BONDS
A tongue-in-cheek expression for "Zombie Bonds."

MUTATIS MUTANDIS
Latin for a necessary change in terminology caused by differing circumstances but without any alteration in essential points. In form, it is an ablative absolute and thus may stand apart grammatically. For example, a municipal Official Statement is—mutatis mutandis—the equivalent of the final prospectus on a registered offering.

The expression literally means "necessary changes having been made" and is often used in foreign translations or comparisons of substantially similar instruments.

MYRA
Acronym: Multiyear Rescheduling Agreements. MYRA are documents created by financial center banks to rearrange and extend repayments of loans made to governments of countries unable to meet their current obligations. To avoid defaults, Poland, Mexico, Brazil, and Argentina sought relief from their debts in the form of lower current payments for longer time periods.

N

N/A
Initials representing "not available." N/A is used to indicate that certain statistical facts (e.g., price, earnings, and the like) are not available or were not provided. It is also used to designate that a certain issue will not be offered publicly.

NABL
See NATIONAL ASSOCIATION OF BOND LAWYERS.

NAKED SHORTING
See GHOST SHORTING.

NAKED SHORT SALE
A quaint NASD expression for a short sale in which no security is borrowed to deliver to the purchaser. The expression is used of incidental intra-day trades (sales) with no backup inventory. The presumption is that the dealer will offset such short positions with purchases that cover and provide securities for delivery.

Otherwise, naked short selling does not fulfill the SEC and industry definitions of a short sale and may be legally or ethically improper.

NANCY REAGAN DEFENSE
The expression is patterned on the former First Lady's ad campaign against drugs. In effect, when an unwanted merger and acquisition suitor tries to take over a company, the proper defense is "Just say no."

NASDIM
Acronym: National Association of Securities Dealers and Investment Managers. This U.K. group oversees and regulates a significant number of securities firms and investment managers not subject to the jurisdiction of London's International Stock Exchange of the United Kingdom and the Republic of Ireland. NASDIM is comparable to the NASD in the United States and is registered as an SRO under the 1986 Financial Services Bill.

NATIONAL ASSOCIATION OF BOND LAWYERS
Abbreviation: NABL. This is a professional group of law firms that serve as bond counsel to municipal issuers. They serve as a source of information to one another and as a lobby for the improvement of municipal securities laws.

NATIONAL ASSOCIATION OF SECURITIES DEALERS AND INVESTMENT MANAGERS
See NASDIM.

NATIONAL COMPANIES AND SECURITIES COMMISSION
See NCSC.

NATIONAL HOME LOANS
Acronym: NHL.
  See HOMES.

NATIONALLY RECOGNIZED MUNICIPAL SECURITIES INFORMATION REPOSITORY
See NRMSIR.

NATIONAL SECURITIES TRADING SYSTEM
See NSTS.

NCSC
Initials frequently used for the National Companies and Securities Commission. NCSC is the Australian counterpart of the SEC in the United States. The commission supervises the securities industry in Australia and insures the financial integrity of its marketplace.

NDFS
Acronym: Next-Day-Funds Settlement. This is the principal method used by the Depository Trust Co. (DTC) to satisfy member participant securities contracts. Payment is in the form of a paper check, which takes approximately 24 hours to clear at a Federal Reserve bank and to be available for use by the broker/dealer.

NEARBYS
In both futures and options markets, this expression signifies the months closest to expiration (options) or delivery (futures). For example, if it is October and the following futures contracts are trading: January, February, March, June, September, and December, in this context, January and February would be "nearbys."

NEAR MONTH
In commodities and futures trading, contracts that will expire (options) or be delivered (futures) in the next available trading month. For example, it is December 21, and call option contracts in ABC are available for January, February, and April expirations. The January contract is the "near month."

NEO

Commonly used abbreviation for "nonequity options." NEOs are puts and calls on other underlying instruments (or investments) than stocks. For example, NEOs are currently being traded on foreign currencies, U.S. government notes and bonds, real estate debt issues, precious metals, and market indexes.

NET BALANCE SYSTEM

This is a cashiering delivery system in which each firm's daily purchases and sales per issue are "netted" to arrive at a single delivery or receipt requirement. Thus, if Prudential-Bache sells 100,000 shares of IBM and buys 90,000 shares on a single market day, it has a net delivery requirement of 10,000 shares.

Under such a system, the clearing corporation notifies participant firms of its net requirements for that day. It also notifies the firm of the contraparty to all trades.

The term is used in contradistinction to a trade-for-trade settlement system.

NET INTEREST COST

Abbreviated: NIC. NIC is the basis for the awarding of competitive bond issues. Thus, the syndicate with the lowest NIC is typically awarded the issue.

There are different methods of computing the cost of interest to the issuer: NIC and TIC (True Interest Cost).

The NIC formula is:

$$\frac{\text{Total interest payments} + \text{Bond discount (or} - \text{Premium})}{\text{Total bond years}}$$

NET LEASE

A long-term commercial property lease in which the tenant promises to pay: (1) a specific dollar amount to the landlord and (2) to pay all the incidental expenses connected with ownership, such as, taxes, utility costs, repairs, and insurance. In effect, the landlord takes care only of the financing charges, if any, on the building itself. In return, the tenant has possession of the property for its use, and possible renewal privileges, tax benefit adjustments, and—in some cases—property appreciation rights.

Often called "triple net lease."

NET MARGINING

Term used in conjunction with the carrying of positions in futures and options on most commodities and options exchanges in the United States. If net margining is permitted, the carrying firm must provide margin or collateral based on the difference between long and short positions. Thus, if a carrying firm has 1,000 long calls and 1,300 short calls on the same underlying, margin would be required only on the 300 net short contracts.

NETWORKING
Term used of a supporting system of information and service sharing among members of a group that have a common interest. Although nothing prevents networking within an individual firm, or by members of a specific group or department, the inference of the term is that the members of the group—who may otherwise be competitors—work together to share information and promote common interests.

Examples are too numerous to mention and are primarily exemplified by trade associations and by informal personal contacts between persons engaged in similar occupations.

"NEW COLLAR" FAMILY
Tongue-in-cheek expression for young investors who are part of a two-worker family. It is not uncommon for such persons to be employed in high-technology fields in a nonmanagement role; thus, they fall somewhere between "blue" and "white" collar status.

Their economic status is such that they can become emerging investors able to start a program of financial planning.

NEW TIME
An International Stock Exchange of the United Kingdom and the Republic of Ireland term for a transaction (popularly called a "bargain" in the United Kingdom completed on the last Thursday or Friday of an account period which, at the request of the buyer or seller, will be carried over for settlement in the following account period. In this way, the buyer/seller will have approximately 12 business days, rather than 1 or 2, to complete the contract.

The ISE total expression is "dealing on new time." It is negotiated and there is a slight charge, which is normally included in the price of the transaction.

NEW ZEALAND STOCK EXCHANGE
This exchange has four regional trading floors (Wellington, Auckland, Christchurch, and Invercargill). Trading is open from 9:30 to 11:00 A.M. and from 2:15 to 3:30 P.M. After-hour trading is permitted for 30 minutes following each half-day session. Regular way settlement is by delivery versus payment, which in many cases may take up to 30 days.

NHL

See HOMES.

NIC

See NET INTEREST COST.

NICS

Acronym: Newly Industrialized Countries. Term used of four Asiatic countries, Singapore, Hong Kong, South Korea, and Taiwan, that developed into economic powerhouses in the 1970s and 80s. Together with Japan, these countries represent the largest segment of the US balance of payment deficit.

NIDS

Acronym: National Institutional Delivery System. NIDS is a central processing system for COD transactions by customers of broker/dealers in the United States. NIDS is operated by the Depository Trust Co. (DTC) and it confirms, affirms, and settles transactions via book entry between executing firms and their COD customers (or their agents or custodians).

NIKKEI STOCK INDEX

An index of the price movement of 225 high-quality stocks traded in the Japanese marketplace (Tokyo Stock Exchange). It is widely followed by persons interested in the economic movements in Japan, and it is considered a barometer of domestic interest in Japanese equities.

The NIKKEI is also linked to redemption values of some international securities.

NIL-PAID SHARES

Term used in allotment letters in the United Kingdom to describe shares during the interim period between the announcement of the offering and the actual subscription date. During this period, the value of the shares can be both theoretical and the subject of supply/demand forces for the subscription rights. As a result, no money is required for the subscription until such time as the market value of the shares is determined.

1992

This is the year in which all tariffs in the European Economic Community (EEC) will be removed. As a result, members of the Common Market in Europe will be granted equal and free access to each other's markets. 1992 is used to designate a time of wide-ranging change in Europe.

In the United Kingdom, in compliance with the Financial Services Act of 1986, European financial services firms will be able to provide services in the United Kingdom if they provide suitable documentation of their compliance.

NNOTC
Official designation for a non-NASDAQ security. In other words, a NNOTC stock is a corporate equity that is publicly traded and is neither listed on an exchange nor traded on the NASDAQ system.

NNOTC stocks are often referred to as "Pink Sheet" issues and, under Schedule H of the NASD bylaws, are subject to special trade reporting requirements.

NOBO LIST
NOBO is an abbreviation for "non-objective beneficial owner." This is a reference to SEC Rule 14b-1(c). Under this rule, an issuer has the right to demand of a nominee the names of actual beneficial owners of stocks, provided the owner does not object to such disclosure.

"NO BRAINER"
1. Trader's term of a customer transaction that can be completed quickly and completely. Also called, to use a basketball term, a "lay up."
2. A reference to an obvious market trend; that is, one that needs neither technical nor market analysis skill to discern.
3. Any investment procedure that is automatically applied without reference to fundamental or market conditions. For example, "Dollar-cost-averaging and constant dollar plans are no-brainers."

NOB SPREAD
Acronym: Notes Over Bonds Spread. A futures contract based on the relationship between the price of Treasury notes and the price of Treasury bonds. A change in the price spread impacts the shape of the yield curve and, it is believed, reflects investor confidence in the direction of the debt markets.

NON-EQUITY OPTION
See NEO.

NON-RESIDENT ALIEN
See NRA.

"NOOKIE"
Sales and trading slang used to identify the common stock of UNC Resources, Inc., a company engaged in uranium mining and nuclear development. The company's former name was United Nuclear Corporation—hence, its nickname.

NORMAL SCALE
Term used of the offering scale of new serial bonds in which the yield on closer maturities is lower than the yield on farther serial maturities or term bonds, or both.

Antonym: INVERTED SCALE.

NOTARIAL SECURITIES
This is the term used in the financial services industry for an issuer's securities if there is no transfer agent. Notarial securities typically arise if an issuer is bankrupt.

Since certificates cannot be immediately re-registered in the name of the new owner, such securities trade with a stock power attached. The name of the previous owner must be notarized on the stock power to constitute good delivery.

NOTES-OVER-BONDS SPREAD
See NOB SPREAD.

NOTIFICATION
This is the simplest form of blue-sky registration for a public offering within a state. To commence the public offering of securities within a state that permits notification, the issuer need only notify the state's securities commissioner.

NOT TO PRESS
See NTP.

NRA
1. Abbreviation for Non-Resident Alien; that is, an individual or institution with no permanent address or place of business in the United States. If such an individual or institution has an account with a US broker/dealer, it must sign a Treasury Department affidavit (W-8) and thus be subject to certain withholding taxes on dividends and interest received (if the security is subject to such withholding).
2. Often used as NR in newspaper bond reporting columns if a security is not subject to withholding for NRAs.

NRMSIR
Pronounced: NURM-SUR.

Acronym: Nationally Recognized Municipal Securities Information Repository, a term created in conjunction with MSRB Rules G-36 and G-8. Beginning in January 1990, all municipal issues of $1 million or more require an Official Statement (which is comparable to a prospectus).

To make sure that Official Statements are kept for records and proper

owner referral, a copy is maintained by the underwriter and a copy is
sent to an "information repository."

NSE
Initials of the Nagoya Stock Exchange. NSE is the third largest of the
Japanese exchanges (after Tokyo and Osaka and like the others is a
membership exchange with both regular and saitori members responsible for exchange activities.

See also SAITORI.

NSTS
Acronym: National Securities Trading System. NSTS is an automated
electronic execution system used by the Cincinnati Stock Exchange, and
it is used to provide members with agency transactions of up to 1,099
shares at the best available ITS quote prices. Under the system, both market and limit agency orders are matched with contra agency orders at the
same price before pairing them against dealer (principal) orders.

NTP
Acronym: Not To Press. These initials may be added as a qualifier on an
execution by a jobber on London's International Stock Exchange of the
United Kingdom and the Republic of Ireland. They signify that the jobber (marketmaker) has sold short to complete the trade and does not
want (nor expect) the buyer to press for delivery of the shares under
threat of buy-in proceedings. The shares will be delivered in the normal
course of business by a later purchase by the jobber.

NUMBER CRUNCHER
See RACCOON.

NYSE RULE 387
Under this rule, the exchange requires that COD/RVP transactions in
DTC-eligible securities be confirmed, affirmed, and settled through the
Institutional Delivery System (ID). Since most institutions use
COD/RVP trades, compliance with this rule is very important for the
efficient completion of such trades.

O

OATS
Acronym: Obligations Assimilables du Tresor, the treasury obligations
of the French government. OATs are now available in the United States
as ADRs, the first such ADRs created for a foreign debt issue. As such,
the ADRs are denominated in U.S. dollars.

The underlying debt obligations are the 9.80s due 1/1/96 and the 8.50s due 6/1/97.

OBLIGATIONS ASSIMILABLES DU TRESOR
See OATS.

OEX
Ticker symbol and common identifier of the Standard & Poor's 100 Index option traded on the CBOE. Both puts and calls are available at five point striking point intervals and with three months traded at any one time: the current month, the subsequent month, and the following month. Options are American style (as opposed to the S&P 500 Option) and thus may be exercised at any time during the life of the option. Settlement is in cash and is based on the deviation of the strike price from the index value times $100. Thus, if a call at 305 is exercised on a day when the closing price of the OEX option is 340, the writer would be forced to pay the holder 35 x $100, or $3,500. The options are used extensively to hedge or moderate systematic market risk.

O'HARE SPREAD
Facetious floor term used on the Chicago trading floors—whether it be CBT, CME, or CBOE—to designate a spread that goes against a trader; thus, if the trader expects the spread to widen, it narrows, and vice versa.

The concept is simple: the trader is now out of capital and goes to O'Hare Airport to fly out of Chicago forever.

OIL PATCH
Broad description of those areas of the United States that are the principal locations for exploration, drilling, pumping, and refining petroleum products and their derivatives. Offshore drilling is also included in the designation. As a general rule, Texas, Louisiana, Oklahoma, California, and Alaska are considered U.S. oil patches.

The term is also used as the location of economic problems caused by a drop in petroleum prices and the effect on the purveyors of other services and property values in these areas. For example, "There has been a dramatic drop in housing prices in the Texas oil patch."

OLD LADY
Affectionate term in the United Kingdom for the Bank of England. The Bank of England has a place in the economy of Great Britain similar to that of the Federal Reserve in the United States. Thus, it acts as a central bank for the issuance of currency and as a regulator of credit and the

money supply in the United Kingdom—although the Bank of England exercises much more moral suasion over credit than does the Fed.

Also called the "Old Lady of Threadneedle Street."

OM

Acronym for the Stockholm Options Market. OM is a publicly owned trading institution overseen by the Swedish Bank Inspection Board (similar to the SEC in the United States).

Founded in 1985, OM trades in Swedish equity options, interest-rate options, Swedish OMX index options, and index forward options. Unlike U.S. options, *only* covered calls and puts are permitted to be written on stock options.

The index options or forwards may be settled for cash or for shares of a Swedish mutual fund.

ONE DECISION STOCK

Term used of the selection of a "blue-chip" stock for permanent inclusion in one's portfolio. The concept is simple: since there is no intention of selling, only a decision to buy need be made.

ONE SHARE, ONE VOTE RULE

Popular term for SEC Rule 19c-4. Effective July 7, 1988, no US exchange or the NASD may list or provide quotations for any issuer that *reduces* the voting rights of existing shareholders. Thus, no-vote stock or less than equal could be issued, but no stock with "super voting rights."

Super voting right stock issued before July 7, 1988, is exempted. IPOs, secondaries, and securities issued to consummate a merger are also exempted, provided they have no greater vote than other common shares of the same issuer.

ONTARIO SECURITIES COMMISSION (OSC)

The OSC is the counterpart of the SEC in the Canadian province of Ontario. As such, the OSC has official jurisdiction over all securities-related registrations and the dealer and agent activities within its borders. In this role, the OSC also includes jurisdiction over the Toronto Stock Exchange (TSE), the largest of the Canadian exchanges.

ON THE CLOSE ORDER

A customer's order to buy or sell a specific amount of a stock on the NYSE as close as is practicable to the closing bell for trading. No assurance may be given that the order will receive the final price, nor that it will be capable of execution.

Generally abbreviated OTC on the order ticket.

ON-THE-HOP
Trading room term for "immediately." Thus, to get the attention of another trader, a first trader may call: "Pick up XYZ broker on-the-hop."

ON THE OPENING ORDER
A customer's instruction to buy or sell a specific amount of a stock on the NYSE, but only as part of the initial transaction for that security on that market day. If the order cannot be executed in this fashion, the order is to be cancelled immediately.

Do not confuse the concept of "On the opening," which is a customer instruction, with the rule that all *market* orders received before the opening must be included in the opening transaction. Limit and stop orders need not be so included.

ON-THE-RUN ISSUES
Government securities trading term used to designate newly issued securities for which the firm intends to make a continuous market. The most popular on-the-run issues are newly issued governments and those with 5–7 year maturities.

OPEN 10 TRIN
A variation of the TRIN index as developed by Peter Eliades, the publisher of *Stockmarket Cycles*, a financial newsletter. This development incorporates 10-day moving average figures into the TRIN calculations, thereby tempering the volatile effect of a single good or bad day into the chart. The net technical effect, however, is the same: entries above one are bullish and entries below one are bearish.

OPERATOR
1. The person who drills, completes, manages, and, in general, oversees the production of oil or natural gas wells.
2. The person who inputs/outputs a computer or other form of electronic equipment.
3. A derisively used term for an overly aggressive salesperson, or a promoter of dubious investments, or who, in a work environment, is overly political and self-seeking, rather than a cooperator with the group.

OPINION SHOPPING
Under SEC rules, every issuer registered with the SEC must have an audit of its books by an independent public accountant. Should that accountant want to "qualify" its findings, management usually reserves to itself the right to seek another accountant for a "clean opinion."

The seeking of a second, more favorable, opinion is sarcastically called "opinion shopping."

OPTION CYCLE

The expiration months normally used for the setting of option series trading. There are three cycles used for equity options:

JAJO — January, April, July, October.
FMAN — February, May, August, November.
MJSD — March, June, September, December.

When a company's options begin listed trading, the options are assigned to a cycle.

In practice, all listed equity options trade: the current month, the subsequent month, and the next month in the cycle. Thus, a stock in the MJSD cycle, if it is before the June expiration date, would trade June, July (next month), and September (next month in the cycle).

Index, debt, and currency options trade continuous months.

OPTION MARGIN

The margin that the buyer of an option must put up, or the margin that a naked option writer must put up and maintain.
1. All long options require a one-time payment of the option premium in full.
2. Short uncovered equity options, if listed, require the premium plus 20% of the underlying if the option is in- or at-the-money.

    If out-of-the-money, the margin is the same, except that it is marked to the market and the out-of-the-money amount is subtracted. However, the minimum is the premium plus 10% of the underlying.

    The same requirements apply to narrow-based index options.
3. Broad-based index options use the same principle, but the initial amount is the premium plus 15% of the underlying. If marked to the market, the minimum is the premium plus 10%.
4. The margin on short straddles and combinations is the margin on the side with the greatest requirement (see #2) plus the premium on the other side.
5. The margin on vertical bullish call spreads and bearish put spreads is the net debit on the spread.

    On other vertical spreads, if the short option is uncovered, the margin is *either* the dollar difference between the strike prices, *or* the margin on the short "leg" (see #2)—whichever is less provided the short call expires at or after the long call.
6. Specific advice is needed on debt and currency options. Similarly, advice is needed on "strangles" (a short combination with the short call covered), or on "ratio writes."

OPTIONSMARKLARE
The name of the options exchange established in Finland to compete directly with the Swedish options exchange (Optionsmarknad, or OM).

The Finnish exchange was organized by three banks, Kansallis, Osake, and Pankki (KOP), and will initially permit the trading of five call options and one index option on Finnish stocks.

ORDER SPLITTING
Term associated with the NASD's Small Order Execution System (SOES). SOES permits the automatic execution of up to 1,000 shares of stocks traded on the NASDAQ/NMS and up to 500 shares of other NASDAQ-traded stocks.

The concept is important because the NASD forbids members from splitting up customer orders into pieces small enough to be executed automatically by means of the SOES system. This is only fair: the market-makers are providing a service for small orders, not a method of breaking up blocks of buy/sell orders.

ORIGINATOR
1. A nonfinancial corporation that is the issuer of a security.
2. A broker/dealer who, in a best-efforts underwriting, does not guarantee to purchase shares it is unable to sell.
3. An employee of a broker/dealer, investment advisor, or fiduciary, who creates an investment position either by developing a security with unique terms (e.g., CATS, MbearS) or by acting as an intermediary between an issuer and a customer.

ORPHAN STOCK
Tongue-in-cheek expression for a company not covered by a research analyst. Hence, its story is never published, and its stock is never recommended. In general, the stock is neglected by investors who tend to follow recommendations made by research analysts.

ORPOS
Acronym: Office of Regulatory Policy, Oversight, and Supervision. ORPOS is a department within the Federal Home Loan Bank Board (Freddie Mac) responsible for establishing loan guidelines, investment policies, and underwriting criteria for member banks of that system.

OSC
See ONTARIO SECURITIES COMMISSION.

OSE

Initials used for the Osaka Stock Exchange, the second largest exchange in Japan and a major participant in stock index market. In terms of national importance however, the OSE is a distant second to the Tokyo Stock Exchange.

OSLO STOCK EXCHANGE

This Norwegian stock exchange is all-electronic and relies heavily upon foreign activity for its existence. It is open on weekdays from 10 A.M. until 3 P.M. although over-the-counter activity may continue as long as there are contra parties willing to trade. Settlement is on the fourth business day after the trade date.

The Oslo Stock Exchange is the smallest of the Scandinavian exchanges.

OUT OF LINE

Term used of the price of a security, either a stock or a bond, that is substantially higher or lower than the price of similar securities trading in the marketplace.

The term may also be used of classes of securities; for example, the current yield on 20-year municipals is "out of line" with the traditional yield spread between municipals and Treasuries.

OUT THE WINDOW

A slang expression used by investment bankers to designate the fact that a new issue sold rapidly and there are not more shares or bonds remaining.

The concept implies that the issue was priced correctly or even slightly below the price that would be indicated by the demand. Of itself, the term does not imply that the aftermarket price for the security caused it to be a "hot issue."

OVERREACHING

An expression used to describe the unethical action of a broker/dealer who executes a transaction as principal at a price that is less favorable than the price that would have been obtained had the broker/dealer acted as an agent.

In the past, dealer markups (markdowns) were not included as a separate entry on customer confirmations; thus, they were to an extent "invisible." New SEC regulations require that dealer markups and brokerage commissions be "broken out" on customer confirmations, and overreaching is less prevalent.

OVERSHOOT

As a verb, transitive or intransitive, meaning to exceed a goal or objective. It is used frequently in both economics and securities research to describe the fact that an economic indicator, economic measurement, or a security price/yield exceeded an anticipated goal. For example, "In the Q3 1989, M-2 overshot the 3.4% growth anticipated by the Fed."

It is also used to explain why the forecasts of economists or analysts were incorrect.

Antonym: undershoot.

OWL STOCK

Clever allusion used of an equity isue that has no active market; that is, the price advertisements for the stock feature an offer but no bid. Thus, when a customer who is long the stock calls up a broker for an immediate sale, the broker legitimately imitates the wise old owl: "Whooo tooo—whooo tooo?"

OVER THE WALL

See BROUGHT OVER THE WALL.

P

P

The fifteenth letter of the alphabet used:
1. Lowercase in newspaper option transaction tables to designate a put; for example, ABC Jan 55 p.
2. Uppercase in newspaper reports of corporate earnings to designate that a security's principal marketplace is the Philadelphia Stock Exchange; for example, East Park Realty Trust (P)
3. As the fifth letter in NASDAQ/NMS listings to designate a convertible preferred; for example, Health Images 0% cv. pfd.: HIMGP.
4. Uppercase alone to designate the NYSE ticker symbol for Phillips Petroleum, a major producer and refiner of oil and related chemicals.

PAC

Acronym: Planned Amortization Class. (Also PACB: Planned Amortization Class Bonds.) PACs are associated with CMOs. CMOs are so established that earlier classes (tranches) generally have a pre-established maturity date with all of the prepayment risk transferred to the residual security. Thus, a mortgage pool with its interest payments and principal repayments are set up in four classes. All payments go first to retire class A, then class B, then class C securities; as a result, any prepayment risk is transferred to the PACs in class D.

PACB
See PLANNED AMORTIZATION CLASS BONDS.

PACIFIC OPTIONS EXCHANGE TRADING SYSTEM
See POETS.

PAINE WEBBER/GAS 100
An index of price performance of selected issues in world markets as determined by Paine Webber Corp. and Global Analysis Systems Corp.

PAIR-OFF
1. Used as a synonym for "offset" in commodities markets; that is, the liquidation of a position by selling the same future month contract.
2. The technique used by exchange specialists to open the market. In a pair-off, orders to buy are so coupled to orders to sell that the specialist who knows whether there is a market balance can determine the proper price at which to open the market.
3. Terminology used in some program-type executions where the executing firm is held to its report. Thus, if there are errors resulting from DKs or QTs, the executing firm assumes such charges and "pairs them off" against the correct amounts.
4. Term used to describe this situation: a client has a long position in a security in one account, and a short position in the same security in another account. A pair-off occurs if the positions and money balances are combined in one account.
5. Term used in connection with the net settlement procedures used by the Depository Trust Co. (DTC), the National Securities Clearing Corp. (NSCC), and other such services. All purchases and sales in the same securities are aggregated daily and settled five business days later with a single delivery or a single check for the pair-off.

PALE BLUE CHIPS
A descriptive term sometimes used of a company whose stock is well on its way to becoming a "blue chip." Traders often refer to such stocks as "second tier" stocks.

P&I
Abbreviations for "principal and interest." The expression is often used by bond traders, salespersons, and institutional customers to describe the typical periodic payments made by issuers of bonds.

If the principal and interest are "stripped" from the bond and sold separately, thereby making them zero-coupons, you will see the expressions: "P only" and "I only."

"PANTY RAID"

A colorful term used to describe a very low bid for a company made by a well-known corporate raider. Concept: the raider is trying "to steal the pants" off the company.

Such a low bid is often followed by a more reasonable bid for the company. For example, in early 1988, Donald Trump made a low bid of $23 per share for the Class A stock of Resorts International only to be followed by a successful bid by Merv Griffin of $36 for these shares.

PAPER

1. Often used to designate short-term commercial paper.
2. Used to designate any debt security of a corporation; for example, AJAX Corp. has both long- and short-term paper outstanding.

"PAPER PROFIT"

See UNREALIZED PROFITS. Also used of unrealized losses.

PAPER TRADING

Hypothetical trading of securities (usually at closing prices and without commissions) often used in gaming situations or as part of a training program. Paper trading can be very helpful in teaching selection and timing techniques to market beginners.

PARALLEL LOANS

See BACK-TO-BACK LOANS.

PARI PASSU

Latin: from Vergil's *Aeneid*, to walk with equal stride, or lock-step. By attribution, to have equal ranking.

The word is used in conjunction with bankruptcy proceedings in the sense that all general creditors have equal ranking in their claim against the assets of the bankrupt corporation.

The term can also be used for any events that seem to be in lock-step; for example, the market is marching *pari passu* with the economy.

PARIS BOURSE

The largest exchange in France and the third largest in Europe.

There are two trading periods per day (9:30 A.M. to 11:00 A.M. and 12:30 P.M. to 2:30 P.M.) but electronic trading is permitted from 10:00 A.M. until 5:00 P.M. and informal trading is permitted until 6:00 P.M. All regular way contracts require month-end settlement through the SICOVAM clearance system.

Deregulation through "le petit bang" (q.v.) mirrors many of the changes in the United States and the United Kingdom.

PARIS MARCH
Slang for a strategy in index options named after the swift, and infamous, German march on Paris in World War II.

The strategy centers on the day before expiration in certain index options. The concept is to sell stocks short while both buying and selling equity call options on the same stocks. The goal is to cause program-type traders into action. This should enhance the short stock positions and the short call options. When done in unison near the close of trading (remember there is no remaining time value), it produces sharp price movements in the indexes and underlying stocks. This, in turn, results in the "march" to describe the near panic of the arbitrageurs.

PARITY
1. The price, exclusive of commissions and taxes, at which the value of the underlying stock is the same as the value of a convertible exchangeable for such stock. For example, a bond convertible into 40 shares is selling at $880 when the stock is selling at $22.
2. In the options market, if the stock is selling at the same price as the option plus its premium it is in parity. For example, a stock sells at $42 when the premium on the 40 call is $2 ($42 = $40 + $2).
3. In the auction market, if the broker with priority has a fill and other brokers can complete all of the remaining order, they are on parity. They will flip a coin to determine which of them will trade with the contra party.

PARITY PRICE FOR AN OPTION
Term used if an option strike price plus the premium equals the market price of the underlying on a call (minus the premium on a put). For example, a stock is selling at $40\frac{1}{2}$ on a day when the premium on the 40 call is 1/2 point ($40\frac{1}{2} = 40 + \frac{1}{2}$). In effect, the in-the-money option has no time value.

Although such situations are not rare, they are most common when an option is deep in-the-money and the time remaining to maturity is short.

PARTICIPANT EXCHANGE AGREEMENT (PEA)
A contract between the option exchanges participating in the linkage of trading and clearance between European and American stock exchanges.

The first PEA was signed in 1987 and links the European Options Exchange and the American Stock Exchange. The PEA included essential information required for disclosure to persons dealing in Major Market Index (XMI) options.

PARTLY PAID STOCK

The term is used in the United Kingdom to describe securities that are bought with a number of installment payments; thus, if the purchaser pays for an offering with a partial payment and the balance is due on specific future dates, it will be partially paid stock.

In this context, "stock" may be either stock or bonds. For example, the British government's bonds are properly called "stock," and this is a preferential financing technique used in their purchase.

PARTNERSHIP DEMOCRACY

An expression variously used in the context of a limited partnership.
1. A provision in the partnership agreement whereby the general partner(s) may exceed a limitation normally imposed upon the business agreement.
2. A provision in the partnership agreement whereby limited partners may, under certain circumstances, vote to discontinue the partnership, or may replace the general partner.

PART OF ROUND LOT

See PRL.

PART-OR-NONE

A term associated with a best efforts underwriting if a minimum sale of the offering is required. In effect, sales before the minimum is reached are held in abeyance (and the money in escrow). When the minimum is reached, these sales are confirmed, the offering is official, and the underwriting continues until it is completed.

If the minimum is not reached, the offering is cancelled and funds are refunded.

Similar in concept to a MINI-MAX offering.

"PASSING THE PARCEL"

A quaint and colorful trading expression from England. In effect, a broker/dealer purchased a block (parcel) of stock from an institutional customer. Before the news of the trade was disseminated, the broker/dealer sold it to another broker/dealer. Thus, the seller and the original purchaser are now "out of the loop," and the new purchaser has all of the risk.

Current SEAQ rules prohibit this practice without proper notification.

PASSIVE INCOME GENERATORS

See PIGS.

PASS THE BOOK
Also PASSING THE BOOK.

Term used by trading firms to describe 24-hour worldwide trading activity. For example, an international brokerage firm has offices in New York, Los Angeles, Honolulu, Tokyo, Singapore, Bahrain, and London. As the day progresses, the "book" (i.e., the firm's inventory and its control) is passed from office to office in a westward direction to be traded successively by the office listed above. In effect, customers can trade on a 24-hour basis by referring their orders to the appropriate trading office.

To be effective, passing the book requires a single financially responsible trading manager.

PAY-IN-KIND SECURITIES
See PIK.

PAY-THROUGH BOND
This is a hybrid security with some characteristics of both mortgage bonds and pass-through certificates.

The issuer uses a pool of mortgages it owns (an asset) and, rather than turn them into pass-throughs (the sale of an asset), it uses them as collateral for further borrowing (thereby creating a bond and a liability for the issuer).

The interest received from the original mortgages is used to pay the holders of the pay-through bonds, while the principal payments are used to systematically retire the bonds.

PAY-UP
1. Used if a mutual fund manager, in exchange for research services, pays a larger commission than usual for the execution of portfolio trades. In effect, the fund is spared the expense of a separate research area.
2. Used if a customer, to acquire a very large block of a security, is willing to pay a price that is greater than the typical market price for the security.
3. In a bond swap, if the price of the purchase is greater then the proceeds of sale, the dollar difference is called a "pay up." Antonym: take out, if the proceeds of the sale exceeds the price of the purchase.

PBN
See PRIME BANK NOTES.

PBR
Used to designate the price/book value ratio in security analysis.

Although the term is not used in the United States—we use market-to-book—it is used extensively in Japan. In Japan, price to earnings is not particularly meaningful because a large amount of the assets of a typical Japanese company may be in the form of nonearning real estate. Yet, it represents a significant amount of the "value" of the company. Thus, in Japan the market value of stocks tends to represent the "liquidating" value of the company, rather than its earning power.

PBW
Older abbreviation for the Philadelphia, Baltimore, Washington Exchange. It is now called the Philadelphia Stock Exchange and its commonly accepted designation is PHLX.

PC
1. Used of a participation certificate; that is, a fractional interest in a pool of mortgages or real estate loans. The holder receives a monthly flow-through benefit of interest and principal repayment.
2. In securities trades, PC stands for "plus commission," which, in practice, means that commissions will be added to purchases and subtracted from sales for services rendered.

P-COAST
An identifier often used for the Pacific Coast Stock Exchange. This exchange is located in California, has trading floors in Los Angeles and San Francisco, and is a registered national exchange.

P-DAY
U.K. terminology for Provisional Authorization Day. On that day in 1988, authorities granted temporary authorization to do financial business in the United Kingdom to certain entities while the details of the 1986 Financial Services Act were being implemented.

PEA
See PARTICIPANT EXCHANGE AGREEMENT.

PEACE DIVIDEND
General term used in fiscal policy for the shifting of priorities from defense expenditures to peacetime expenditures. Thus, in the United States, a peace dividend would see some of the funds in the $300 billion defense budget shifted to education, housing, and other needed consumer items. Generally, the peace dividend does not result in lowered taxes—although it did following World War II.

PEARL
Allusion to a "gem" of an investment that is a lucky find, as is a pearl in an oyster.

The term is also used to designate the premier holding in a portfolio; for example, "That stock is the pearl of all of my holdings."

In both meanings, the term implies diligence, some luck, and a lot of patience.

PEDESTRIAN PERFORMER
An expression used of a stock that achieves average performance both in its operations and in market performance.

In this context, "pedestrian" means commonplace; that is, a foot traveler, as opposed to a runner, a rider, or a "high" flier.

"PEEK-A-BOO"
U.K. slang for an unscheduled offering of new securities in the Euro-marketplace.

Because there are no filing requirements, the actual offering can take place shortly after the decision to bring the security to market. In such circumstances, the critical consideration is favorable market conditions, which as a window of opportunity may open and close quickly. Thus, the expression "peek-a-boo market conditions" is also used.

PEER REVIEW ORGANIZATION
See PRO.

PEE-WEE STOCKS
Slang for stocks above the "penny stock" category but decidedly below good quality and investment grade ("blue-chip") stocks.

They are considered second tier stocks and usually are the last to rise in bull markets and the first to fall in bear markets.

"PENNY STOCK RULE"
See SEC RULE 15c2-6.

PENSION PARACHUTE
Term used to describe the dedication of excess assets in a pension plan to the benefit of pension plan participants in the event of a change in control in the underlying corporation. Thus, the pension parachute serves to enhance the interests of the plan participants while at the same time serving as a "poison pill" in the event of a hostile takeover attempt.

PENSION REVERSION

The act of terminating an overfunded defined benefit pension plan and reclaiming the surplus assets. In practice, the plan is cancelled, the plan purchases fixed annuities to cover employee's entitled benefits, and the surplus is reclaimed by the corporation to become part of its assets. Usually, the cancellation of the defined benefit plan is accompanied by the substitution of a defined contribution plan for the continued benefit and retirement planning of the employees.

The courts have decided that plan termination is not covered by ERISA rules; thus, many firms with excess pension plan values have used this procedure.

PEOPLE PILL

A term used to describe a defensive strategy that may be used in the face of a hostile takeover attempt. Under a "people pill" defense, current management announces that, if the takeover is successful, the managers will resign *en masse* and thus leave the company directionless.

PER

1. Acronym: Post Execution Reporting. PER is used on the American Stock Exchange and, through it, members can direct market, limit, and odd lot orders to the specialists at the various posts. Details of the execution reports are made directly to the members without their physical attendance at the post.
2. Used outside the United States to designate the price earnings ratio; in the US, "P/E" is the more common expression.

   PER is numerically expressed as the quotient of the price per share divided by the earnings per common share; for example, 10, 12.5, or 15.

Also called the "multiple."

PERCENTAGE RISK ADDITION

See PRA.

PERCS

Acronym: Preferred Equity—Redemption Cumulative Stock. This Morgan Stanley innovation was tailor-made for Avon Products, Inc., at a time when it was about to reduce its common dividend by 50%. Holders of common shares could exchange for PERCS and would retain their old dividend but from a preferred share. The exchange worked well. Sufficient common shareholders elected to receive PERCS and thereby took a lot of potential selling pressure off of the common when the payout crisis became known.

PERFORMANCE INDEXED PAPER
See PIP.

PERFORMANCE PLUS
A Shearson Lehman Brothers servicemark for a CD issued by a commercial bank (thus, amounts of $100,000 or below were FDIC insured). Under the "performance plus" concept, the CD holder had a choice: *either* a fixed rate of interest for the life of the CD, *or* a return based on the performance of the S&P index during the life of the instrument.

The "Performance Plus" CDs were sold by Shearson through its network of retail brokerage offices.

PERLS
Acronym: Principal Exchange-Rate-Linked Securities. PERLS are a Morgan Stanley product designed for insurance companies seeking higher rates of return on foreign investments in exchange for controlled foreign currency risks.

The instrument is a debt security denominated in U.S. dollars and with interest paid in U.S. dollars, but the *repayment* of principal is linked to the performance of the U.S. versus the Australian dollar; thus, if the Australian dollar is stronger than the U.S. dollar at maturity, redemption will be at a premium.

Thus far, only Sallie Mae (Student Loan Marketing Association) with its strong credit rating and short-term repayment period (three years) has made a successful offering of PERLS.

PERPETUALS
A U.S. term for a debt issue without a maturity date. The Canadian Pacific 4s are an example and are the only such bond traded in the United States. The reason: the IRS has never ruled whether or not such interest payments are deductible before taxes; if the IRS was to make an adverse ruling, such securities would be construed as equity securities, because they are perpetual and have a fixed rate of return similar to a preferred stock.

In the United Kingdom, such securities are called "irredeemables." Irredeemables have no maturity date, but they are redeemable by the issuer at its option; in effect, they are similar to a callable preferred stock.

"PERUVIAN BONDS"
A derogatory term for a worthless security. The term originated in the 1930s when the government of Peru defaulted on its bonds and created great financial losses for retail and institutional investors.

PETS
Slang for "perpetual floating rate notes" innovated in 1986 by Citicorp. Many variations have since been created.

The core concept includes three ideas: (1) interest was pegged to LIBOR, (2) there was no specific maturity date on the bonds, and (3) the holder had a put option permitting redemption of the bond.

Later PETS have had some maturity date assigned thereby giving the issuer greater control on the open-endedness of the original concept.

PHANTOM INCOME
Income that must be reported as taxable income for the tax year that has no corresponding cash flow with which to pay the tax.

The term applies in certain limited partnership situations and particularly to zero-coupon bonds (except Series EE or nontaxable municipals) that are not held in a tax-sheltered account. The price of such zeros must be adjusted upward (accreted) each year according to the economic experience of the holder. This accreted amount is taxable on an annual basis, despite the fact that there is no cash flow to the customer.

PIG
Acronym: Passive Income Generator. The Tax Reform Act of 1986 originated the term passive income and losses to describe income that comes from business enterprises in which the customer has no substantial management control; for example, an interest in a limited partnership.

Many customers had limited partnership interests that provided passive losses. Such losses would have to be carried forward unless they could be offset by passive income. Hence the term: a limited partnership interest that provided sufficient passive income to offset such losses.

"PIGGYBACKING"
The term is used in the securities industry to describe the unethical practice whereby a salesman uses knowledge or market information provided by a customer to effect trades in his or/her personal account. Using such tips provided by customers is considered an inherent conflict of interest and may violate securities laws.

PIK
Acronym: Pay-in-Kind. PIK is used of securities in which the issuer has the option of paying interest in cash or in the form of other securities. The payment decision is totally at the option of the issuer.

Such PIK securities are typically debt obligations used in conjunction with an LBO. During the first few years, there will typically be either a PIK payout or no payout. Later, cash payments will begin as the company begins to manage the leveraged debt.

PIN

1. Acronym: Personal Identification Number, a unique series of numbers assigned by the SEC to all public corporations registered with the commission under the '34 act. This number is used when filing periodic SEC reports through the use of the EDGAR system.
2. Ticker symbol for Public Service Company of Indiana, a large utility listed for trading on the NYSE.

PINC

Acronym: Property Income Certificate. PINCs are permitted in the United Kingdom under the provisions of the 1986 Financial Services Act.
PINCs are real estate securities with two components:

1. Entitlement to a portion of the rental income from the underlying property.
2. A share in the property's management company created to control the property and collect the rental income.

PINK SHEET ISSUE

An equity security that is neither listed on a stock exchange nor traded on the NASDAQ quotation system.

Pink sheet issues include (but are not limited to) penny stocks, straight and variable preferreds, and ADRs. Trade activity by NASD members may be subject to special reporting requirements under Schedule H or the NASD's bylaws.

The "pink sheets" are published by the National Quotation Bureau, a subsidiary of the Commerce Clearing House, a large commercial printing concern.

PIN-STRIPED PORK BELLIES

A somewhat derogatory term used for index futures contracts in stock market indexes. The term arose when such futures contracts were initially offered by the Chicago Mercantile Exchange (CME) because the contracts were traded in the pit next to the pit where contracts in pork bellies (bacon) were traded.

PIP

Acronym: Performance Indexed Paper. PIP is a Salomon Brothers product linked to the performance of the West German Mark. This is a commercial paper program where Salomon interposed itself between issuer and investor. The issuer is guaranteed a fixed interest-rate expense; the investor is guaranteed a rate that can vary according to fluctuations in the foreign currency to which it is linked.

If investor interest develops, this concept could be expanded to other underlying currencies.

PIPELINE THEORY
Tongue-in-cheek term used for an IRS taxation privilege accorded to regulated investment companies. Under this privilege, neither the net investment income from dividends and interest nor net capital gains is taxable to the investment company; instead, these distributions (even if reinvested) become the annual tax obligation of the fundholder.

At present, 98% of the net investment income must be distributed by the fund. There is no minimum distribution requirement on net capital gains, although in practice most investment companies distribute 100% of such gains.

Also called the "conduit theory."

PIR
Acronym: Professional Investor Report. PIR is a Dow Jones news service publication for traders and arbitrageurs. The service is by private wire and alerts viewers to rumors and information about issues undergoing unusual volume or price activity.

PITCH
London's International Stock Exchange of the United Kingdom and the Republic of Ireland term for the location of where a dealer (jobber) maintains a continuous market for specific stocks. In the United States, such locations are called "posts."

Physically, the pitch is one of the faces of the hexagonal booths that are located on the floor of the ISE.

PLAM
Acronym: Price-Level Adjusted Mortgages. This is a term developed by Housing and Urban Development (HUD) to help homebuyers afford mortgages in the early years of their acquisition of a home. The interest level was pegged at 4% in 1988. The difference between the pegged rate and the market rate (e.g. 10%) is adjusted in one of two ways:
1. Monthly payments rise as the loan matures.
2. The difference is added to the principal amount due (negative amortization).

PLANNED AMORTIZATION CLASS
See PAC.

PLATINUM PARACHUTE
An obvious takeoff based on the concept of a "golden parachute"—only better! The concept involves two ideas:
1. A payoff for an executive who loses his or her job because of a corporate merger on unfriendly acquisition.

2. The payoff is sufficiently large to assure the executives of a "safe landing" as they either retire or look for another position.

PLASTIC BONDS
Nickname for asset-backed debt securities collateralized by accounts receivable arising from VISA and MasterCard charges.

Various names have been used for such asset-backed debt securities: Salomon Brothers calls them "CARDS" Citibank calls them "Citi-Credit Card Trusts."

PLAYER
1. Any person who likes to speculate by the frequent purchase and sale of securities.
2. Any person who becomes involved in takeovers and LBO situations. For example, "The arbitrageurs are major players in the takeover game."

PLAYING THE MARKET
A loosely used term to designate someone who buys and sells stocks frequently; in effect, the person uses the stock market as a game.

The term originated in the mid-1920s when the stock market seemed to go only upward and buying and selling stocks became a game. Although the seriousness of investment risk has become more well known, the term is still used.

PLC
1. In the United Kingdom, an abbreviation for Public Liability Company; plc is analogous to "corporation" in the United States in that the owners have their liabilities limited to the money they have invested in the business enterprise.
2. The stock symbol for Placer Development, Ltd., a Canadian mining company listed on the American Stock Exchange.

PLUM
Slang for anything that is particularly desirable.

The term may be used as a noun. For example, "That investment is a plum." Or it may be used as an adjective. For example, "That is a plum job."

The word is derived from the delicious fruit of the same name.

PLUNGER
Descriptive name for a speculator who tends to concentrate his or her assets in single transactions; thus, a person who puts all investment capital in one speculative investment or makes a series of speculative

investments involving all, or almost all, of investible assets is a plunger. An example: "Mr. Jones became a plunger and put all of his speculative money into long sugar futures."

PMI
See PRE-MEMBERSHIP INTERVIEW.

PMP
See PRIMARY MARKET PROTECTION.

POB
Acronym: Public Oversight Board. The POB is a division of the SEC Practice Section of the AICPA. This board is composed of distinguished individuals from outside the accounting profession. The POB monitors the audit activities of AICPA members and publishes statistical reports regarding them for public and SEC inspection.

PODM
Acronym: Put Option Deutsche Marks. PODM is a conventional option, European style, that permits the holder to deliver a fixed amount of West German marks at a fixed price in terms of U.S. dollars on a predetermined date in the future.

POETS
Acronym: Pacific Options Exchange Trading System. POETS is a program that encompasses order routing, automated execution, and market quote updates for equity options processed on the PSE. POETS is designed to handle quickly and efficiently retail-type orders and to compete effectively with other option exchanges. A by-product of the system: it facilitates trading by marketmakers and recordkeeping by exchange board brokers.

PO/IO
See IO/PO.

POISON PUT
A quaint term for a provision in a bond indenture that permits the bondholder to tender the security to the issuer at par (or at a premium, as determined) if: (1) there is a hostile takeover proposal or (2) the bond is downgraded by a national rating service. It is presumed that this provision will discourage an unsolicited takeover.

POLICYHOLDER LOAN BONDS
See DEATH-BACKED Bonds.

POLISHING THE ELEPHANT'S TOENAILS
Colorful British expression for work that is a waste of time and effort.

The term is most often used in the context of securities litigation in which lawyers (solicitors, in Britain) use an inordinate amount of time preparing a case and the time, in practice, does not seem justified in the results of the case.

POLITICAL STOCK
See ELECTION STOCK.

POM
1. NYSE ticker symbol for Potomac Electric Power, a large utility corporation serving the mid-Atlantic area of the United States.
2. See PUBLIC ORDER MEMBER.

PORCUPINE DEFENSE
Colorful name for a strategy designed to thwart a hostile takeover attempt. The metaphor arises from the fact that those who attack a porcupine often come out the worse for wear because they come out wearing its quills.

PORTAL
Acronym: Private Offerings, Resales, and Trading through Automated Linkages. This is an NASD term for the ability to trade private offerings using the automated quotation services of NASDAQ.

Such service is available only to sophisticated institutions, financially qualified investors (accredited persons), and to selected foreign investors. Thus, PORTAL gives some liquidity to what was in the past a highly illiquid market.

PORTFOLIO INSURANCE
Generic term used to describe a kind of insurance of portfolio values by tracking a market index and the corresponding purchase/sale of index futures. Thus, portfolio insurance is a self-established hedging technique versus stock holdings. When the market declines by a predetermined amount, index futures are sold; when the market rises, index futures are bought. In effect, the portfolio manager has set up the situation whereby a loss in one instrument will be offset by gains in the other, thereby coinsuring the portfolio.

PORTFOLIO SYSTEM FOR INSTITUTIONAL TRADING
See POSIT.

POS

Acronym: Preliminary Official Statement. Both the Preliminary Official Statement and the Final Official Statement are similar in purpose to the Preliminary and Final Prospectuses on a registered offering. There are these principal differences: municipal issuers need not publish either statement; and, in recent years, a number of municipal issuers have published a preliminary official statement but not a final official statement because of the size of these documents and the cost of publication. In this latter case, the principal underwriter (or dealer) is required to send a copy of the preliminary official statement (or summary thereof) to the original purchaser in lieu of the final official statement, as required in the rules of the MSRB.

POSIT

Acronym: Portfolio System for Institutional Trading. POSIT is an experimental computerized trading system that endeavors to trade entire portfolios between institutional investors without benefit of an intervening central marketplace.

In effect, the system functions as an exchange between subscribers. Overages in dollar amounts are executed by Jeffries & Co. in formal exchange transactions. The dollar proceeds would go to the firm with the larger portfolio value.

POSITION RISK ADDITIONS

PRA is a process employed by English broker/dealers in the calculation of their net capital requirements. Unlike the U.S. procedure, which is based on a "haircut" of the current market price, British brokers must add a specified percentage to reflect the degree of potential risk maintained in the position. This addition is called "PRA."

POSITION TRADER

This is a term associated with "upstairs trading" by member firms for their own account. The persons who evaluate the potential risk/reward of the position and make the market decisions to buy or sell for the firm's proprietary security positions are called "position traders."

POSTING A LEVEL

Expression used by issuers of short-term paper as they endeavor to borrow money at the best possible rate.

Thus, commercial paper borrowers endeavor to find an interest rate, in comparison with U.S. T-bills, CDs, and LIBOR at which they can attract short-term capital. Once found, this standard, or level, becomes the norm at which other comparable borrowers will endeavor to attract short-term money during that time frame. The process of establishing a norm is called "posting a level."

PPM
See PRIVATE PLACEMENT MEMO.

PR
A commonly used abbreviation for preferred stock. The other commonly used abbreviations are PF and Pfd.

PRA
See POSITION RISK ADDITIONS.

PREARRANGED TRADING
An arrangement between two or more commodities exchange members to buy and sell between themselves at predetermined prices. Thus, their transactions are not at risk but are done for their own personal economic reasons. Usually such reasons pertain to taxes.

Prearranged trades violate industry rules and may be fraudulent.

PREDATORS' BALL
The tongue-in-cheek name for an annual conference of junk bond (high-yield bond) issuers and buyers sponsored by Drexel Burnham Lambert, at one time the premier underwriter of such bonds. The macabre name for the conference was based on the fact that many of the attendees were directly involved in many of the mergers, acquisitions, LBOs, and hostile takeovers of the 1970s and 1980s.

PREFERRED EQUITY—REDEMPTION CUMULATIVE STOCK
See PERCS.

PRE-MARKET, THE
A British term for the active trading of proposed new issues before they are actually offered for public sale. The practice is condoned in the United Kingdom for nonexchange members, but it is fraught with financial risk.

In the United States, the practice is not permitted for securities "in registration," but it is similar in concept to the U.S. trading on a "when issued" basis of exempt securities before they are actually offered.

PREMEMBERSHIP INTERVIEW (PMI)
Under Schedule C of the NASD bylaws, an applicant for membership must be first interviewed by officials of the district office where the applicant's principal office will be located. Among the documents that the

applicant must submit at this meeting are: a copy of its SEC BD Form (Broker/Dealer form), a copy of its written supervisory procedures, and a copy of its financial statements.

PRER
This is an abbreviation for "pre-refunded," a municipal bond identifier for a debt security that is fully collateralized by U.S. Treasury issues. In effect, the outstanding municipal debt is guaranteed by a pool of funds equal to the debt and having a maturity that is the same as that of the municipal debt.

Other abbreviations are used for "pre-refunded," and occasionally the abbreviation ETM (escrowed to maturity) is similarly used.

Pre-refunded securities may have a maturity that is equal to the earliest call date of the original municipal issue.

PRESENT VALUE OF A DOLLAR
The amount of money required right now to become a dollar at a time in the future at a given rate of compound interest over a given number of years. The formula is the reciprocal of the Future Value formula (q.v.). It is:

$$\frac{1}{(1 + R)^n}$$

Where n is the number of compounding periods, and R is the compounded rate of return.

Thus, to achieve $1 if money is invested at 7% over 5 years would require:

$$\$0.71298$$

PRICE-LEVEL ADJUSTED MORTGAGES
See PLAM.

PRICING
Securities industry term for the establishment of a value for the sale of a security. The term applies:
1. To the determination of the price at which a public offering will be made; for example, the pricing meeting.
2. To the determination of the value at which proprietary securities will—after the statutory "haircuts"—be carried in the determination of net worth of the broker/dealer.

PRIMARY MARKET PROTECTION (PMP)
This term refers to the protection that regional exchange specialists must provide to customers if they accept an order that is "away from the

market." Generally, if a transaction occurs on the issue's primary exchange (usually the NYSE) at the customer's price or better, the regional specialist must guarantee at least a partial execution of the limit order.

PRIME BANK NOTES (PBN)
PBNs are debt obligations of good-quality bank holding companies associated with the major banks in the chief financial centers of the United States.

PRINCIPAL
1. The face amount of a debt security. The term is applicable even if the security is a zero-coupon bond.
2. Any person—including an individual investor, an institution, or a broker/dealer—who buys or sells a security for its own account and risk.
3. A person associated with an NASD broker/dealer who is actively engaged in that firm's securities or investment banking business. Such a person may be a sole proprietor, a partner, a corporate director, or a manager of an office of supervisory jurisdiction.
4. Any person who authorizes another—often in writing—to act as his or her agent in a transaction or a business. For example; "Tom Jones is principal in that power of attorney account."

PRINCIPAL EXCHANGE-RATE-LINKED SECURITY
See PERLS.

PRINCIPAL ONLY/INTEREST ONLY
See IO/PO

PRIVATE MARKET VALUE
Often used as a synonym for liquidating value, as opposed to its value in a stock market.

The term became necessary because many LOBs are "asset plays" in which parts of a company will be resold in private negotiations with the owners of on-going businesses. In effect, the advisability of the merger or LBO will be decided by the price at which the portions of the company can be resold in a private transaction.

PRIVATE OFFERINGS, RESALES, AND TRADING THROUGH AUTOMATED LINKAGES
See PORTALS.

PRIVATE PLACEMENT MEMO

Initials: PPM. A PPM is similar to a prospectus for registered offerings in that it discloses the pertinent facts about the private placement. Remember: for a placement to qualify as "private," the purchasers must have sufficient information to make an informed decision. Such a memo would undoubtedly have pertinent information about the issuer, the limited or nonexistent marketability of the issue, and what is going to be done with the funds raised by the issue.

PRIVATISATION

An English term for the sale to the public of shares in what had previously been government-owned enterprises. In the 1980s, Margaret Thatcher's government sold shares in British Airways, British Telecommunications, British Gas, and British Petroleum.

In a similar fashion, the Japanese government sold shares in Japan Air Lines and in Nippon Telephone and Telegraph.

PRL

Exchange terminology for "part of a round lot."

The term is associated with the sale of a part of a round lot (odd lot) in conjunction with a round lot; for example, the sale of 225 shares involves two round lots of 100 shares plus part of a round lot (25 shares).

Such a designation is required on exchange-directed orders to point out that (1) the odd lot differential should not be charged and (2) that the odd lot (PRL) is to be transacted at the same price as the round lot(s).

PRO

Acronym: Peer Review Organization. A PRO is an SEC-recognized accounting firm with authority to examine other accounting firms that certify financial statements of publicly traded securities.

Under SEC Regulation S-X, the purpose of "peer review" is to make sure that the audit of such publicly traded firms comforms to generally accepted account standards (GAAS).

A body of three independent individuals oversees the work of the PRO.

PROFESSIONAL INVESTOR REPORT

See PIR.

PROFILE A CUSTOMER, TO

Expression used by sales and administrative personnel to describe the act of soliciting customer background information. Profiling results in the fulfillment of one of the basic requirements of financial service: to "know the customer." As a general rule, profiling is done by registered representatives (RRs) who alone among brokerage personnel are permitted to solicit buy and sell orders for securities.

PROGRAM TRADING

A general term for any endeavor by a portfolio manager to replicate the movement of a popular index and to use this in the management of the account.

Usually program trading is accomplished by the use of a computer to (1) either measure the index or (2) to initiate trades—or both. Program trading may be a hedging (offset or position before the fact) technique, or an arbitrage (profit-capturing) technique.

There is currently much controversy about program trading and whether it inordinately increases market volatility.

PROGRESSIVE TAX

General term applied to any system of taxation where the tax bracket (marginal rate) increases as the dollar value of the tax base increases. In the United States, both income and estate taxes are progressive taxes.

Antonym: regressive tax, where the rate remains the same for all persons.

PROPRIETARY

1. Securities and other assets of a broker/dealer as well as those of its principals that are pledged as capital contributed to the organization.
2. Anything owned by a proprietor.
3. A product or service covered by a patent or by a trade or service mark.
4. As an adjective in conjunction with an account: the broker's inventory—either long or short—used in securities trading.

PROTECT PREFERRED

A new form of convertible preferred that sets a specific price that the common is to achieve by a certain target date. If the common fails to reach that price, there is a special dividend equal to the shortfall. The purpose of the security is to enhance shareholder value by giving predictability to the stock.

PSBR

Acronym: Public Sector Borrowing Requirement. PSBR is an important segment of the British budget. Because Britain has a socialized health program and other government-sponsored public benefits programs, PSBR is an important indicator of the United Kingdom's fiscal policy for the year.

PSDR
Acronym: Public Sector Debt Repayment. PSDR is an important segment of the British budget. PSDR gives an insight into the British government's ability and willingness to repay its annual public services debt, rather than refund it through further borrowings. Thus, together with PSBR, PSDR gives an insight into the net change in the public debt of Britain.

PUBLIC OVERSIGHT BOARD
See POB.

PUBLIC UTILITY DISTRICT
See P.U.D.

P.U.D.
A common abbreviation used in listings of municipal bonds for a Public Utility District. A P.U.D. is generally established as a quasi-governmental agency or authority within a municipality organized to provide citizens with water, gas, or electricity.

The initials (or the full expression) will also appear on the face of bond certificates, Official Statements, or tombstones accompanying bond issues of the P.U.D.

PUFFING
Term used to describe the act of bragging or exaggerating the qualities of an issue or the fortunes of the issuer. The noun form of the concept is "puffery."

Puffing, or puffery, in research publications, in sales literature, or in communications with clients is considered promissory and thus lacking in "truthfulness and good taste" as required by the NASD and NYSE rules for communicating with the public. As such, it may also violate federal securities laws.

PTA
Common abbreviation for peseta, the principal currency of Spain. All securities traded on Spanish stock exchanges are denominated or traded in pesetas.

Plural: Ptas.

PUBLIC, THE
1. Used in opposition to market professionals, who are often called "market insiders."
2. Used derisively of the small investor who is considered to do exactly the opposite of the sophisticated investor by buying at the top, selling

at the bottom. This concept is at the heart of what is called the "odd lot" theory: do the opposite of the public and you will invest smartly.
3. Used without "the" as an adjective in distinction to private; for example, the stock is now public, or the company went public with the information.
4. Used extensively as an adverb in such expressions as "publicly traded," "publicly known," and so on.

PUBLIC LIABILITY COMPANY
See PLC.

PUBLIC ORDER MEMBER
Acronym: POM. A POM is a participant in the British options market who is neither a marketmaker nor a member of the London Options Clearing House (LOCH). A POM (1) buys and sells English listed options on his own behalf or (2) as an agent on behalf of his clients. In order to do so, the POM must appoint a member of LOCH to act on its behalf.

PULLING IN THEIR HORNS
Term used of market professionals—although it can be used of any investor—when they take a defensive position in the marketplace. Such defensive positions may be the transference of risk through sales, or the hedging of positions through options or futures. For example, "Traders were pulling in their horns during the session by extensive profit taking. . . ."

The term was originally used when bullish sentiment was offset by bearish sentiment, but now the term can be used when any aggressive trading (long or short) is moderated by offsetting activities.

PULL THE PLUG
Colorful expression used to describe the dissemination of unfavorable information about a company, or the act of making a decision that adversely affects others. The analogy: removing the plug from a basin of water causes a vortex of water to rapidly go down the drain. For example, "The company's announcement that it was laying off workers in its Midwest plant quickly pulled the plug on speculative activity in the stock."

Pulling the plug usually results in an immediate lack of demand for a stock, coupled with a large amount of supply from sellers. Generally, there is a dramatic drop in the price of the underlying security.

"PUMP AND DUMP" OPERATION
Slang used by securities fraud prosecutors to describe the activity of "penny stock" promoters who "hype" low-priced or worthless stocks to investors by high-pressure tactics.

A "pump and dump" operation may result in large losses for gullible investors and huge profits for the promoters. SEC Rule 15c2-6 prohibits such fraudulent operations, and recent NASD rules also apply to "penny stock" promotions.

PUNT
1. Slang in the United Kingdom for a gambler or speculator. Thus, a punter is a handicapper; that is, one who takes the opposite side of a bet. For example, "Investors are anxious to buy LMN, but there are plenty of punters around to take their money."
2. Used as a verb to signify a delaying tactic. The analogy is with the game of football, where a punt transfers the ball to the opposing team at a worse field position. For example, "If you want a prediction of the market activity for that stock in this year, I'll have to punt."

PUPPY TAX
A colorful term for the turnover tax levied on transactions on the Stockholm Stock Exchange. The tax is a 0.30% levy on brokered transactions and is equally split between buyer and seller.

The term originated when the Swedish finance minister jocularly referred to the brokerage community in Sweden as "finance pups."

PURE PLAY
Term that designates a speculation in the stock of a single company with the company, in turn, engaged in a single business. In effect, the speculator is "putting all his eggs in one basket." Hence, the term denotes concentration as opposed to diversification.

PUT ON
1. In the United Kingdom, the term is used when a customer has authorized a broker to act on his or her behalf. For example, "I had my broker put on a buy for me."
2. In the options market, the act of establishing an options spread; that is, the purchase and sale of options of the same class. For example, "The time seemed right to put on a bull spread on ABC."
3. To dissemble or to fake; for example, "His illness was a put on." By derivation in the securities industry, any fraud or deceit perpetrated against the contra party to a trade.

PUT THROUGH
1. In the United States, as a verb: to complete or to effect. For example, "I was able to put through the buy order."
2. In the United Kingdom, the use of an intermediary on a loan. For example, "Jones and Co. acted as a put through on the loan from Smith & Co. to Reilly & Co."

3. The simultaneous sale and repurchase of the same security through the same broker on the same exchange. In the United Kingdom, this is permissible to establish a new price for the owner's portfolio. In the United States, such an activity is called a "wash sale" and is illegal.

PYRAMID, TO

As used in the finance industry, to pyramid means to accumulate further holdings in a security by borrowing against the increasing paper profits of a position. For example, to use the buying power of a margin account to accumulate more shares of the original purchase is a form of pyramiding.

Pyramiding can be extremely successful if the underlying asset continues to rise in collateral value; but—like a house of cards—pyramiding can quickly become unprofitable if the underlying falls in value and the borrower is overextended and must be liquidated to reduce the loans.

The term is also used in real estate and commodities trading.

Q

Q

Seventeenth letter of the alphabet:
1. Used uppercase before the ticker symbol on Consolidated Tapes A and B to designate the stock of a company that is in bankruptcy and will be liquidated or reorganized.
2. Used as the fifth letter in the symbol of a NASDAQ/NMS stock to signify that the company is under the protection of federal bankruptcy laws. For example, WOWIQ is the symbol of World of Wonder, Inc., a company that is under Chapter 11.

Q1, Q2, Q3, Q4

Used by security analysts and newspaper financial reports to designate the operating results of a company during successive three-month periods. Thus, Q1 means the first quarter of the fiscal year, Q2, the second quarter, and so on.

Q-RATIO

A measurement of a company's hidden assets in relation to its market value.

Q-ratios are particularly important in Japan where many assets— particularly real estate and stock ownership in subsidiaries and other companies—are carried at cost. Thus, traditional price earnings ratios in Japan are at an average of 50+ to 1 (with worldwide averages about 12 to 1) and seem to make the market overpriced. On a Q-ratio basis, however, if the hidden assets are factored into the consideration, the prices do not seem overinflated.

QUACK
This seemingly derogatory term is part of the floor lingo on the exchanges. It designates a trade made at a quarter of a point. Thus, "Forty-four and a quack" means 44¼. It is used in the noisy environment of the floor to keep the trade from being confused with a trade at 44¾.

QUALIFICATION
1. The recognition by an SRO (q.v.) of registration status of an individual either through waiver or examination. For example, "John Jones is recognized by the NASD as a registered representative," or "Peter Smith qualified for registration as a financial principal."
2. The act of registration of a particular security for sale under the blue-sky laws of an individual state.

QUALIFIED LEGAL OPINIONS
A conditional opinion by bond counsel about a proposed municipal issue.

If the bond counsel has any reservations about the enabling legislation for the issue, its taxability/nontaxability under federal statutes, or the existence of prior restrictive covenants that would impede this issue, their opinion will be "qualified." If there is no question on these three points, the opinion will be unqualified.

The terms are used exactly as they would be in ordinary parlance. For example, "The office party was an unqualified success," or "I have some qualifications about the feasibility of this plan."

QUANT
A shortened expression for a market research technician who makes financial decisions only in terms of quantitative measurements. In practice, a synonym for a "number cruncher." The term is derogatory.

Effective securities research requires both quantitative and qualitative judgments about a company and its performance.

QUIET PERIOD
The term used to describe the time between the initial public offering of securities and the earliest date when the underwriters may write and disseminate research material about the company.

The quiet period is required by SEC rule, and its purpose is to let the stock settle into portfolio-type accounts (as opposed to trading accounts) based on the merits set forth in the prospectus. In effect, investors should not be swayed by dealers and traders who have a vested interest in the security.

R

R

Eighteenth letter of the alphabet used:

1. Lowercase in older copies of stock option transaction tables to signify that no transactions took place in that market session in a given option series.
2. Uppercase as the fifth letter in a NASDAQ/NMS entry to designate a subscription right. For example, RABTR stood for Rabbit Software Corp. subscription rights. Such usage is limited to the life of the rights.
3. Uppercase as a single letter, R is the ticker symbol of Rothschild Holdings, Inc., the parent corporation of L. F. Rothschild, a prominent broker/dealer.

RABBI TRUST

Nickname for a retirement vehicle used to protect the financial benefits that have already accrued to present executives of a company bought out in a hostile takeover. Deferred compensation, for example, is corporation-funded but administered by an independent third party (a commercial bank or trust company) without fear that successor managements will default or appropriate the assets.

RACCOON

Slang expression for a number cruncher; that is, an analyst who does only quantitative research. The allusion is to the rings around the eyes of raccoons and the rings around the eyes that number crunchers get from endless hours in front of their computer screens.

RACING THE TAPE

Jargon used to describe the unethical practice of transacting personal business in front of and because of a transaction about to be entered by a customer. Thus an RR buys in anticipation of a large buy order to be entered by a customer to profit from the activity caused by the customer's buy order. The same concept also applies to sales.

RAINMAKER

Slang for a big producer—either an RR or an investment banker—who brings new business to the broker/dealer. As such, the rainmaker brings profit to the firm and receives additional personal compensation.

RAMP

The U.K. equivalent of what in the United States is called a "corner." A ramp, or corner, arises when an individual, or group of individuals working in concert, control so much of a security or commodity that they, in effect, control the trade price.

Ramp, or corner, usually implies that individuals or groups provide the price control; if the price control is done by groups of governments, the word *cartel* is used.

"RAMP UP" FINANCING
British term for the use of convertible preferred shares as a form of capital financing. The concept centers on this: a shareholder starts with a senior security and, as the company prospers, the shareholder can convert and thus become a common shareholder of the company.

RANDOM WALK
A market philosophy that states there are no special techniques to outperform the market—just luck, and enough random selections. Theoretically, throwing darts at the listing of stocks in the financial pages of the newspaper will provide as much return as those who use complicated strategies.

This is obviously an oversimplification, but it has been shown that an increase in the number of random selections made of stocks does substantially reduce the standard deviation (the degree of risk) in terms of nonsystematic risk in a portfolio. To this extent, therefore, it does seem that portfolio diversification improves the chances for a random walker.

RANGE
Unless otherwise qualified, the term means the opening, the high, the low, and the close of a security for a specific trading session.

The term is variously used to give the high and low for a week, a month, or 52 weeks. Currently, newspapers tend to give the daily and 52-week ranges. Opening prices are often omitted from the range.

RATCHET COMPENSATION
An incentive compensation program whereby management receives additional remuneration in the form of salary, cash, stock options, and the like in terms of its ability to reach certain preset revenue or earnings figures for a year or other period.

The analogy is with a ratchet, which goes forward but not backward.

R-DAY
Term used by the Association of International Bond Dealers (AIBD) to designate April 3, 1989. On this day and following, it has been agreed that all international bond trades will be reported within 30 minutes following execution. The report will be made to the association, which—as a registered investment exchange (RIE) and recognized by the Securi-

ties Investment Board (SIB)—has been authorized to receive these reports.

"READY MARKET"
A market in which there exist bona fide bids and offers, reasonable liquidity, and prompt settlement for securities trades.

The term is important because it is used by the SEC in its net capital rule (15c3-1) to describe the value to be given to portfolio securities in measuring capital requirements. The value must be reasonably related to the last sale price in bona fide competitive markets.

REAL ESTATE MORTGAGE INVESTMENT CONDUIT
See REMIC.

REALIZED PROFITS AND LOSSES
Completed transactions for which the taxpayer must accept tax accountability. Most investors pay their security tax obligations on this basis; thus, there is no "taxable event" until long positions are sold or short positions covered at a profit or loss.

Not all gains or losses need be realized to cause a tax obligation. Tax advice is needed on certain forms of "phantom income," and on certain required "marks to the market" required by federal tax statutes on zero-coupon bonds and certain "spreads" in commodities.

REALS
Composite term for Real Yield Securities. REALS are a Morgan Stanley innovation. Basically, the security is a debenture with a 2.75% coupon. However, this coupon is adjusted quarterly and pays at a rate keyed to the government's consumer price index. In effect, the debenture holder gets a quarterly payment, as opposed to a semiannual payment, that is inflation adjusted to give a "real" return.

REAL YIELD SECURITIES
See REALS.

RECAPS
See RECONFIRMATION AND PRICING SERVICE.

RECOGNIZED INVESTMENT EXCHANGE
See RIE.

RECONCILEMENT OF OUT-TRADE NOTICES
See ROTN.

RECONFIRMATION AND PRICING SERVICE

Popularly known as RECAPS, this is a security valuation service overseen by the National Securities Clearing Corporation (NSCC). Under this service, the NSCC marks members to the market for transactions that have been compared but not cleared on settlement date. In this way, there is financial integrity in all contracts, both cleared and as yet uncleared.

The service was originally set up for municipal bond contract fails but now includes fails in corporate securities as well.

RECOURSE

A financial term that describes the ability of a lender to hold the borrower of money responsible for losses in the event of a default in connection with that loan. Thus, the term *recourse loan* or *nonrecourse loan.*

Recourse loans are often taken out by limited partnerships (DPPs) to leverage the enterprise. In this event, the lender has recourse against the assets of the partnership (but not against the assets of the limited partners). In other situations, the recourse may be limited to a percentage of the assets.

REDS

See REFUNDING ESCROW DEPOSITS.

REDUCTION-OPTION LOAN

Acronym: ROL. ROLs are a form of mortgage financing in which the borrower is allowed a one-time opportunity during the second through the fifth year to match current mortgage interest rates. If elected, these new rates are fixed for the remainder of the mortgage. Usually the reduction is permitted only if rates have dropped more than 2% in any one year.

In effect, the mortgage holder is given an opportunity to take advantage of lower rates. Such an adjustment is cheaper than refinancing the mortgage.

REDUNDANT

Although the term is basically an adjective and means dull or repetitious or useless, in the United Kingdom the term is also used as a noun to signify someone who has been laid off from a job because of economic forces (as opposed to being fired for cause). For example, "Jim is redundant as a result of the merger of his firm with British Ford."

REFUNDING ESCROW DEPOSITS

Acronym: REDS. REDS are a First Boston innovation designed to enable municipal securities issuers to lock in future financing rates. The sale proceeds of these securities are invested in short-term Treasuries which, at maturity, are used to refund an earlier dated issue of a municipal security. At that time, these deposits will then represent ownership in the new tax-exempted refunding bonds.

REGIONAL INTERFACE ORGANIZATION
See RIO.

REGLEMENT LIVRAISON DE TITRES
See RELIT.

REGRESSIVE TAX
1. The opposite of a progressive tax; that is, a tax that decreases as the tax base increases. For example, if the tax on one gallon of gasoline were 10 cents and on two gallons of gasoline were 19 cents, the tax would be regressive.
2. Any tax that affects the poor as much or more than it does the rich. For example, the payroll tax (Social Security) affects all persons equally on the first $51,300 of wages (1990), but those who make over that amount pay a lower percentage of wages on their total earned income.

REGULAR WAY TRANSACTION
General term for the settlement date of a *secondary* market transaction unless other terms are negotiated.
1. In the United States, regular way transactions in stocks, municipal, and corporate bonds is the fifth business day following the trade date in clearing house funds.
2. In the United States, transactions in money market securities, Treasuries, and agencies are on the next business day in "good money"; that is, federal funds. Listed options, by exchange rules, settle on the next business day; clearing house funds are acceptable.
3. Regular way settlement on foreign exchanges is usually made by the "account period" (a fortnight in the United Kingdom), the end of the month, or on a specific day following the trade date.

In the United States, primary market transactions are generally made on a "when issued" basis.

REGULATED INVESTMENT COMPANY
Acronym: RIC. RIC is a tax code term. In general, a regulated investment company is eligible for a tax exemption as a corporation *if* it fulfills certain requirements. The tax is paid by the fundholder on an annual basis.

To qualify as a RIC, these are the principal requirements:

1. The fund must be registered with the SEC.
2. The fund must be "diversified."
3. The fund must be "domestic."
4. 90% of the fund's total income must come from dividends, interest, and capital gains (of which no more than 30% may be short term)
5. The fund must distribute at least 98% of its "net investment income." The term *conduit theory* is used to describe this tax exemption.

REGULATION D
A generic name for a series of SEC rules that describe the various ways in which an offering of securities may qualify as a "private placement."

One of the most important definitions given in Regulation D is that of "accredited investor"; that is, those institutional and individual investors who are not included in the upper limit of 35 persons to whom a private placement may be sold because of their sophistication or income/net worth qualification.

REGULATORY FLEXIBILITY ACT
Acronym: RFA. RFA is a federal law that requires each governmental agency to consider, in the course of proposing substantive rules, the effect those rules will have on "small" entities. In this context, the law defines *small* as a business or organization that is independently owned and operated and not dominant in its field.

RELATIONSHIP SHARES
It is common for Japanese companies to own substantial amounts of other companies to enhance the business relationships between the companies. Such shares are called "relationship shares"; and it is taken for granted that such shares will be held as a permanent investment and that they will never appear in the public market. It is said that such shares show sincerity and respect; in practice, such shares seriously restrict the "float" and act as a barrier to uninvited takeovers.

RELIT
Acronym: Reglement Livraisons de Titres. RELIT is an automatic clearing and settlement system featured exclusively on the Paris Bourse. This system formalizes trade comparisons and completes settlement procedures on the fifth business day following execution. RELIT is also linked directly to the bourse's central depository, SICOVAM.

REMEDIAL POISON PILL
An offshoot of the original poison pill concept that mandated purchase rights for shareholders if a hostile suitor acquired as little as 20% of a company.

The "remedial" poison pill contains the same purchase rights but, in addition, allows the prospective suitor to convene a stockholder's meeting with as little as 1% of the target company's stock. The suitor (bidder) must furnish an investment banker's "fairness opinion" and pay for one half of the cost of that meeting.

REMIC
Acronym: Real Estate Mortgage Investment Conduit. REMICs are vehicles for financing real estate mortgages through multiclass pass-through instruments. Unlike MBSs and CMOs, which generally pool mortgages of similar characteristics, REMICs permit the aggregation of multiclass mortgages to collateralize debt issued by corporations, partnerships, or trusts.

REMP
Acronym: Real Estate Mortgage Product. The term *REMP* is a generalization used to classify such investments as collateralized mortgage obligations (CMOs), real estate investment trusts (REITs), Ginnie Maes (GNMAs), midget, and other "pass-through" investments.

RÉMÉRÉ
Using French franc-French government bonds as collateral, this is a reverse repurchase agreement in which the customer buy-back is not assured in advance. Thus, it is a conditional agreement, but not an obligation, to repurchase the bonds.

REOPENING
1. The resumption of trading in an exchange-listed security after trading was previously suspended on that market day. For example, "Trading in LMN was halted at 10:03 A.M.; the reopening did not occur until 3:30 P.M.
2. If an issuer offers debt securities at various times with the same terms as the original offering (i.e., maturity and coupon interest rate), each subsequent offering is called a "reopening." The term is most frequently used of government securities, both U.S. and U.K.

RESCHEDULED LOANS
A euphemism for a loan renegotiated to forestall default and bankruptcy. Because bankruptcy is so expensive and presents problems both for debtor and creditor, it is often advisable to "reschedule" the loan. Thus, a 10% 14-year loan, with the consent of both parties, could be rescheduled into a 30-year 9% loan.

RESIDUAL INTEREST BONDS
See RIBS

RESTRICTED INTERNAL MEMO
Acronym: RIM. Technical term for a document prepared by a broker/dealer for dissemination only to its salesforce. Usually a RIM is an educational marketing tool prepared for the salespersons who will distribute the issue. Because of regulatory restrictions, RIMs may not be sent to customers or other prospective buyers.

Such documents will always be headed "For Internal Use Only," and this restriction must be scrupulously maintained.

RETAIL CD
Common expression for a bank certificate of deposit of $100,000 or less.

In general, such certificates are nonnegotiable, subject to penalty for early withdrawal, and covered by deposit insurance (FDIC).

The term is used in distinction to *jumbo CD* (more than $100,000). "Brokered CDs" are purchased by retail customers in amounts under $100,000 through a broker/dealer. Such brokered CDs are insured but are paid only simple interest.

RETAIL PRICES INDEX
Acronym: RPI. RPI is a monthly index of consumer prices based on a weighted basket of food, clothing, and shelter in the United Kingdom. The RPI will show inflationary and deflationary trends in the British economy and is prepared by a governmental agency.

REVERSE BID
English terminology for a takeover attempt in which a listed company makes a bid to buy out the holders of a private concern. No approval is required of the public stockholders because it is felt that such an acquisition will add to the product line and profit of the public concern.

REVERSE LBO
Media term for a public sale of a company after a leveraged buyout was used to take it private. Generally, the motivation for such a resale following a purchase is an anticipated profit if the shares are again sold to the public.

REVERSE SPINS
SPINS are acronyms for Standard & Poor's 500 Index Notes. SPINS were originally offered by Salomon Brothers in 1986 and were a *call* option on a rise in the S&P index after August 20, 1986. Meantime, the holder got a 2% nominal rate of interest payable semiannually.

Reverse SPINS were the opposite: a *put* option on the S&P index after September 14, 1987, to run until the maturity of the notes on September 14, 1990.

As with the original offering, the holder—in a worst case scenario—got a 2% annual rate of interest plus a full return of principal.

REVERSE YIELD GAP
A U.K. term for a yield curve on gilts where the return on those government securities is greater than the rate of return on UK equities. If investment return is commensurate with risk, such a reverse yield gap would mean that the risk on gilts is greater than the risk on equities—certainly an anomaly.

In this concept, *yield* means total return; generally, the interest yield on gilts is less than the dividend yield on equities.

RFA
See REGULATORY FLEXIBILITY ACT.

RIBS
An acronym for Shearson Lehman Hutton's Residual Interest Bonds. It is a class of municipal security issued in conjunction with select auction variable rate securities (SAVRS). The municipal issuer contracts to pay a fixed sum of tax-exempted interest semiannually split among two classes of debt securities holders, SAVRS and RIBS. The holders of SAVRS receive a variable amount, determined by Dutch auction (q.v.) every 35 days, while the holders of RIBS receive what is left over. Thus, if rates decline in the municipal market, the RIBS' holders benefit greatly. If rates increase, they suffer!

RIC
Common abbreviation for Registered Investment Company. An RIC is a corporation (or Massachusetts trust) registered with the SEC under the Investment Company Act of 1940 and subject to all of the regulations appropriate to investment companies.

Domestic investment companies are required to register if they are face amount certificate companies, unit investment trusts, or management companies (either closed- or open-end management companies). Holding companies and other companies whose principal occupation is the management of corporations—as opposed to the management of money—are not permitted to register. Open-end management companies are popularly called "mutual funds."

RIDING THE TAPE

The simplest form of technical analysis: speculators are buying stocks that are rising and selling stocks that are falling, and they are using the ticker tape to tell them when to do this.

An expanded form of this technique arises when speculators buy stocks that are "in vogue" and sell stocks that are falling out of vogue.

RIE

Acronym: Recognized Investment Exchange. In the United Kingdom, an RIE is any organized body that provides a market framework within which specific transactions can be effected.

An RIE, under the Financial Services Act of 1986, is expected to provide facilities whereby the market price of an investment may be established in an open and fair way. In and of itself, an RIE need not be a place (it could be electronic) nor need it be an SRO. Part of the concept of an RIE is the ability not only to establish a fair price but also to disseminate the price to users of the marketplace.

RIGGING THE MARKET

A slang expression for price manipulation. In practice, such manipulation occurs if buyers in concert push prices up, or sellers in concert push prices down—for their own benefit. In practice, neither direct buying nor selling is required; rumors will often cause the appropriate effect to occur.

The term is also used of *imputed* manipulation; thus, following the two October crashes (1987 and 1989) many small investors were convinced that market insiders and sophisticated money managers manipulated the market to the disadvantage of the small investor.

RIM

See RESTRICTED INTERNAL MEMO.

RIO

Acronym: Regional Interface Organization. RIO is used of a limited participant member of the Midwest Securities Trust Co. (MSTC). The sole purpose of this limited form of membership is to have transactions cleared by MSTC but ultimately settled (*flipped* is the slang term) at another clearing agency that is electronically linked with MSTC.

ROAD SHOW

An issuer's presentation, made either in person or by a representative, to sophisticated investors. It highlights the features of an upcoming issue and publicizes the strengths of the company.

Also called: DOG AND PONY SHOW.

"ROBINSON CRUSOE WEEK"

A colorful and literary allusion to the novel by Daniel Defoe and is used to refer to a very dull and listless market. The term originated in the United Kingdom, and to devotees of the novel it means a week that "is waiting for Friday"—Crusoe's manservant—and for the end of the listless week!

In the United Kingdom the term has the added connotation that the British market is waiting for economic news from the United States (much of which appears on a Thursday here), which will have a market effect on Friday in Britain.

ROL

See REDUCTION OPTION LOAN.

"ROLLER COASTER" SWAP

Colorful expression for a transaction in which two parties exchange interest payments on identical principal amounts, and the principal amounts are self-amortizing. The self-amortizing effect may result from sinking fund payments or other scheduled payments. For example, two parties could exchange the same principal amount of GNMAs for sinking fund bonds; the yield may be the same but the paydown may vary. Thus, as with other interest-rate swaps, the liabilities could be fixed versus "floaters," or any combination thereof.

ROLLING BIG BANG

A term used on the Amsterdam Stock Exchange to classify certain reforms adopted by the ASE to regain lost institutional business and to compete more effectively in international marketplaces. The term was coined to mimic the "big bang" that occurred when London's International Stock Exchange initiated its reforms on October 27, 1986.

ROLLING COVERED WRITE

A description of a continuous covered call writing program on an underlying position in the stock (or a convertible).

The concept is simple: following a covered write (but before its expiration), the writer makes a closing purchase followed by another covered write on the same underlying security. Thus, the writer voids the previous obligation, gains a second (and third, and so on) premium, and extends the time of the obligation to deliver the underlying.

However, such a program of rolling covered writes is not a "gold mine"—it requires proper timing, avoidance of unprofitable commissions from turnovers, and monitoring of premiums received and paid.

ROLLING PUT

Term used of the put feature on certain bonds. At specified times in the future, the holder may put the bond to the issuer at par (or at a premium). However, if the bond is not put at the first available put date, the holder must wait for the second (or the third) date to put the bond. Thus, unless put at a specific date, the holder has only two recourses: sell in the market at prevailing prices, or wait until the next put date.

ROSOKU-ASHI

A popular Japanese term for a way of charting price movements. The term in Japanese means "candle chart."

Using graph paper, *price* is the vertical measurement; *time* is the horizontal measurement. Thus, time versus price will make a rectangle. If the price is upward, the rectangle will be left white; if price trend is downward, the rectangle is shaded.

In effect, it is easy to identify upward moving stocks from downward moving stocks. The time frame may be extended to cover longer periods.

In the following illustration, A is the high, B is the open, C is the close, and D is the low. C is the critical measurement, and, as a result, white blocks signify stocks that have risen (closed high) and shaded blocks signify stocks that have fallen (closed low).

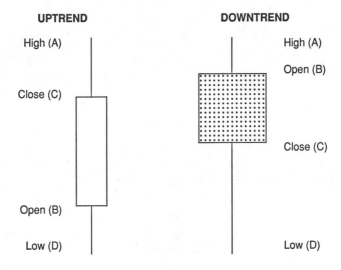

ROTHSCHILD RULE

When asked about the secret of his financial success, the founder of the Rothschild dynasty is said to have replied: "Buy cheap, sell dear."

Obviously, such a secret is a tautology because one either bought cheap or one did not. As such, the saying became popular on Wall Street in the expression: "Buy low, sell high."

ROTN
Acronym: Reconcilement of Out-Trade Notice. ROTN is an abbreviation for a form submitted by clearing corporations to brokers involved in transactions that cannot be compared because of discrepancies in trade terms.

On trade plus one (T + 1), this notice of an out-trade is sent to the floor for reconciliation so an agreement can be reached by trade date about the terms of the trade.

ROUNDTRIP
1. A purchase followed by a sale (or a sale followed by a purchase) of a security, commodity, or currency (a) during a relatively short period of time that (b) resulted in a net zero position in the underlying. For example, "The client did a roundtrip in March silver futures."
2. Before the time of commission negotiations (May 1, 1975), a reduced commission schedule for clients who bought and sold (or sold short and covered) within a relatively short period. Originally, this was 30 days; later, it was reduced to 14 days.

RP
1. A commonly used abbreviation for Repurchase Agreement. Repurchase agreements are used by securities dealers to finance inventory. They are also used by the FOMC in its endeavor to fine-tune the economy.
2. An acronym for remarketed preferred stock (q.v.), originated by Merrill Lynch for its institutional and corporate customers.

RPI
See RETAIL PRICE INDEX.

R + 1, etc.
A technical designation used by industry operations departments to designate "RECAP date plus 1." The enumeration continues: plus 2, plus 3, and so on.

This procedure is used to count the elapsed days since a broker/dealer submitted to the NSCC for a reconfirmation and repricing of a fail with a contra dealer member of the clearing corporation.

RTC
1. NYSE ticker symbol of Rochester Telephone Company, a large communications company located in upper New York State.
2. The designator of the Resolution Trust Company, a legal entity established by Congress in 1989 to salvage failing thrift institutions in the United States. It is funded by the Treasury Department through the issuance of bonds.

RULE 97
A NYSE rule that limits a member's proprietary activities in a stock on the same day after it has completed a block transaction to facilitate a customer's order.

RULE 390
A famous NYSE rule that requires, with some exceptions, a member's execution of NYSE-listed securities only on the NYSE floor. Its principal exceptions have been used in connection with a domestic customer's transactions in Europe before the exchange opens and in Asia after the exchange closes.

RULE 535 SECURITIES
London's International Stock Exchange rule that applies to the Unlisted Securities Market (USM) and certain exempted transactions for securities:
1. Principally traded outside the United Kingdom and Ireland.
2. Of small, local nonlisted companies that have been given permission to trade in the USM.
3. Of mineral exploration companies that have not been in existence long enough to qualify for listing.
4. Of suspended issuers, but only to cover shorts and to liquidate estates.

RULE OF 19
A stock market theory that uses as a predictor of market direction the sum of the P/E ratio of the S&P 500 Index and the nation's inflation rate. If the sum is less than 19, the indicator is bullish; if the sum is greater than 19, the indicator is bearish. And, the greater the deviation from 19, the stronger the message.

"RULER" STOCKS
Street slang for companies whose earnings growth seems to rise in a straight line year after year through good times and bad. The description is factual and does not indicate whether the results are from good management or good luck.

RUMP
Colorful English term for the remnant securities in a rights offering (or offering of warrants) that are not subscribed to by current stockholders. The "rump" is purchased by stand-by underwriters at prices that represent a bargain, compared to current market prices. The underwriter can then resell the securities to customers for a profit.

RUN-OFF
1. The execution and publication on the consolidated tape of transactions that occurred on the floor during the 30 seconds of the final bell.
2. Term used to describe a series of declining prices either in individual securities or the market in general during a relatively brief time. For example, "There was a run-off in the market this afternoon between 3:30 and 4:00 o'clock."

RUSH WITHDRAWAL TRANSFER
See RWT.

RUSSELL 1,000
A stock market index developed by the Frank Russell Co., an investment advisor located in Tacoma, Washington. The index is composed of 1,000 of the largest equity capitalized US corporations in terms of market value. Because the smallest company in this index has a capitalization of about $250 million, the index has particular tracking appeal for large hedge funds and investment companies.

The Russell 2,000 on the other hand, is composed of 2,000 of the smaller publicly traded US companies.

RUSSELL 3,000
A stock market index developed by the Frank Russell Co., an investment advisor located in Tacoma, Washington. This market barometer is comprised of 3,000 of the largest U.S. companies in terms of market capitalization and represents about 98% of the U.S. equity market.

RUST BELT
A broad descriptive term used of the states of Pennsylvania, West Virginia, Ohio, Indiana, and Illinois. The allusion is to several facts: these states are the principal manufacturing states for iron in the United States; the factories in which the iron is fabricated are, in many cases, old and "rusty"; and the workers who manufacture iron and steel have suffered a number of economic hardships in recent years because their factories are noncompetitive.

RV

Acronym: Recreational Vehicle. Such RVs generally fall into three general categories: (1) travel trailers, (2) motor homes, (3) and van conversions.

There are several publicly traded stocks whose issuers manufacture such vehicles. Receivables for such RVs often form the collateral for asset-backed securities.

Many states place the initials RV prominently on the registration plates for such vehicles.

RWT

These initials stand for Rush Withdrawal Transfer. RWT is a special service provided by the DTC upon the request of member firm customers and the payment of a special fee. Through automation, a C.O.D. customer can obtain upon payment of a $22.50 processing fee urgent physical delivery of certificates purchased with clearing house funds.

S

S

Nineteenth letter of the alphabet used:
1. On the consolidated tapes, a transaction in round lots of 100 shares; for example 3s = 300 shares.
2. In older option newspaper tables, to signify that a specific series was not listed for trading.
3. In the stock table of the newspaper, following the name of the stock, to signify that within the past year there was a stock split or dividend that increased the number of shares by 20% or more. For example, Boeing s.
4. As the fifth letter in NASDAQ/NMS listings to signify shares of beneficial interest.
5. As the NYSE symbol for Sears, Roebuck & Co., a major U.S. retailer.

SABRES

Acronym: Share-Adjusted Broker-Remarketed Equity Securities. SABRES are a Smith Barney innovation designed to function like commercial paper, or medium term notes, but is, in reality, a preferred stock. The stock is puttable to the issuer at par any time after a minimum 46-day holding period.

SAEF

Mnemonic for SEAQ Automated Execution Facility. SAEF is an offshoot of SEAQ (Stock Exchange Automated Quotation) system of the International Stock Exchange in London.

SAEF will enter electronically and execute small buy and sell orders on the London exchange. It is modelled after the NYSE's DOT system. If successful, the SAEF system will be expanded to execute larger orders.

SAIF
See SAVINGS ASSOCIATION INSURANCE FUND.

SAITORI
Name given to a category of membership on the three major stock exchanges in Japan.

Saitori members act as intermediaries for regular members of the exchanges, in a manner similar to that of the $2 brokers on U.S. exchanges. They are not permitted to trade for personal or firm accounts, but they are permitted to report transactions electronically to securities firms and to news offices.

SALES WRAPPER
Term used of a broker/dealer's promotional material employed to accompany a prospectus. Technically, that material may only be a restatement of the information in the prospectus but, because it may be a more interesting synopsis, it is preferred by many firms marketing the new issue.

SALOMON–RUSSELL GLOBAL EQUITY INDEX
A joint effort by Salomon Brothers and the Frank Russell Company to gauge market performance of 1,572 equity securities traded in 23 different countries.

The base of the index represents approximately 81 percent of the capitalization of the participating marketplaces. The index is heavily skewed to the Russell 1,000 (q.v.) of important U.S. stocks because the index emphasizes liquidity and actively traded stocks in world markets.

SANTA CLAUS RALLY
Jocular title for the anticipated year-end rally in the stock market. Historically, there has tended to be a year-end rally in anticipation of buying by institutions in early January as they receive pension fund contributions from employers.

SAO PAULO STOCK EXCHANGE
Pronounced San Pau–loo, as in book. The largest and most volatile of the South American stock exchanges. Most private sector securities in Brazil are traded there.

Trading is permitted between 9:30 A.M. and 1:00 P.M. on business days, with no after-hour trading permitted. Settlement is on the third business day following the trade date.

SAPCO

Acronym: Single Asset Property Company. A U.K. issuer whose sole asset collateralizing a security listed on the U.K. exchange is a single building (or a group of buildings consolidated to serve as a single asset). SAPCOs can now legitimately offer both equity and debt issues against such collateral.

SATURDAY NIGHT SPECIAL

This colorful merger and acquisition term is used to describe a quick and unexpected bid by a raider to acquire control of a company. A "Saturday night special" is designed to act fast, while the stock market is closed, to gain control before management can muster its defenses.

United Kingdom equivalent: dawn raid.

SAUCERS

Acronym: Sovereign Australian Currency Enhanced Securities. Saucers are a Bankers Trust Eurobond offering with a currency option attached. The issuer sells the bond but retains the right (an option) to redeem the bond in either US or Australian funds. The option is selected just prior to the redemption date.

SAVINGS ASSOCIATION INSURANCE FUND

An arm of the Federal Deposit Insurance Corporation (FDIC). SAIF was created under FIRREA (Financial Institutions Reform, Recovery, and Enforcement Act of 1989) to insure depositors' savings accounts, up to $100,000, at savings and loan institutions.

SAVRS

An acronym for Shearson Lehman Hutton's Select Auction Variable Rate Securities, a class of municipal security issued in conjunction with residual interest bonds (RIBS). The municipal issuer contracts to pay a fixed sum of tax-exempted interest semiannually, split among two classes of debt securities holders, SAVRS and RIBS. The holders of SAVRS receive a variable amount, determined by Dutch auction every 35 days; while the holders of RIBS receive what is left over. Thus, if rates decline in the municipal market, the RIBS' holders benefit with an increased portion of the residual interest. If rates increase, the RIBS holders suffer with a smaller portion of the interest pool. SAVRS have a prior claim to the available interest.

SAX

Acronym: Stockholm Automated Exchange. SAX is a fully automated trading system in Sweden's largest financial center. SAX is also fully compatible with trading systems in Copenhagen, Oslo, and Helsinki.

SAX was designed and installed by Tandem Computers (US) and is linked by the Ericsson Information System so member brokers can trade from their offices, rather than be present on the floor of the exchange.

SAX is similar in function to SEAQ on the International Stock Exchange in London.

SCA

See ALL SUBSEQUENT COUPONS ATTACHED

SCARLET LADY OF WALL STREET

Colorful nickname for the New York and Lake Erie Railroad, a major East Coast transportation system of the 19th century. The railroad was so called because of the many major stock manipulations during this era between Cornelius Vanderbilt and Daniel Drew. Many investors found themselves on the wrong side of the market and lost a great deal of money in these manipulations.

SCHEDULE C OF THE NASD BYLAWS

A section of the NASD bylaws that sets forth the registration requirements and procedures for membership. In summary, the minimum registration requirements for a member organization call for at least two persons to be registered as principals, one of whom must be qualified as a financial and operations principal (FINOP).

SCIN

Acronym: Self-Cancelling Installment Note. A SCIN is an estate tax-savings technique for persons who do not expect to survive the minimum of 15 years required for a GRIT.

Under a SCIN, an asset is sold to an heir for an installment note with the proviso that the liability is cancelled upon the seller's death. The buyer pays a premium for the self-cancellation privilege and a market rate of interest for the installment notes. If the seller dies before the sale is completed, only the asset value above the installments already paid to that date are included in the estate.

SCR

Initials standing for Safe Custody Receipt. An SCR works in much the same way as an ADR; that is, the receipt for the security is bought and sold just as though it were the underlying security. Dividends on the underlying security are received through the custodian.

Unlike ADRs, where the actual certificates are held in the foreign branches of American banks, SCRs represent certificates held in safekeeping by the U.K.'s Talisman system.

SCRIP

1. In the United States, it was not uncommon in the past for a corporation to issue partial shares, or scrip. Such scrip could be "rounded up" by the payment of a subscription fee, or the partial share could be sold in the marketplace. It is no longer a common practice.
2. In the United Kingdom, the term is *scrip issue* and is used when a corporation makes a stock split. A stock split, or capitalisation issue, results in more shares outstanding but no more capital in the treasury of the company.

SCRIPOPHILY

Pronounced: scri–pop´-fily. The hobby of collecting old stock and bond certificates. Such certificates have no value except for their rarity as collectors' items. Many, however, have great artistic interest because of engravings, coloration, or calligraphy.

SD

See STATUTORY DISQUALIFICATION

SDFS

Acronym: Same-Day-Funds Settlement. SDFS is a method of settlement used by the DTC for certain securities transactions. Same-day funds are federal funds ("good money") and are paid—if both parties to the trade are properly collateralized—for transactions in US government securities, short-term municipal notes, medium-term (commercial paper) notes, collateralized mortgage obligations (CMOs), auction rate preferred issues, and certain other instruments.

Other DTC transactions are settled on the fifth business day following the trade date.

SDRT

Acronym: Stamp Duty Reserve Tax. SDRT is a levy imposed by the British government on transactions in equity securities in the United Kingdom. There is no duty if both the seller and buyer are domiciled outside the United Kingdom.

Technically, stamp duty is a re-registration tax paid on secondary transactions by the *purchaser;* thus, it is not unlike the SEC fee paid on exchange transactions in the United States by the *seller.*

SEAQ AUTOMATED EXECUTION FACILITY
See SAEF.

SEASONED
1. Descriptive term used of an issue that was distributed to a large number of holders and now trades frequently with good liquidity in the secondary market. For example, "With 30–40,000 shares trading each day, LMN is now a seasoned issue."
2. Used of Eurodebt issues that were originally issued for sale outside the United States and which were not registered with the SEC. If such an issue is actively traded for a period of time (i.e., "seasoned") it may be purchased by sophisticated U.S.-domiciled investors without violating US securities laws.

The term is also used as a participial noun; for example, *seasoning.* "That issue needs a bit more seasoning before I would make a major investment in it."

SEASONED MORTGAGE
A real estate loan older than 30 months. Thus, a mortgage that has been outstanding 30 months or less is considered to be "unseasoned."

SEATS
Acronym: Stock Exchange Automated Trading System. SEATS is an electronic trading system used to coordinate trading activity on the different marketplaces known collectively as the Australia Stock Exchange.

SECONDARY DOOMSDAY VALUE
For purposes of determining capital gains tax liability in the United Kingdom after April 6, 1982, all purchase transactions are adjusted to the English retail price index to establish a basis cost. Investors, therefore, are not penalized just because of inflation when they sell.

The dates of reference and the benchmarks are different, hence, "secondary."

SECOND-ROUND FINANCING
Colorful term used to designate product development costs for a relatively new business concern.

These funds are generally provided by the same venture capital firm(s) that provided the original seed money for the new business. Invariably, such capital contributions are made in exchange for equity in the company.

SECPS
Acronym: Securities and Exchange Commission Practice Section. SECPS is a division of the AICPA.

SECPS is comprised of CPA firms that conduct almost 90% of the audits of publicly traded firms. Its goal is to make sure that those companies comply with the SEC's financial reporting requirements and procedures.

SEC RULE 15c2-6
Popularly known as the "penny stock rule," this is an attempt by the SEC to cut down investor fraud in the marketing of low-priced securities. The rule establishes a suitability test, and a "cooling off" period for shares selling at less than $5 if the company has less than $2 million in tangible assets. There is an exemption for low-priced shares that are exchange-listed or NASDAQ-traded.

SEC RULE 15c2-11
This rule prohibits a broker/dealer from submitting quotations for publication in any quotation medium unless it has in its records such specific information about the issuer as would normally be required to make an intelligent investment decision. The rule outlines the kinds of information required.

In effect, the broker/dealer not only has to know its customers, it has to know its companies if it is to act as a marketmaker.

SEC RULE 19c-4
See ONE SHARE—ONE VOTE RULE.

SEC RULE 237
A rule, under the Securities Act of 1933, that enables nonaffiliated holders of an issuer's unregistered securities to sell relatively small amounts publicly in nonbrokered transactions, provided they have owned the securities five years or more.

SECULAR TRUST
Secular, from the Latin *saeculum,* meaning long term. A secular trust is a form of deferred compensation on which the tax rate is frozen at 28%. The amount deferred is immediately taxed at 28%, and the trust pays an annual tax of 28 percent on dividends and interest received and realized long-term capital gains. New funds can be deposited into the trust after the 28% tax is paid.

The trust is qualified under ERISA and is so established that it cannot be appropriated in the event of a hostile takeover. Because taxes are paid on a current basis, there is no further obligation when funds are distributed.

SECURITIES & INVESTMENT BOARD
See SIB.

SECURITIES ASSOCIATION (TSA), THE
The Securities Association is the successor to the merged London Stock Exchange and the International Securities Regulatory Organization (ISRO). As a new SRO, the Securities Association will have administrative responsibility for the combined membership, including business authorizations and capital compliance oversight, under SIB rules.

SECURITIES DEALERS ASSOCIATION OF JAPAN
See JASD.

SECURITIES EXCHANGE OF THAILAND (SET)
Located in Bangkok, the SET is a prominent Asian exchange. Trading is conducted daily from 9:30 until 11:30 A.M., with settlement on the third business day after trade date.

SET is dominated by local banks and cement companies and there is a strict limitation on the extent of foreign ownership of companies listed on the exchange. In fact, share transfers are halted when this limit has been reached.

SECURITIES INDUSTRY COMMITTEE ON ARBITRATION
See SICA.

SECURITIES INFORMATION CORPORATION
Initials: SIC. SIC is a private firm that works under contract for the SEC to serve as a clearinghouse of information about lost, stolen, or missing securities. SEC Rule 17f-1 sets the provisions for compliance by broker/dealers and banks.

SECURITY TRADERS' ASSOCIATION OF NEW YORK
See STANY.

SEDOL
Acronym: Stock Exchange Daily Official List. SEDOL is similar in concept to CUSIP in the United States. It is a seven-character number assigned to each of about 6,000 issues admitted to trading on London's International Stock Exchange. Thus, SEDOL is used as an identifier for comparing, clearing, and settling transactions made on the ISE floor.

"SEED MONEY"

Term used by venture capitalists for the initial expansion of new corporations. This may involve building a plant, further exploring a process of manufacturing, or initial marketing endeavors. In exchange for the seed money, the venture capitalists take an equity interest in the enterprise.

SEER

A prophet or oracle, thus a person with great foresight. The term is used in the financial industry to describe someone who makes accurate predictions about the market's movements. Many technical, market, and economic analysts have deserved reputations as "seers" and their suggestions are eagerly followed.

The term is similar in concept to *gnome*. Gnome, however, emphasizes the expertness of the person; seer emphasizes the predictive ability of the person.

SEE-WEE

Phonetic expansion of the NYSE ticker symbol CWE, Commonwealth Edison Corporation. It is used by floor traders to designate trades in the stock of that large electric utility that services the Chicago area.

SEGREGATION ACCOUNT 100

This is a special account at the DTC for shares of communications and maritime issues held by members for foreign owners.

Because there are legal limitations on the extent of foreign ownership of most of these issues, DTC used to require registration of beneficial ownership and would not hold such certificates in street name. Now, such securities may be held in nominee name if they are put into this special account where foreign ownership is readily identified.

SEGREGATION OF INFORMATION PRINCIPLES

A popular term for the internal rules within member firms whereby confidential information obtained from issuers by investment banking and research employees is kept secret from sales and trading personnel who might be tempted to use it illegally.

The concept of such separation of information within the firm is also known by the colorful term *Chinese wall.*

SELECT AUCTION VARIABLE RATE SECURITIES

See SAVRS.

SELF-CANCELLING INSTALLMENT NOTE

See SCIN.

SELF-REGULATORY ORGANIZATION
See SRO.

SELL A BEAR
Colorful English expression for a short sale. The term originated in the 18th century when bear skins were actually traded. A person who sold skins before the bears were actually caught in anticipation of a drop in bear skin prices was said to "sell a bear." Thus, short sellers anticipate a drop in prices and are said to be "bearish."

"SELLING AWAY"
A euphemism for the illegal practice whereby registered representatives (RRs) conduct business that is not recorded on the books and records of the employing broker/dealer while utilizing the reputation and facilities of their employer.

The private placement of securities and the sale of questionable tax shelters are examples of "selling away" that have been discovered in the past. Registered representatives are agents of the broker/dealer, and the broker/dealer has a right to know and approve the business done by its employees.

"SELLING THE ORDER FLOW"
A colorful expression that describes the handling of large institutional orders for securities. Thus, upon receipt of a block trade, a member firm will often shop the order with other customers to see if there is a contra order. This will facilitate the trade and lessen the risk to the broker/ dealer if it must take the other side of the trade; or to the customer if a larger order is "dumped" on the auction market or on the third market (the over-the-counter market).

SELLING THE SPREAD
A term used in the options and futures marketplaces to describe the simultaneous *purchase* of a contract in a nearby month and the *sale* of a contract in a far out month. In options, if the strike price is the same, the far out month should have a larger premium than the nearby month and the person "selling the spread" receives a credit for the difference in the premiums. In the futures market, particularly if it is a "carrying charge market," there should also be a net credit.

SEPON
Acronym: Stock Exchange Pool Nominees. SEPON is a common pot of securities on an issue-by-issue basis in which stock exchange members may have a specific interest as a partner participant, based on their daily trade activities.

SEPON is not unlike the DTC's use of a nominee pool, under the common nominee name of CEDE, in which member security interests are registered.

SEQUAL
A melding of the terms SEAQ and QUALITY transactions.

The program is still a pilot. The concept is to have an on-line computer matching system for trades in non-British equities. Under SEQUAL, within five minutes of the trade, the details are displayed within the system to the participants for comparison and confirmation. Once done, the trade is "locked in" and subject to settlement and transfer of the underlying securities.

SERIES 7 REGISTERED
Industry term used to describe an employee of a member broker/dealer who has qualified to be a registered representative by passing an NYSE/NASD 6-hour industry examination.

The term is also used of persons who previously qualified and thus were "grandfathered" and did not have to take the Series 7 examination. In certain circumstances, the NASD will also waive the exam for persons with extensive industry experience.

SERP
Acronym: Supplemental Executive Retirement Plan. SERPs are enhanced pension plans for key executives. Because of ERISA rules regarding "top-heavy" plans, they are usually not funded by company contributions; instead, they are funded by the employees themselves. On the other hand, they are not under the control of an acquiring group in case of an unfriendly merger.

SES
Initials for the Stock Exchange of Singapore. Trading is conducted on three separate trading sessions on each working day, and settlement is on the fifth business day following the trade date. "Fails" are not condoned.

SESDAQ
Acronym: Stock Exchange of Singapore Dealing and Automated Quotation System. SESDAQ is similar to NASDAQ in the United States. Second tier stocks (i.e., those that do not qualify for listing on the SES) are traded through SESDAQ. In this way, SESDAQ acts as an adjunct to the floor trading on SES.

SET
See SECURITIES EXCHANGE OF THAILAND.

SET-ASIDE
An expression developed in the 1980s to describe the percentage of underwritten securities reserved for minority broker/dealer organizations. Set-asides are typically found in municipal issues where minority-run broker/dealers may have influence on the underlying issuers, but they are now beginning to show up in corporate underwritings, also.

SETTLEMENT DAY
The day on which payment and transfer of security requirements (if any) must be met.
1. In the United States, settlement day is based on trade date. In general, it is the fifth business day following trade date for secondary trades in stocks and bonds. The exceptions are governments, agencies, and listed options that settle on the business day following trade date.
2. In the United Kingdom, settlement day is based on the account period, a two-week period in which all trades are "netted." It is usually the seventh business day following the end of the account period.
3. In other countries, there are fixed days for settlement. The Italian exchanges are an apparent exception because long delays are the rule. Such delays seriously impede the efficient running of these exchanges.

SGB EFFECT
European term derived from the aborted attempt to take over the Societe General de Belgique in 1988. Because of the bad aftereffects, many companies have adopted antitakeover measures modeled after the "poison pill" measures in the United States.

SHARE-ADJUSTED BROKER-REMARKETED EQUITY SECURITIES
See SABRES.

SHARE REPURCHASE PUTS
See #SHARPS#

SHARKWATCH SERVICE
A computerized information service offered by Georgeson & Co., a well-known proxy solicitor in the financial community. This service is able to detect unusual trading activity in an issuer's stock and, through careful analysis, determine the identity of someone who may be accumulating the stock in advance of a proxy contest or tender offer.

232

#SHARPS#
Acronym: Share Repurchase Puts. This is a Merrill Lynch innovation designed to assure equal treatment of all shareholders and to discourage arbitrage activities. It is an alternate to corporate self-tender offers or large stock repurchase programs in that a put option is attached to shares that can be exercised by the holder at any time before expiration. By knowing in advance how many shares—and at what price—may be repurchased, the issuer has greater operating flexibility, and un-friendly corporate takeovers are discouraged.

SHEARSON LEHMAN WORLD INDEX
Shearson and Quantum Matrix work together in the preparation of this measurement of international market performance. This global index stresses total return, rather than simple price movements, of the se-lected issues.

SHERIFF
Colorful term used to describe a CBOE member who is empowered to ensure the forced liquidation of a position at the request of a clearing member organization. If the equity of an options trader (or an options member organization) falls below the margin requirement of its clear-ing firm, that firm may immediately demand more collateral *or* the liq-uidation of established positions to reduce its financial exposure. Its sur-rogate, which is known as the "sheriff" or the "leg breaker," oversees completion of this liquidation.

SHINJINURI
Japanese term for a high risk or "go go" trader; that is, a free-wheeling speculator who plays with the most volatile issues in the market. Need-less to say, when such persons are successful, they make huge sums of money; when wrong, the results are catastrophic.

SHOCK ABSORBERS
Colorful term for a number of temporary measures adopted by the secu-rities and commodities marketplaces to avoid the disastrous volatility of October 19 and 20, 1987. Some of these measures include trading halts if certain indicators are up or down by a specified number of points; re-strictions on the automatic trading systems (e.g., D.O.T.); the elimina-tion of proprietary program trading; and limitation on the entry of or-ders marked "on the close."

Also called "circuit breakers."

SHOPPING THE STREET
Colorful expression used to describe the practice of canvassing other dealers and marketmakers to determine the best bid/offer available before executing an order.

SHORTFALL
1. Verb. The act of failing to meet a financial objective.
2. Noun. The amount by which a planned financial objective is not met. For example, "There is a shortfall of $10 million in the city's budget." Also, "The company will have a shortfall of 10% in meeting its marketing objectives."

"SHORT-SHORT" TEST
To qualify as a regulated investment company, the IRS requires that an investment company acquire no more than 30% of its gross income from the sale of securities held less than three months. This is to prevent short-term trading as a normal pattern of investing.

This prohibition and its measurement is called the "short-short" test or the "short 3" test.

SHORT-STOP ORDER
This is a multiple instruction order for stock exchanges. It requires a short sale at the market, but only if someone else first makes a transaction at or below the memorandum price (the "stop" portion of the order). The short sale, as usual, requires an uptick.

"SHORT THEIR BOGEY"
Quaint expression used by fixed income portfolio managers.

The term means that the portfolio manager has portfolio maturities that are shorter than the fixed income index on which their performance will be based. This will result in a better performance than the index only if the yield curve is inverted (short-term rates are higher than long-term rates); otherwise, it will result in a poorer performance for the portfolio.

SHORT 3 TEST
See "SHORT-SHORT" TEST

SHOSHA
Japanese term for the giant trading houses; for example, Mitsubishi, Mitsui, C. Itoh, and Nichimen, which specialize in international export-import dealings as intermediaries for other Japanese industrial concerns and which, as a result, are the principal players in foreign exchange and foreign currency futures trading in Japan.

SHOW-IN BUYER/SELLER
Trading language used to designate a possible large buyer/seller in a particular security. Thus, the trader feels that if a contra party makes its presence known, the trader will be able to generate a large order.

SIB
Acronym: Securities and Investments Board. SIB is a quasi-governmental body established under the Financial Services Bill (1986) in Britain to oversee and regulate various forms of investments in the United Kingdom.

Although the SIB is, in many ways, similar in function to the SEC in the United States, SIB is more independent and less political.

SIC
See SECURITIES INFORMATION CORPORATION

SICA
Acronym: Securities Industry Committee on Arbitration. This is a private body that established and monitors compliance with an arbitration code for individual complaint cases involving customers and securities firms.

SICAV
Acronym: Societes d'Investissement a Capital Variable. SICAV is one of two types of mutual funds found in France. SICAVs are organized as corporations and are required to invest a minimum of 30% of their assets in French bonds. The remaining 70% may be invested in other forms of securities, either French or international.

A variation on the SICAV: the "monory" (equity) SICAV has 30% in French bonds, 60% in French stocks, with remaining 10% in other investments.

"SIDE CAR" RULE
Colorful name for Rule 80A of the NYSE. In effect, this rule governs the use of the DOT system in times of great market volatility. If the S&P 500 has declined 12 or more points (about 96 points on the DJIA), institutional orders of a program type are routed into a separate file for five minutes so individual customer orders may have time priority. After five minutes, the institutional orders are eligible for execution.

The term *express lane* is also used of the fact that individual orders are given precedence over institutional orders in this circumstance.

SIGNIFICANT ORDER IMBALANCE
A stock exchange term sometimes used if trading is halted because the market is demoralized; that is, there is a wide spread between bid and offer, or the bid side of the market has suddenly disappeared. As a rule of thumb, for example, a spread of 10% or 3 points, whichever is lower, between the bid and offer on stocks selling below 100 (10% or 5 points for stocks above 100) would be a "significant order imbalance."

This imbalance may apply either to the opening or the reopening of the market. In addition, trading may be halted because of pending news, and following the news there may be a "significant order imbalance."

SICOVAM
Acronym: Societe Interprofessionelle pour le Compensation des Valeurs Mobilieres. SICOVAM is similar in function to the DTC in the United States in that it holds certificates in nominee name so they can be cleared and transferred. SICOVAM was set up under French law and, in effect, has created a certificateless (book entry) society for French broker/dealers, banks, and other financial institutions. SICOVAM is also linked with many foreign clearing corporations so they may take part in the internationalization of the French securities markets.

SIMEX
Initials of the Singapore International Monetary Exchange, a prominent futures exchange in the Orient. SIMEX has futures contracts in foreign currencies and is linked with the Chicago Mercantile Exchange (CME). SIMEX also trades futures contracts in the popular Nikkei Index of Japanese stocks.

SINC
A tongue-in-cheek term from the 80s to stand for: Single Income No Children. This term describes a couple in which one person works and the other goes for an advanced professional degree; for example, MBA, JD, MD, and the like.

SINGLE ASSET PROPERTY COMPANY
See SAPCO.

SINGLE-PREMIUM LIFE INSURANCE
A form of whole or universal life that is marked by:
1. A one-time payment in full of all premiums.
2. A fixed death benefit.
3. Tax sheltering of the internal growth of the policy.
4. Some direction of investment values within the policy.
5. A minimum restriction on loans against the policy.

Most recent tax law changes have severely restricted policy loans before age 59½. Now, to be eligible for such policy loans, the premium must be paid over seven years.

SINGLE PROPERTY OWNERSHIP TRUST
See SPOT.

SITUS
Acronym: System for Institutional Trading of Unregistered Securities. SITUS was a plan initiated by the American Stock Exchange to foster trading by foreigners and US institutions of unregistered (with the SEC) securities of large, high-quality, foreign issuers. Such securities were originally issued outside the United States or in private placements. SITUS facilitates the trading of such securities without the need to register them in the United States. It has not been approved by the SEC.

"SIZE OUT" A BROKER
Term used in the auction market on exchange floors if a broker is trying to "cross" a block. The broker usually waits for another broker to trade in the crowd. This trade takes care of the broker with time *priority*. Now the broker with the "cross" can freeze out the other brokers because his or her order is the largest. This floor rule is termed *precedence;* that is, getting an execution by virtue of the size of the order.

"SIZE THE BOOK"
Term used by block trading organizations when they effect block trades on the floor. In effect, the floor broker asks not for a quote and size but asks to get an insight into the size of limit orders above (if buying) or below (if selling) the current quote. In this way, the floor broker can ascertain the quantity and price at which the block can be effected. The block, if executed, must include all limit orders capable of execution at the transaction price. Thus, if the lowest offer is 75 and the block trade (a buy) is made at 75¼ everyone whose shares are taken will get 75¼.

"SKID"
Floor traders' nickname for the shares of Standard Oil of California. The nickname is a play on the NYSE ticker symbol for the stock: SD.

SKIPPIES
A play on the acronym: School Kids with Income and Purchasing Power. Skippies are an important marketing force. Not only do they spend (and often invest) their own money, it is estimated that they influence 40–60% of the fashion buying in their families.

"SLAM DUNK"
From basketball: an unopposed and forceful score. By analogy in mergers and acquisitions: an unopposed corporate takeover.

SLEAZE BAG
See DIRT BAG.

SLEEPING LEVEL, THE
Colorful expression often used when giving financial advice, particularly if the person is already invested. If there is a drop in the market, the investor is counseled to sell a sufficient amount of his or her holdings so he or she may sleep quietly at night. This is the investor's mental level of comfort.

The expression is also used before the investment. For example, "Mr. Jones, 100 shares of this stock should not disturb your sleeping level."

SLGS
Acronym: State and Local Government Series. SLGS is pronounced "slugs."

SLGS are private offerings of U.S. government securities to municipalities that enable them to pre-refund their outstanding debt in compliance with IRS and Treasury Department regulations. Such issues are often labeled PRE-REF or ETM (Escrowed to Maturity) on dealer offering sheets.

SLIPPAGE
Metaphor from the science of mechanics where it means the loss of work because of inefficiencies in a system.
1. In the United States, a shortfall in projected revenues or sales from a predetermined plan. For example, "The company's sales caused a slippage in anticipated earnings."
2. In the United Kingdom, the consumption of available capital faster than anticipated. Thus, it may be difficult to obtain further capital from investors. For example, "Eagle Industry's plant was not completed with the proceeds of its initial public offering. This slippage may make it difficult to successfully offer a second block of stock."

SLOB
1. Slang expression used by salespersons and traders for the common stock of Schlumberger, Ltd. The jargon is derived from the NYSE ticker symbol for the stock: SLB.
2. Acronym: Secured Lease Obligation Bonds. SLOBs are the modern-day equivalent of mortgage bonds; that is, a bond secured by specific real property.

In effect, the proceeds of a bond issue are used to build a utility plant. The plant is then leased to the utility with lease payments equal to the bond debt service over the life of the bond (interest and principal). If there is a default, the bondholders become general creditors for the amount above the resale value of the plant.

SMA
See SPECIAL MEMORANDUM ACCOUNT.

SMART MONEY
Term ascribed to those investors who seem to do the right things at the right time.

Smart money, for example, appears to be able to profit both from good markets (they are long) and bad markets (they are short).

The term is also used of individual investment decisions. For example, "At this time and with this yield curve, the smart money is in one to two-year CDs."

Needless to say, the term is also used as a substitute for the proverbial *they*. For example, "They say that . . ." becomes "Smart money says. . . ." This latter usage may not be suitable or ethical.

SMM
See SUPPLEMENTAL MARKETMAKER

SMMEA
Common abbreviation for Secondary Mortgage Market Enhancement Act of 1984. SMMEA encourages access by home buyers to capital market financing. For example, it places highly rated mortgage-backed securities on a par with government agency securities in terms of several, otherwise restrictive, regulatory requirements. Thus, mortgage-backed securities are exempted from the seven-day settlement rule for purchases under Regulation T of the Federal Reserve. (MBS settlements are generally on one day per month.)

SNOWBALLING
Generally used as a verbal noun (a gerund) to mean:
1. The establishment of a market trend that induces an ever-increasing number of investors to trade on the same side of the market. For example, "The program trades in the early afternoon caused snowballing as the market slid continuously downward."
2. The incessant triggering of stop orders from the specialist's book as one set of trades sets off others. For example, "Snowballing increased as the buy stops at 59½ caused a wave of short selling."

SNUGGING
Nautical term: to haul in and tighten sails in preparation for a storm.

Thus, as a metaphor, when the Federal Reserve, the agency responsible for the control of credit in the economy, tightens credit either through raising the interest rate or lowering available credit. For example, "The Federal Reserve anticipates a rise in inflation and as a result is snugging available credit."

SOCIÉTÉ INTERPROFFESSIONALLE POUR LA COMPENSATION DES VALEURS MOBILIERES.
See SICOVAM.

SOCIETES d'INVESTISSEMENT A CAPITAL VARIABLE
See SICAV.

SOCIETY FOR THE PROMOTION OF INSIDER TRADING
See SPIT.

SOCIETY FOR WORLDWIDE INTERBANK FINANCIAL TELECOMMUNICATIONS
See SWIFT.

"SOES-ED"
Pronounced "so–sed." From SOES, the NASD's Small Order Execution System.

SOES automatically executes many orders to buy/sell for 1,000 shares or less against available firm quotes made by marketmakers on the NASDAQ system. Thus, if a marketmaker is *slow* in changing his or her quotes on the NASDAQ system, the marketmaker may get an execution at a price that he or she really does not want. For example, a complaint by one marketmaker to another: "I was SOES-ed on my last trade in ABCD; I received 57¼ instead of 57½, and thus I lost $250."

SOFE
Acronym: Swedish Options and Futures Exchange. Located in Stockholm, SOFE is the principal exchange in Sweden for the trading of SX 16 (Swedish Index) and the SX 16 (Swedish Index Futures) contracts.

SOFFEX
Acronym: Swiss Options and Financial Futures Exchange. SOFFEX was founded by the Zurich, Geneva, and Basel exchanges and five major Swiss banks.

SOFFEX will trade options on 14 Swiss companies and will also trade futures contracts for interest rates on Swiss government bonds.

"SOFT BULLET" ASSET-BACKED SECURITY
A debt obligation collateralized only by credit card receivables. Thus, there is no other guarantee of performance on the bond except the principal amount received from the credit card debtors.

SOFT CURRENCY
Used in opposition to "hard currency"; that is, any currency backed, to some extent, by gold, a substantial trade balance, a large and steady GNP, or by realistic purchasing power.

"Soft currency," on the other hand, has no backing in gold, or has an unrealistic exchange rate in terms of actual buying power. The Chinese yuan, the Russian ruble, Argentina's austral, Brazil's crusado, and Israel's shekel are classic examples of soft currencies.

Soft currencies usually mark "closed economic systems" or countries with a severe flight of capital because of uncontrolled inflation. Countries with severe soft currency problems tend to be marked with large "black markets."

"SOFT FOR NET"
Colorful U.K. term for what in the United States are called "soft dollars"; that is, the customer pays the broker in "hard commission dollars" and the brokerage firm bears the cost of research services to that customer. This is what is known as "soft dollars."

In the United Kingdom, the practice is acceptable for all broker /dealers except marketmakers.

SOFTING
English jargon for the practice of paying in "soft dollars." For example, a broker/dealer with excess computer time does research and provides computer services to an institutional money manager. The institutional money manager indirectly pays for the services by directing commission business to the broker/dealer. The institution pays in "hard dollars"; the broker/dealer rebates part of the commission/markup in "soft dollars" (the services rendered for no apparent payment).

SOFT PUT
A special arrangement between a purchaser and an underwriter of an issue enabling the buyer to sell the security back to the underwriter (a) at a prearranged price, (b) within a specific time period, (c) but usually only on specific dates within the effective period. An example of the latter could be on the date when the issuer will reset the rate on a "floater."

The issuer is not involved in this transaction because it is not a party to the guarantee.

SOGO SHOSHAS
Japanese term for those trading firms that are prominent in the futures markets. The term literally means "conglomerates."

The role of the sogo shoshas on the Japanese commodities exchanges was similar to that of the "locals" who trade for their own accounts on US commodities exchanges. In recent years, negotiated commissions and decreased liquidity on the Japanese exchanges have reduced the importance of the sogo shoshas.

SOKAIYA
Japanese term for a person who tries to extort money from public corporations by a threat to disrupt their stockholders' meeting. Such gangsterism is not condoned by public officials but it is a recognized way of corporate life in Japan.

SOLD
Past participle of the verb *to sell*. Sold is used to accept a bid, and thereby completes a transaction. For example, a broker/dealer (or a specialist) bids 59½ for 1,000 shares. By saying "sold" the contra broker accepts the bid and contracts to deliver 1,000 shares at 59½ to the broker/dealer.

SOL SPREAD
A term used in the futures markets in the United Kingdom. A SOL spread involves the purchase of short-term gilt futures and the sale of long-term gilt futures. The strategy will be profitable if the spread narrows because the yield curve flattens.

"SOUR" BOND
Slang for a debt issue that is in default on its interest or principal payments. Such a bond has a very low rating and will be deeply discounted in the marketplace; in effect, it has gone "sour."

SOUTH KOREA STOCK EXCHANGE
South Korea is one of the "Asian Tigers" that has prospered in recent years. This growth has been manifested in the value of its industrial stocks, and it has caused the role of the South Korea Stock Exchange to expand. At present, foreign investors are not permitted direct access to Korean markets; this will change, however, in 1991.

There are two scheduled trading sessions on weekdays and a half-day session on Saturdays. Settlement is on the third business day following the trade.

SOVEREIGN AUSTRALIAN CURRENCY ENHANCED SECURITIES
See SAUCERS.

"SOX 'N STOCKS"
Tongue-in-cheek term used of Dean Witter Reynolds, a large U.S. broker/dealer, because the firm is owned by Sears, Roebuck & Co., the largest retailer in the country.

SOYLAND BONDS
Quaint term for the debt securities of Soyland Power Cooperative, Inc. The debt of this rural electric utility cooperative is actually placed into trusts deposited with and serviced by the National Rural Utilities Cooperative Finance Corporation, a not-for-profit organization founded to facilitate financings for farmland power requirements. Its guarantees for repayment of principal and interest are, in turn, guaranteed by the US government.

SPAGHETTI OPTIONS
A facetious term used of the proliferation of option products introduced by the various exchanges. The allusion is a bit farfetched: like cooked spaghetti thrown against a wall, some will stick (and these options will be successful) while others drop to the floor, dry out, and become useless.

SPANISH BOLSA
Common name for the Madrid Stock Exchange. Trading is by open outcry during the hours of 10 A.M. and 1 P.M., with negotiated trading for the next three hours. Settlement is made on the Wednesday after the week in which the trade was made.

SPECIAL AGREEMENT TRANSACTION
An infrequent form of transaction on the Tokyo Stock Exchange that permits settlement within 14 days of the trade. Its original purpose was as a convenience for investors in remote areas of Japan. With the advent of securities depositories and book-entry re-registration, such trades are now outmoded.

SPECIAL BID/ASKED QUOTE
A Japanese market term that is used when there is an imbalance of buy /sell orders. The special quote is used (higher bid *or* lower offer) to attract contra parties into the marketplace and thereby eliminate the imbalance. The special quote may change every five minutes, either higher or lower, until supply and demand are again in balance.

SPECIAL MEMORANDUM ACCOUNT (SMA)
The SMA is an ancillary bookkeeping record used in conjunction with a client's margin account. In the account are noted excess margin, dividends and interest received, deposits of cash, and a portion of the proceeds of long sales. In this way, the SMA becomes a line of credit that may be extended by the broker to the customer for cash withdrawals, withdrawals of securities, or the purchase of additional securities without the need to deposit further margin into the account.

Formerly known as the "special miscellaneous account."

SPECIAL MONEY TRUST
See TOKKIN FUND.

SPEL–BOND
Acronym: Stock Performance–Exchange Linked Bond. This bond was introduced by Mitsui & Co. (USA) as a Euromarket debt instrument. The key feature is that the redemption value at maturity is linked to the *upward* movement of the NYSE's Composite Index. Thus, holders will receive a premium if the index value is greater on maturity date than it was on issue date. For this reason, many call these bonds "bull bonds."

SPINS
Acronym: Standard & Poor's 500 Index Subordinated Notes. SPINS is a Salomon Brothers product that gives subscribers a four-year call option on the S&P Index, with settlement made in cash on maturity date. Investors receive a nominal rate of periodic interest, but at maturity are entitled to the par value amount of difference between the SPIN value at issuance and the SPIN value at maturity. (The August 1986 unit exchange ratio was 3.75 per $1,000 bond.)

In effect, this product assumes features of debt, equity, and options marketplaces.

SPIT
Acronym: Society for the Promotion of Insider Trading. While it may seem to be a facetious organization, in actuality it is a legitimate society in New Zealand. There, insider trading is not illegal, and market participants are accustomed to ferreting out inside information to use in their trading.

SPLIT COUPON BONDS
A euphemism for a debt instrument that begins life as a zero-coupon security and, at a specified date in the future, starts paying a fixed interest rate as set forth in the indenture. This was a popular form of debt offered in the late 1980s on behalf of corporate and municipal issuers.

SPLIT-TERM REVERSE MORTGAGE
Such mortgages provide monthly loans using the borrower's home as collateral. It is like a fixed-term reverse mortgage in concept, but the split-term permits longer time periods, and also permits lump-sum loans in addition to periodic loans. Both forms of reverse mortgages defer repayment until the borrower moves or dies.

SPLIT TRUST
The U.K. equivalent of what in the United States is known as a "dual fund" (investment company). Such dual funds arise when an investment company's share capital is divided into two classes: income shares that get all dividends, and capital shares that get all capital gains. Thus, the income shares reflect the dividends from all of the capital, while the capital shares reflect all of the gains (losses) from all of the capital.

SPONSORED SPINOUT
The concept is this: a company establishes a new company for the exploitation of a new and specific business opportunity. While the new company is owned (and often managed) by the parent company, it is not uncommon for additional shares to be offered to new investors to increase capital. Although it may be looked at as a conglomerate, there is a "corporate shield" that protects the parent from the debts of the spinoff.

Also called "sponsored spinoff."

"SPOOK"
Verbalized slang identifier of the Standard & Poor's index options and futures contracts traded on major option and commodity exchanges.

The word play derived from the original S&P 500 Index Option and its symbol: SPX. In practice, the term is used not only of the S&P 500 Index Option but also of the S&P 100 Index Option (OEX) and the futures contracts. All are jocularly called "spook contracts."

SPOT
Acronym: Single Property Ownership Trust. In the United Kingdom, SPOT is the issuer of unit investment trust shares whose sole underlying asset is a single property generating rental income and prospective gains.

In this regard, SPOT is similar to a SAPCO. The principal difference: SPOT owns *and* manages the property and thus provides shareowners with steady rental income.

SPOUSAL IRA
An individual retirement account opened in the name of a nonworking spouse. Under the IRS rules, the total annual amount that may be con-

tributed is $2,250. This amount may be divided in any way the spouses see fit, provided no more than $2,000 is contributed to either party's account.

Whether or not the contribution is tax deductible depends on the income of the spouses and whether or not the working spouse is covered by another qualified plan.

SPOUSAL REMAINDER TRUST
A pool of assets created under a legal agreement. Ownership of the assets passes to a spouse after a fixed number of years. In the interim, income from the assets is dedicated to the welfare of a third party, usually a child (or children).

Tax advice is needed both for *inter vivos* and testamentary trusts because of tax law changes.

SPRAYING THE MARKET
Slang in the exchange community for the DOT (Designated Order Turnaround) system and its ability to enter at almost the same time orders for many securities; in effect, the orders are "sprayed" all over the market.

Although such spraying by DOT facilitates arbitrage in program trading situations, or permits the sale (or purchase) of a "market basket" of securities, it is blamed for unusual activity and volatility.

See also CIRCUIT BREAKER and "SIDE-CAR RULE" as partial remedies for such activity in the marketplace.

SPREADS
Acronym: Spread Protected Debt Security. A Morgan Stanley servicemark of a technique used to market the Transcontinental Gas Pipeline $8^{1}/_{8}$s of 1/15/97. The security had a put feature enabling a one-time redemption two years after issue date if the issue was not trading at least at $132^{1}/_{2}$ basis points above the U.S. Treasury $7^{1}/_{4}$s of 11/15/96. In effect, as the name suggests, the bond is guaranteed a spread over Treasuries two years after issue date.

SPX
Identifier and ticker symbol for the Standard & Poor's 500 Index class of option traded on the CBOE. Settlement is made in cash and is dependent on the closing price of the S&P 500 Index on the day before expiration. As an European-style option, the SPX may only be exercised on the day before expiration.

246

SQUARE TRANSACTION

Term used of a transaction in stocks/bonds where the broker/dealer buys and sells an equal amount. In effect, the broker/dealer takes no risk position subject to market volatility.

Also called a "natural."

"SQUEEZE OUT"

Term used of a merger/acquisition technique that tends to discriminate against most stockholders in the acquired corporation. Under a "squeeze out," a soliciting group with 10% or more of the corporation gains effective control of a corporation through an offer of cash and junk bonds to the remaining stockholders. Using the company's assets to secure the debt, it—in effect—converts the company's stockholders to creditors of questionable status while assuming absolute control of management.

SRO

1. In the United States, the term means "Self-Regulatory Organization." An SRO is a national securities exchange, a registered securities association, or a registered clearing agency that oversees and regulates the conduct of its members. SROs derive their authority from the SEC.
2. In the United Kingdom, an SRO is a "Self-Regulating Organisation." They are empowered under the Financial Services Bill of 1986 to oversee and regulate members of authorized trade associations that choose to register with them. There are many SROs in the United Kingdom, all subject to oversight by the Securities and Investments Board (SIB).

SSAP 15

The term means Stipulated Standards of Accounting Practice, and the abbreviation stands for procedures used to calculate taxes on corporate income in the United Kingdom.

Although similar in concept to the Financial Accounting Standards Board (FASB) in the United States, the practices in the United Kingdom are more flexible. This often results in two companies with similar earnings having divergent tax consequences and thus different price-earnings ratios in securities analysis.

STABILIZE

Term frequently used by market technicians to designate that a previous trend (either up or down) has reversed itself, either temporarily or permanently.

STALE BULL/BEAR
Slang expression for an investor with a long-term long (or short) position in a stock. Thus, a "stale bull" is someone who has held a long position for a long time. The time period is relative. The opposite is true of a "stale bear."

STALE QUOTE
Term often used of a quote for a derivative product (an option or a future) that has remained unchanged while the price of the underlying has changed. Thus, if the premium for a short-term 50 call remained at 3 while the price of the underlying had gone from 50½ to 51, the quote on the call would be considered "stale."

STAMP DUTY
An English tax on equity securities payable by a person transferring ownership in a British company. The stamp duty is payable only if the transfer occurs in the United Kingdom.

Purchase and sales made during the same account period are not subject to tax. Transfer of an ADR is similarly exempt from tax because the re-registration takes place outside the United Kingdom.

STAMP DUTY RESERVE TAX
See SDRT.

STANDARD & POOR'S 500 INDEX SUBORDINATED NOTES
See SPINS.

STANDARD DEVIATION
Statistical term that designates the deviation (on average) of two thirds of the samples from the mean of the sample. Also abbreviated S/D.

To illustrate, during the past 60 years, the average annual compounded return on the 500 stocks of the S&P Index is +12.1%. The standard deviation, however, is +/− 21.2%. Thus, two thirds of the time, a random selection of *one* stock will fall between − 9% and +33%.

Standard deviation gives an insight into the unpredictability of a financial event, and thus an insight into the risk inherent in the choice. To lower this statistical risk of selection, the use of diversification within the portfolio is recommended. With 8 or 9 stocks in the portfolio the S/D is lowered to +/− 8%.

STANDARD MARGIN
1. Used in the futures industry to designate the good faith deposit required when a customer initiates purchase or sale positions. The good faith deposit differs by commodity and whether or not the cus-

tomer is a commercial or speculative account. The margin is released when the customer closes the position.

2. Sometimes used in the securities industry to designate the initial margin required by the Federal Board or the NYSE when a customer buys or sells short a security.

STANY

Acronym: Security Trader's Association of New York. STANY is a membership group that meets for social, instructional, and lobbying purposes and is composed of persons in the New York City area who trade securities. STANY is affiliated with NSTA (National Security Trader's Association.

STAR

1. Acronym: Short-Term Auction Rate, a money market preferred stock issued by the Lincoln National Corporation. As with most such issues, the rate is reset each 49 days and has a put feature.
2. Euphemism for a successful investment. Generally, a "star" is one whose profits are such that they repay all prior losses.
   Also called a "GEM" or a "PEARL" (q.v.).

STATED RATE AUCTION PREFERRED STOCK
See STRAPS.

STATUTORY DISQUALIFICATION
Often abbreviated as SD, this is a list of offenses set forth in the Securities and Exchange Act of 1934 that would prohibit someone from qualifying as an associated person of a broker/dealer.

The NYSE and the NASD have adopted similar provisions in their rules or bylaws to disqualify persons from membership.

STEEL-COLLAR WORKER
Tongue-in-cheek term that reflects the increased presence of automation in manufacturing. The "steel" refers to metal robots that replace human workers in many automated industries.

"STEENTHING"
A questionable practice whereby a floor broker undercuts another order by the minimal amount and, after getting an execution, claims parity for a larger amount with the order that formerly had a time priority at that price. This practice is often possible in stock option contracts—although ethically inappropriate—because of exchange rules regarding priority, parity, and precedence in verbal bids and offers.

STEP-DOWN FLOATING RATE NOTE
A three- to five-year security with a changeable interest-rate payment pegged periodically to the prevailing commercial paper rate *plus* a declining adjustment in interest for each year of life. Thus, the rate may be the competitive commercial paper rate plus 0.25% the first year, 0.20% the second year, and so forth.

"STICKERS"
Industry jargon for prospectus supplements. Such supplements may be required because material information has changed between the time of the printing of the prospectus and the time of the actual offering of the security. Such information may be printed on small "stickers" that are appended to the prospectus.

The term is not used of "supplemental information" that often accompanies the prospectuses of investment company shares. Because such securities are in constant registration and information changes, many mutual funds print a standard prospectus and a supplement of additional information. Both are sent to customers. The supplement is periodically updated.

"STOCK CLEANING"
Name of an innovative financing technique used by the Algemene Bank Nederland (ABN) in its takeover of Exchange Bancorp in Chicago. ABN placed privately 9.4 million ordinary shares with *no* dividend in 1989 in exchange for 7.5 million ordinary shares entitled to a 1989 dividend (in effect, making a stock dividend before the fact). ABN then sold the shares entitled to a dividend publicly on a worldwide basis. The net result was an immediate increase in bank equity with no outlay of new funds in 1989.

STOCK EXCHANGE AUTOMATED TRADING SYSTEM
See SEATS.

STOCK EXCHANGE DAILY OFFICIAL LIST
See SEDOL.

STOCK EXCHANGE OF SINGAPORE
See SES.

STOCK EXCHANGE POOL NOMINEES
See SEPON.

STOCK FUTURES 50
This is a futures contract traded on the Osaka Stock Exchange (OSE). It is an equity-related futures contract indexed to the component issues. Unlike most such contracts, it settles not for cash but for physical delivery of the underlying package of its 50 component stocks.

STOCKHOLDER
A person, either real or legal, with a proprietary participation in a corporation. This interest, in most cases, is represented by a certificate that, in the case of public corporations, is freely transferrable.

STOCKHOLM STOCK EXCHANGE
This bourse is located in the capital of Sweden and is the largest bourse in Scandinavia.

Trading hours are from 10:00 A.M. until 2:30 P.M. without any restrictions on after-hour trading. Settlement is on the fifth business day following trade date.

There is an onerous transfer tax on Swedish shares; for this reason most international companies buy shares outside Sweden. Leading Swedish companies are also listed in London and New York.

STOCK JOCKEY
Colorful expression for a registered representative(RR) who generates a significant amount of commission dollars from the short-term trading of customers' accounts. Such activities often take place in accounts over which the RR has discretionary authorization.

As a general rule, the term is pejorative.

STOCKWATCH AUTOMATED TRACKING SYSTEM
See SWAT.

STOCK PERFORMANCE EXCHANGE-LINKED BOND
See SPEL-BOND.

STOCK RECORD BREAK
The term is used of any out-of-balance situation in a firm's recordkeeping of securities that are its responsibility. In effect, there is a position debit without a corresponding credit—or vice versa. Such "breaks" must be reconciled quickly, because the older they are the more difficult they are to reconcile; in addition, such "breaks" can have an adverse effect on the member's capital requirements.

Also called a "break."

STORY BONDS
Debt securities of corporate issuers rumored to be takeover targets. Unlike the stocks of these companies, however, which usually go up in value, the debt securities of these issuers usually decline because the takeover will usually raise the amount of debt and lower the quality of other outstanding bonds.

"STORY STOCKS"
Slang term for any stock whose market value is more dependent on a story (either real or fictitious) than on its balance sheet figures.

At the end of bull markets, story stocks abound as the market looks for a favorite; thus, an abundance of story stocks often presages a downturn in the market.

In the 1980s, the term was also applied to companies about whom there was a rumored takeover or a financial restructuring.

"STOX IN A BOX"
Slang for a form of illegal price manipulation. Such manipulation may occur during the original distribution of a "penny stock." The scam involves a partial withholding of the original offering by the underwriter, thereby lowering the supply. Later, when the artificially lowered supply causes the price to rise, the underwriter carefully releases the "stox in a box" at inflated values.

STRAPS
Acronym: Stated Rate Auction Preferred Stock. STRAPS are a Goldman Sachs' innovation made to appeal to investors in both fixed and variable rate preferred shares. Investors in STRAPS are entitled to the 70% "dividend received" exclusion for corporate investors. Dividend payments are at a fixed rate for five years and at a variable rate thereafter.

STRATEGY
1. Any defined plan for profiting from investments or groups of investments; thus, dollar cost averaging and/or diversification may be called "strategies."
2. A synonym for asset allocation. In this sense, the asset allocation may be recommended for all of a firm's customers; for example, "At present, our strategy is based on a portfolio of 65% stocks and 35% bonds."
3. The approach to investing that is specific to a customer. For example, "Mr. Jones, at your age and with your investment objectives, your main strategy should center on capital preservation for income." Although *strategy* and *tactic* are often used interchangeably, strategy tends to be longer-term and tactic shorter-term in scope.

STRONG HANDS
Industry term for investors who are likely to hold for the long term.

Originally, the term was used to mean institutional investors; that is, persons with sufficient funds that they are not forced to sell in down markets.

With the advent of program trading and the increased turnover of institutional portfolios (40% of the ownership versus 80+% of the trading), the term is no longer centered on long-term holding.

STRUCTURING DEPOSITS
An SEC euphemism for the deposit of cash (or cash equivalents) into customer accounts in amounts just short of $10,000. By doing this, the reporting requirement to the Treasury Department is avoided.

The Treasury Department requires notification of all transactions in cash, or cash equivalents, in amounts of $10,000 or more to prevent the illegal "laundering" of money. "Structuring" occurs when the amounts are purposely kept below $10,000 to avoid the reporting requirements.

STUB STOCK
Street slang for small amounts of publicly held stock left outstanding after a reorganization, tender, or merger.

Often, because of the large amount of debt assumed by the company, the actual net worth of the stock is negative. In this case, the value of the stock, if any, may be quite volatile.

"SUCKER" RALLY
Slang for a general rise in prices in the midst of a bear market. It is often characterized by falling volume along with rising prices.

So called because sophisticated investors do not buy at such times, only "suckers" who are lured into the situation for illusory quick profits.

SUGGING
English slang for "selling under the guise of. . . ."

This practice is of questionable ethics and suggests that customer purchases are solicited on the occasion of a forthcoming research report. The concept is this: buy now on the rumor and have an immediate profit when the actual printed report is published.

Perhaps from the Scottish "soughing" (pronounced "suffing"), meaning to spread a rumor.

SUITABILITY
A broad industry term that signifies that a firm, or registered representative, recommendation is appropriate in terms of the customer's investment objectives, financial capabilities, and other portfolio holdings.

The term *suitable* is used not because a recommended investment is the "best" but because—all things considered—it is not inappropriate. Often customer "risk tolerance" is the best determinant of suitability.

All SROs have arbitration facilities for customers who consider that they have been given unsuitable recommendations. As with many financial decisions, there are some wrong answers but many right answers.

SUNRISE INDUSTRY
Broad term used to describe businesses engaged in promising areas of the economy. At the present time, companies engaged in high technology, genetic engineering, pharmaceuticals, and waste disposal, for example, are considered to be in "sunrise industries."

SUNSET INDUSTRY
Broad term to describe businesses engaged in mature areas of the economy that are declining and may be phased out by rising technology. At the present time, coal mining, steel production, heavy machinery, commercial railroading, and automotive manufacturing are suffering a decline.

"SUNSHINE" TRADER
Street slang for a "fair weather" marketmaker. In other words, a broker/dealer who is willing to make an active two-sided market in those stocks that are going up in price. When the price starts to fall, the broker/dealer is unwilling to continue marketmaking activities.

"SUNSHINE TRADING"
Slang for the execution of large trades in the public marketplace made with prior notification to interested prospective customers. The practice is somewhat suspect because it is felt that the advance notice could frighten away contra parties to the transaction.

SUPER PO
See SUPER PRINCIPAL ONLY BOND.

SUPER PRINCIPAL ONLY BOND
Term used of a collateralized mortgage obligation (CMO) stripped of its interest payments but inclusive of a planned amortization class (PAC) or a targeted amortization class (TAC).

These latter features lead to a disadvantageous impact on the residual class of securities in a CMO if interest rates change significantly. Such a Super PO is more volatile than ordinary POs in the face of interest-rate changes.

SUPERSHARES
Written "SuperShares." Name given to an investment trust that provides interested parties with a chance to participate in market trends without using portfolio "insurance."

Subscribers' monies are divided into two mutual fund pools: money market issues and stock portfolios. Holders can swap their interests into a trust issuing equity index units. The units, listed on the NYSE, can then be broken into four types of SuperShares, each with a different objective:
1. Downside Protection (falling market).
2. Indexed Income (slight falling market).
3. Money Market Income (flat market).
4. Upside Appreciation (surging rising market).

SUPERSINKER
Slang for debt securities that will be retired faster than would normally be expected by the use of sinking fund deposits. For example, a bond issue that uses a sinking fund to retire a debt in 3–5 years, rather than the usual 15–20 years, would be an example of a "supersinker."

SUPER VOTING RIGHT
Management-accorded privilege permitting a select class of shareholders a greater voice in corporation management than another class of common stocks. Before the SEC implemented its "one share—one vote" rule, the use of a "time-phased" super voting right was a popular defense against a hostile takeover.

Under the "time-phased" concept, when an unwanted suitor acquired a specific percentage of stock, a new class of voting stock was initiated for earlier shareholders. This stock carried a greater voice in corporate affairs, thereby discouraging the prospective predator.

SUPPLEMENTAL EXECUTIVE RETIREMENT FUND
See SERP.

SUPPLEMENTAL MARKETMAKER (SMM)
A category of member of the CBOE authorized to assist lead marketmakers (LMMs) in expediting the opening rotation in OEX Index options.

The SMM is appointed on a week-to-week basis by the exchange's Market Performance Committee. The SMM is required to accept previously agreed-to portions of customer order imbalances in specific OEX

Index series. The SMM works closely with the LMM in specific series of OEX options.

SUPPLY-SIDE ECONOMICS
See LAFFER CURVE, THE.

"SUPPLY-SIDERS"
A school of economic thought that holds that a cut in tax rates plus a concomitant cut in government spending is the best way to stimulate the economy. The central concept is based on the idea that, by giving people increased amounts to spend, more jobs will be created and the economy will expand. This, in turn, will provide more income for the government for needed social programs.

SURPLUS INSURANCE
Term used in conjunction with the management of pension fund assets. The concept: the manager uses arbitrage and stock and index futures but only to hedge the amount whereby assets exceed expected benefit obligations. In effect, it is a form of portfolio insurance, but only with the balance sheet surplus of the pension fund.

SWAG THEORY
Acronym: Scientific Wild Ass Guess. This facetious vulgarism is part of the lingo of the Street. The term is a take-off of WAG Theory (q.v.).

Typical usage could be as follows: "People are talking of a drop in interest rates, but I don't see it happening. According to the SWAG theory, when that happens, one really should go into short-term debt instruments."

SWAPTION
A combination of "swap" and "option"; that is, an option on a swap transaction. A swaption gives the purchaser the right, but not the obligation, to enter into an interest-rate swap at a preset rate within a specified time.

The swaption writer assumes the obligation of providing the swap, but the writer can hedge the risk through certain offsetting transactions.

The swaption purchaser pays a premium to the writer for the privilege.

SWAT
Acronym: StockWatch Automated Tracking System. SWAT is an NASD computer program designed to identify abnormal trading patterns for OTC; that is, NASDAQ-traded securities. The program sets

performance parameters; that is, price and volume figures. Activities that substantially exceed those parameters are investigated.

"SWEEPING THE STREET"

The term is used in conjunction with corporate takeovers and signifies that the person endeavoring to take over acquires large blocks of stock in a relatively short time period before the knowledge of the takeover is generally known. In this way, the initiator gets most of the stock before his or her intentions are known and the price of the stock becomes exorbitant.

SWIFT

Acronym: Society for Worldwide Interbank Financial Telecommunications. SWIFT is a European version of CHIPS in the United States. SWIFT is a telex system between most European banks to facilitate customer transfer of deposit funds among the banks.

SWINGS

Acronym: Sterling Warrants into Gilt-Edged Stocks. SWINGS are customized options to buy or sell a specific British government security; for example, a warrant to buy (a call), or a warrant to sell (a put) a specific gilt (the 8¾s of 1997, for example) during a specific period.

Although such warrants may be for longer periods, generally they are for one year or less.

SWITCHING

1. Used as a synonym for a swap; that is, a sale of one security and the purchase of another.
2. The substitution of one security for another as collateral in a margin account. This substitution may be effected by the physical substitution of one security for another, or the sale of one and the purchase of another.
3. A salesman's recommendation that a customer sell one mutual fund (for which a sales charge has been paid) and the purchase of a second fund with a second sales charge. This practice is also called "twisting" or "churning."
4. In the currency markets, the purchase of a spot currency contract together with its sale in the forward market.

SWOON STOCK

A term associated with illiquid OTC equity markets. For example, at the first sign of bad news, or even a rumor, the bid for the stock disappears and its price collapses. In effect, the price swoons, or faints away.

It would not be unusual for such a stock to lose 50% of its resale price in one day because there are no bidders.

SX INDEX OPTION
A put/call option based on an index of the 16 largest company stocks traded in Sweden. It is a European-style option traded on the Stockholm Stock Exchange.

SYNDICATE CONTROL NUMBERS
Unlike US underwritings where syndicate members are bound to make a fixed-price offering, European syndicates are not so bound. They must follow the manager's instructions, and sometimes those price limitations are surreptitiously broken. If the European syndicate manager can force all initial clearing through a single entity (e.g., CEDEL) and record distributed certificate numbers, it can control the offering prices at which syndicate members sell the security.

SYNERGY
From the Greek: *syn,* meaning together, and *ergon,* meaning work; that is, working together.

In recent years, the term has become a "buzz-word" for increased harmony and efficiency, often through a merger of companies or forces. For example, "The merger of A and B has given the combined company a synergy in its assault on market share." Or, "The addition of our new marketing department has given advertising a synergy it did not have before."

SYNTHETIC DEBT
Nickname for debt securities that arise when a broker/dealer strips interest payments from principal payments. By so doing, the broker/dealer hopes to satisfy the needs of different customers at a greater profit than if it had sold the debt as one piece.

In effect, the debt becomes two zero-coupon bonds with the dealer responsible for directing payments to the two parties.

SYNTHETIC MORTGAGE AGREEMENT
A one to five-year contractual commitment between a customer and a broker/dealer in which the customer receives the cash flow from a GNMA security with a specific coupon and maturity date. In return, the customer pays the broker/dealer the prevailing LIBOR interest rate plus a negotiated spread. At the end of the period, the customer can choose to buy the GNMA security or walk away from the deal by paying

258

the difference between the GNMA values on a current and forward basis. In effect, the agreement is simply a financing procedure with an interest in a mortgage-backed security.

SYSTEM FOR INSTITUTIONAL TRADING OF UNREGISTERED SECURITIES
See SITUS.

T

TAA
See TACTICAL ASSET ALLOCATION.

TAC
Acronym: Targeted Amortization Class. TACs are associated with collateralized mortgage obligations (CMOs) and, specifically, the class of CMOs to which the risk of prepayment of principal is transferred. Usually the TACs are the last and second last of the classes to mature, with earlier classes having relatively stable maturities.

TACTIC
A short-term military maneuver designed for a specific objective. In general, a tactic is part of an overall strategy.

Thus, in the financial services industry, a tactic is part of an overall strategy to achieve the customer's financial objectives. For example, "Mr. Smith, we have discussed your overall strategy of capital growth. I would suggest two tactics that will help you achieve this goal. We will recommend (1) stocks with a low market-to-book ratio and (2) stocks with low price-to-earnings ratios. In this way, your portfolio will be value-oriented and should produce long-term capital growth."

TACTICAL ASSET ALLOCATION
Often abbreviated TAA. Term coined by institutional portfolio managers to describe changes in investment strategies based upon their view of the upcoming market. The term refers to the percentage allocation of assets; that is, the amount of the portfolio in cash, in bonds, or in equities. In anticipation of a downswing in the equities markets, the manager may opt to have more assets in the form of cash and short-term bonds.

TAIWAN STOCK EXCHANGE
Located in Taipei, the capital of Formosa (Latin: beautiful, Chinese: Taiwan), this exchange is one of the smallest and one of the most active of

the world's exchanges. Trading is from 9:00 A.M. until noon six days a week. Physical settlements are made on the third business day following the trade date. Foreigners may not deal directly on the exchange, but they may transact through a Taiwanese nominee.

TAKE OFF

1. Verb: to begin flight; thus, by metaphor, a strong rise in the market or in the price of an individual stock. For example, "At 11:00 A.M. the market took off."
2. In the United Kingdom, the cancellation of an order previously given to a broker to execute.
3. In the United States, the removal of a print from the consolidated tape. This may be done only if buyer and seller agree and a floor official concurs.

TAKEOVER ACTIVITY

A term used to generally describe a market where stock trading appears to be marked with a large number of buyouts, mergers, tender offers, hostile offers, consolidations, and other actions that accompany mergers and acquisitions. For example, "Volume today was 150 million, of which a third seemed to be takeover activity."

If this activity marks a long time period, a common synonym is "mergermania."

TAKING A BATH

Slang for the loss of a significant sum of money either by an individual or by groups of investors. For example, "Investors in ABC took a bath today when the company announced negative earnings for the quarter."

The word is of unknown origin and is informal, but it may arise from the days of piracy. When ships were overtaken, the crew was often set adrift or forced into the water to prevent pursuit.

TALISMAN

Acronym: Transfer Accounting Lodgement for Investors, Stock Management for jobbers. TALISMAN is an International Stock Exchange (in London) procedure similar in function to the DTC (Depository Trust Co.) or CNN (Continuous Net Settlement) in the United States.

All ISE transactions are settled through TALISMAN by physical delivery, although book-entry balances are established each day for jobbers (specialists). Actual money settlements are made approximately every two weeks according to the account period.

TAMRA
Acronym: Technical and Miscellaneous Revenue Act of 1988. This act was passed by Congress to correct certain technical errors in previous tax laws.

TAMRA requires that losses and gains on foreign currency options and futures be considered ordinary income or ordinary income losses. It also decrees that the wash sale rule apply to options and futures as well as to the underlying securities. Interest on Series EE savings bonds, currently tax sheltered, is also tax free in most cases if used for educational purposes.

TAN-ITSU-YAKUJO
See ITAYOSE TRADING.

TAPE IS LATE
Industry expression used when the consolidated tape is reporting transactions one or more minutes after they take place on the floor. Although the tape can run faster, it will be too fast for the human eye, so the tape is programmed to use no more than 900 characters per minute.

The consolidated tape often adjusts for lateness by having digits deleted from the prints. Usually the price digits are deleted first; then, if the tape continues late, the volume digits are deleted.

TAPE-WORM
A term used of boardroom habitués; that is, persons who sit hour by hour mesmerized by the activity of the tape, philosophical comments on the market, and who in actuality do very little trading.

The term originated in the days when there was an optical projection of the actual tape, or a mechanical reproduction of the tape in brokerage offices. Today most stockbrokers have such price information electronically reproduced at their workstations.

"TAP" SYSTEM
Metaphor for the system whereby the British government distributes gilts. The Bank of England, as marketing agent for the government, sells gilts little by little as the government directs. In effect, the Bank of England can turn off or on the supply of gilts whenever it thinks the time is right. Hence the metaphor "tap."

TARGETED AMORTIZATION CLASS
See TAC.

TARGETED INDEX MATRIX

Abbreviated TIM. TIM is a Salomon Brothers' customized bond index of selected debt securities. TIM is designed for bond portfolio managers who want to track certain duration/quality parameters.

The matrix starts with Salomon's Broad Investment Grade Bond Index of mortgage/corporate issues. It then adds other statistics for bond duration so it, in effect, becomes a multitracking vehicle to meet the specialized needs of various portfolio managers.

TAURUS

Acronym: Transfer and Automated Registration of Uncertified Stock. TAURUS was developed by London's International Stock Exchange to computerize the process of transferring share ownership for securities organizations and their customers. TAURUS is an offshoot of the TALISMAN system (q.v.).

TAX-EXEMPT DIVIDEND SERVICE

See TEDS.

TAX-EXEMPT ESOP NOTE SECURITIES

See TEENS.

TBRs

Treasury Bond Receipts, a proprietary product of Shearson Lehman Hutton similar in nature to Merrill Lynch's TIGR and Salomon Brothers' CATS. In effect, TBRs are stripped Treasuries that become zero-coupon bonds.

T-DAB

Acronym: Treasury Debt Automated Bill recording system. T-DAB was originated in 1978 to maintain the ownership records of T-bill holders when "book entry" became prevalent. The system has been superceded by TREASURY DIRECT (q.v.).

TEASER RATE

Used in conjunction with adjustable-rate mortgages (ARMs), the teaser rate is a particularly low rate of initial interest used to attract mortgage loans. The teaser rate may be valid for a year or two but then it returns to usual ARM rates. Generally, usual ARM rates have a cap and a floor and an annual maximum/minimum change. It is not uncommon for ARMs to feature balloon maturities.

TECHNICAL POSITION
The term is used to designate the net positions, long or short, of dealers and marketmakers in specified securities.

Technical positions are short term and, as such, can dramatically effect supply and demand—hence price—in the marketplace.

TEDDY-BEAR PAT
Merger and acquisition jargon for the initial contact by a raider to a target issuer. The "teddy-bear" pat may be a seemingly innocent letter or telephone call designed to frighten management into submission. If the raider is given no encouragement, the raider can back off without further publicity.

TEDS
Acronym: Tax-Exempt Dividend Service. This is a DTC service whereby eligible holders of Canadian securities on deposit with the DTC can receive dividend and interest payments without deduction for the Canadian withholding tax.

Revenue Canada (their IRS) has approved this program and Canadian transfer agents can make unrestricted payments to the DTC nominee.

"TED" SPREAD
Term used of the interest rate difference between U.S. T-bills and Eurodollar futures contracts.

The spread reflects the price difference between these two instruments and thus is reflective of credit concerns in the United States and Europe. The spread tends to widen as interest rates rise and narrow as they fall.

"TEENIE," A
Trading slang for $1/16$th of a point (0.0625 cents). Sixteenths are used in option trading for options selling below $3, for subscription rights, and occasionally for short-term municipals.

Popularly called a "steenth."

TEENS
Acronym: Tax-Exempt ESOP Note Securities. TEENS are a Salomon Brothers debt product designed to provide eligible investors with a 50% tax exemption for interest received. It is a seven-year note that evidences a loan taken out by a corporation from a bank, insurance company, finance company, thrift institution, or mutual fund—all of whom would be eligible to receive tax-preferred interest income (50% exemption) if the loan proceeds are used to finance a contribution to the

issuer's employee stock option plan (ESOP). The corporation lends the proceeds to the plan's trustee who, in turn, uses the proceeds to purchase shares in the company for immediate deposit into the plan. Since the employer's ESOP contribution is also tax deductible, both the issuer of the note and the lender receive tax benefits.

TEL AVIV STOCK EXCHANGE
Israel's largest exchange for stocks and bonds, but a relatively inactive exchange. The government strictly regulates all activity on the exchange. Sessions are held from Sunday to Thursday from 10:30 A.M. to 3:30 P.M. Settlement is for the business day following trade date.

TELESCOPING
An alternate term for a *reverse split*. A reverse split is used by a corporation if there are many shares outstanding and the market price of the shares is relatively low. Thus, a company with 100 million shares outstanding with a market price of $3 could cause a reverse split so there would only be 10 million shares outstanding. If the shares are selling at a reasonable multiple to earnings, such a reverse split could cause the new shares to sell at or about $30 per share.

TEMPORARY RESTRAINING ORDER
Popularly initialed as TRO.

TROs are a court-issued document that prohibits the continuation of a specified activity, which is deemed to be harmful, until an investigation and due process of law are completed. Thus, the owner of property builds a fence across a road because he contends that there is no "easement." A person who has been using that road for 20 years contends that there is an easement. A court could grant a temporary restraining order against the fence until the matter is properly adjudicated.

"TENBAGGER"
Common term used by security analysts to describe the multiple of return they expect on a particular stock. Thus, a "tenbagger" anticipates a 10-fold return on invested capital; a twentybagger, a 20-fold return; and so forth.

Analogy with baseball to measure the number of bases a hit produces: a one-bagger, two-bagger, and so forth.

10b-5 LETTER
Named after the SEC rule, such a letter is used by lawyers in conjunction with a municipal underwriting. A 10b-5 Letter is written by a municipal issuer to a prospective underwriter. It attests to the authenticity

of the information presented and further promises the issuer will not employ any manipulative devices in the sale of the security.

10-UP RULE
Popular name for an option exchange requirement imposed on specialists and registered option traders whereby they must be in a position to bid or offer at least 10 contracts on either side of the market on the exchange marketmaking computer screen. Generally, the 10-up rule applies only to the near month—although individual exchanges may require the 10-up rule to apply to other series' expiration months. The rule is intended to provide both depth and liquidity to options markets.

TERMS
Acronym: Top Efficiency Reliable Maturity Securities. TERMS are a Salomon Brothers innovation in the special mortgage-backed securities market. TERMS are issued by thrift institutions and protect an investor against premature call of the bond.

If the thrift institution becomes insolvent, the trustee promises to sell the mortgage collateral and replace it with Treasury securities. In effect, the mortgage-backed security is "defeased" instead of redeemed.

"TEXAS HEDGE"
A tongue-in-cheek expression based on the traditional optimism that is associated with Texans. Thus, in a bull market, a "Texas hedge" means that a speculator buys everything before it becomes more highly priced—instead of hedging current holding against a possible drop in prices.

"TEXAS PREMIUM"
A term used to describe the extra interest offered by relatively insolvent savings and loans to lure added deposits in the wake of the drop in real estate prices in Texas and in other states in the "oil patch" (q.v.).

The drop in real estate prices went hand in glove with the drop in oil prices. For example, "You can get 8% CDs in the East but you can get a Texas premium in the Southwest where CDs are earning 9.5%."

THETA
An options analyst's term used to describe the change in premium for an option versus the change in the number of days to expiration. Thus, as the time to expiration shortens, one would expect the time value to shrink toward zero for out-of-the-money options, and toward the intrinsic value for options that are in-the-money.

Do not confuse with DELTA, which is the differential calculus for the difference in the premium compared to the difference in the price of the underlying. DELTA tends toward one as the option approaches expiration; THETA tends toward zero as time expires.

THIRD-PARTY GIVE-UP
A *give-up* is the term used to describe a trade by member firm A for a customer of member firm B (or a customer of another office of member firm A). In effect, the *executing* firm is required to share part of its commission (mark up/mark down) with another firm.

If the other firm is outside the trading loop (i.e., a third party being rewarded for research and other services), the present term is used.

Needless to say, a "third-party give-up" must conform to federal, industry, and NASD rules.

THIRD WORLD COUNTRY
A euphemism for any nation that is not one of the 10-or-so developed countries, nor a member of the Eastern European/Communist bloc. Thus, a country whose average per capita income is substantially below the average of either of these two blocs.

The term may be pejorative; thus, in one recounting, Mexico could be considered a "Third World" country in that it does not fit into either category. On the other hand, Mexico's per capita income is too high to be considered a "Third World" country.

See LESS DEVELOPED COUNTRIES.

THREE-LEGGED BOX SPREAD
In betting, a box is a four-position or nine-position bet that cannot be without a winner (although the net result may be a slight loss).

Thus, a "three-legged box spread" has three of the four positions needed to "box" the market, but one position is missing. Here is a "three-legged box":

Long October 40 call   Short October 40 put
Long November 45 put

The short November 45 call is missing to "complete the box."

THREE-STEP-AND-STUMBLE RULE
"Invented" by Edson Gould, this "rule" is a sort of axiom in technical analysis.

Simply stated, this rule says: There will be a major market decline if the Fed raises the discount rate three times in a row.

THREE-WAY TICKET
Term used in the days before negotiable commissions.

In the days of fixed commissions, institutional customers could reward firms for good research (whose block handling capabilities were deficient) by directing orders to members of regional exchanges with the proviso that parts of the commission be directed to one or more other firms.

The practice did not altogether die with negotiable commissions.

THROUGH-PUT
A Spanish term used to describe an "off-Bolsa" transaction. We would call it an "OTC trade."

Under Spanish law, a large trade done outside exchange trading hours can be done by a registered broker and not reported.

TIC
See TRUE INTEREST COST.

TICK
1. The minimum variation that may occur in the trading of particular securities. Thus, stocks, corporate bonds, and most options trade in variations of 1/8th. Municipal bonds trade in minimum variations of 1/16th (usually 1/8th). Governments and agencies trade in 1/32nds, although trades in 1/64ths are also permitted. The term is not used of bonds that trade in basis points (yield to maturity).
2. Any report of a transaction. An allusion to the old ticker tapes.
3. The relative value of a transaction in terms of the previous transaction; thus, up-tick, down-tick, plus-tick, minus-tick, zero-plus tick, zero-minus tick.

TICKET
1. In the United Kingdom, slang for the authorization to work in the financial services business. For example, to be associated as a jobber (specialist) or as a broker/dealer associated with one of the SROs.
2. The written form of buy/sell instructions received from the customer. For example, "To enter a ticket."
3. The authorization to enter and take a regulatory examination.
4. Any investment suggestion that patently fits the needs or objective of a customer. For example, "That's the ticket."

"TICKETS IN THE DRAWER"
The practice of hiding losing trade tickets from the management of the firm so the firm cannot hedge itself against loss.

This unethical practice can severely compromise the net capital requirements of the member firm.

TIE-IN SALE

An unethical prearranged trade between a member firm and a customer, or vice versa. For example, if a member firm were to allocate shares of a new issue to a customer *on the proviso that* the customer buy even more shares in the aftermarket, it would be a "tie-in sale." The prohibition arises because such a tie-in is basically unethical and manipulative of the price of the stock.

TIFFE

Acronym: Tokyo International Financial Futures Exchange. TIFFE is a new exchange. It is similar in function to LIFFE in England. At the time of its inception, TIFFE traded three contracts: a three-month Eurodollar, a three-month Euroyen, and a yen/dollar currency future.

TIGHT BID/OFFER

A quotation with a spread (difference) equal to the minimum trading variation. Thus, if the minimum variation were $1/8$th point, a tight bid (offer) would be one where the spread was $1/8$th point.

TIM

See TARGETED INDEX MATRIX.

TIN PARACHUTE

An extension of the "golden parachute" usually reserved for senior management. Under this antitakeover measure, not only senior management but also middle management gets a cash payment (often equal to $2^{1}/_{2}$ times annual compensation) in the event of an unfriendly takeover.

TINT

Acronym: Treasury Interest Payment. TINTs are the interest components associated with a stripped government security.

The term is used in conjunction with the reconstruction of the original stripped Treasury bond. To do this, both the principal (corpus of the bond) and the TINTs must be so "reassembled" that all components of the original bond are accounted for.

TOCOM

Acronym: Tokyo Commodity Exchange for Industry. TOCOM is the largest of the Japanese exchanges for the trading of metal futures.

TOHKI
Japanese word for speculation. The term has bad connotations for individual Japanese investors and, as a result, the government prohibits retail-type market participants from engaging in the practice.

TOKKIN
A tokkin is a separate legal entity whereby corporate funds may be invested and yet kept separate from the corporation for tax and holding period purposes. For example, if Hitachi were to deposit a sum of money with a special money trust, it could give investment instructions and remain the beneficiary of the growth and income from the trust. Japanese regulations require that the identity of the beneficiary be revealed to the executing broker when these funds are invested.

Also called "special money trust."

TOKYO INTERNATIONAL FINANCIAL FUTURES EXCHANGE
See TIFFE.

"TOM AND JERRYS"
Slang for securities issued by Deutsche Bank and whose redemption values are linked to the performance of the FAZ Index over a five-year period. These securities are also nicknamed "bull bonds and bear bonds" because they offer investors a way to speculate on future price trends in German stocks.

TOOTHLESS NOTES
Term used of an installment sale contract that has no penalty should the buyer of the securities defer or default on the promised payment.

TOP EFFICIENCY RELIABLE MATURITY SECURITIES
See TERMS.

TOPIC
Acronym: Teletex of Price Information by Computer. TOPIC is a video information developed by the ISE that provides business information on a timely basis. It is a subscription service providing up-to-the-minute price information on U.K. equities, options, gilts, and selected international issues, and on other business news.

The service can be effected by linkage with any IBM PC terminal.

TOPIX
Acronym: Tokyo Stock Price Index. TOPIX is a measure of performance of selected Japanese stocks traded on that exchange. Futures contracts are based on TOPIX.

TOPPING OUT
A market technician's term to signify the apparent final rising value for a security (or market in general). In and of itself, "topping out" does not imply a decline in the stock. The stock may go sideways before it goes higher, or lower. The term *consolidate* is used if the technician feels that a sideways movement will be followed by higher prices; the term *stabilize* is used if the sideways movement will be followed by a reversal of the upward trend. A market technician, for example, could say: "LMN is in a near-term topping pattern. We anticipate that the stock will plateau during its distribution phase. After that we expect a consolidation to even higher market values."

"TOP-UPS"
A U.K. term for the issuance of debt securities with a significant number of warrants attached. The warrants are detachable soon after issuance and, if exercised, would greatly expand the number of shares an unwelcome suitor would have to purchase in a takeover attempt. Thus, "top-ups" are intended to protect the company from a hostile takeover.

TORONTO STOCK EXCHANGE 300 COMPOSITE INDEX
An index of 300 actively traded stocks listed on the Toronto Stock Exchange. It is also called the "TSE 300" and is the basis for a futures contract.

TOUCH, THE
Colorful English term for the marketmaker's spread. Thus, if the quote were 275 p. bid and 285 p. offered, the "touch" would be 10 p.

T + 1, T + 2, ETC.
T stands for trade date. Thus, T + 1 means the business day following the trade date; so with T + 2, T + 3, and so forth.

In practice, the term is used of the sequence of events leading from the trade to settlement. Thus, T + 1 is comparison day; T + 2 confirmation of the trade (and an endeavor to clear up DKs); and T + 5 is settlement date.

The expression is in constant use in operations and in the clearing of securities.

TRADE-FOR-TRADE SETTLEMENT SYSTEM
A method of cashiering, clearing, and delivery whereby settlement is arranged between buyer and seller on a separately identifiable basis. This method is slow and cumbersome and generally inefficient.

Industry usage is toward a "net settlement" system, or the use of an intermediary, such as DTC, to effect trade settlements.

TRADES
Acronym: Treasury Reserve Automated Debt Entry System. TRADES is a computerized program of recordkeeping for government obligations designed to eliminate certificates. The identities of the beneficial owners are preserved by means of computerized third-party commercial accounts maintained on the books of a District Federal Reserve Bank. The system can accommodate a large volume of trades, such as that generated by bank and nonbank government securities dealers.

TRADE-THROUGH
Term that designates a trade on one market while another market has a more favorable quote on the same security. Thus, a trade on exchange A at 58 when exchange B was offering the same stock at 57 would be an example of a trade-through.

TRADING ON A SHOESTRING
1. A trader who uses little personal capital in day-to-day trading activities. Such a trader uses borrowed capital to leverage his position.
2. Any customer who trades with little margin.

TRAFFIC TICKET RULE
Term associated with NYSE Rule 476. Under this rule, the NYSE has power to obtain summary judgments against members or their employees for relatively minor and undeniable offenses. This avoids long adjudication or even litigation. Under this rule, the exchange may levy (and the member accept) fines of $25,000 to $100,000.

TRANCHE FUNDING
Term associated with private financings and corporate buyouts. For example, the newly reorganized company secures additional capital for future investment, but the timing and amount of this future financing is determined prior to the takeover.

TRANCHETTE
Term used in the United Kingdom to describe the sale of additional gilts by the Bank of England with the same maturity and interest rate as an already outstanding issue.

In the United States, this procedure is called "reopening a Treasury issue."

TRANSLATION RISK
A colorful and descriptive term for the risk of currency exchange and the value of assets on the balance sheet of international companies. Thus, Royal Dutch, a Netherlands company, publishes its balance sheet in

Dutch florins, despite the fact that its assets are distributed throughout its worldwide production and marketing network.

As the value of world currencies change, the "risk of translation" is great because some assets may go up and some down.

TRAX
Code name for a trade comparison and confirmation system developed by the Association of International Bond Dealers (AIBD) to facilitate the matching and subsequent settlements of Eurodollar securities. TRAX provides members with an almost on-line comparison system for trading.

TREASURY BOND RECEIPTS
See TBRs.

TREASURY DIRECT
A book-entry securities system that permits private investors to maintain perfected interests in U.S. Treasury issues directly on the records of the Bureau of the Public Debt.

TREASURY DIRECT is the successor to T-DAB for Treasury securities issued after July 1, 1986.

TREASURY NOTE
Popularly called "T-note." T-notes are intermediate-term (2, 4, 5, 7, and 10-year maturities) issued by the U.S. Treasury to finance government expenditures. T-notes are available in book-entry or registered format. Interest is paid semiannually. T-notes are noncallable and generally have minimum denominations of $1,000.

There are active secondary markets for T-notes, and prices are generally given both in points and 32nds and as yield to maturity (basis price).

Owners who are nonresident aliens are not subject to withholding on most recent issues of T-notes.

TREASURY RESERVE AUTOMATED DEBT ENTRY SYSTEM
See TRADES.

TRIGGER
1. Any event that is the occasion for a second event. For example, a trade at or through a stop price "triggers" the stop and the order becomes a market order. In this sense, *activate* and *elect* are synonyms for triggers.
2. In corporation finance, a "poison pill" tactic whereby the acquisition of a set percentage of a company's stock automatically causes certain changes to take place in other outstanding shares. For example, the

other outstanding shares are given subscription rights for many new shares at bargain prices. Thus, the acquisition "triggered" the changes in the other shares.

TRIN
Popular name for a short-term trading index developed by Richard Arms, a journalist at *Barron's* in 1967.

Find the quotient of advancing issues divided by declining issues on the NYSE. Then, find the quotient of advancing volume on the NYSE. Finally, divide the first number by the second to find the TRIN (*Tr*ading *In*dex). TRIN numbers above one are bullish; below one are bearish.

TRO
See TEMPORARY RESTRAINING ORDER.

TRUE INTEREST COST
Abbreviation: TIC.

This is a municipality's calculation of its real interest cost to issue debt. TIC considers, on a semiannual basis, the time value of proceeds received versus the obligation to pay creditors both interest and principal.

TIC, also called "Canadian Interest Cost," is an alternative method to NIC (q.v.) for the awarding of competitive bond issues.

TRUTH-IN-ISSUANCE ACT
Descriptive explanation of the Securities Act of 1933, which requires disclosure of the material facts about new issues of nonexempt securities offered for public sale.

There are severe penalties, both civil and criminal, for persons who fail to register such public sales or who fail to include the material facts, or omit material facts, from the registration statement and prospectus for such issues.

Also called the "Truth-in-Securities Act."

TSE
1. Toronto Stock Exchange. The largest of the Canadian stock exchanges for the trading of stocks and options. The TSE is linked electronically to stock exchanges in the United States.
2. Tokyo Stock Exchange. The largest of the stock exchanges in the Orient and the originator of 80% of all securities trades in Japan.

TSE 300
See TORONTO STOCK EXCHANGE 300 COMPOSITE INDEX.

TSY

Common abbreviation for any of the negotiable forms of Treasury securities: bills, notes, or bonds. It is not used of Series EE bonds.

For example, on an order ticket: Buy 300M TSY 9s of '99. Translation: Buy $300,000 (face value) of the U.S. Treasury notes/bonds with 9% coupons that will mature in 1999.

TUNNELS

See CYLINDERS.

TURNING A CORNER

1. Any decisive move in a person's life.
2. Used of persons and corporations who have survived a crisis and for whom the future looks prosperous. For example, "Ajax has had a number of poor marketing years, but it seems that in 1990 they have turned a corner and are back on track."

12b-1 FUND

Number of a paragraph in the Investment Company Act of 1940.

Under paragraph 12b-1, a mutual fund—if properly registered with the SEC—may charge certain costs against the income of the fund if these costs are to be used for advertising, certain general corporate purposes, and for distribution fees to reward securities salespersons. As a result, the expense ratios of such 12b-1 funds are generally higher than the expense ratios of other funds.

Generally, 12b-1 funds have no up-front sales charge, but most have a "deferred contingent sales charge" if the client prematurely redeems shares of the fund.

The prospectus will explain both features of 12b-1 funds.

TWINS

A Salomon Brothers product. The product is a six-month warrant that entitles the holder to purchase $1,000 face value of the U.S. Treasury 7³/₈s of May 1996 at a discounted price. The discounted price is based on an index of U.S. dollar versus German deutsch mark values. In effect, the warrant will appeal to investors who consider that the U.S. dollar will fall in value versus the DM during the life of the warrant.

TWO-SIDED PICTURE

Jargon for an OTC marketmaker in NASDAQ securities who accepts orders to buy and sell at prices equal to (or slightly away from) the current market. For example, "We have a two-sided picture in Apple Computers" means that the marketmaker is showing bids and offers at those prices.

2,000 SMALL STOCK INDEX
A barometer of stock market performance developed by Frank Russell Co., an investment advisor in Tacoma, Washington.

It is part of the Russell 3,000. The 1,000 stock index contains about 90% of the dollar value of the top 3,000 publicly traded stocks in the United States. The 2,000 stock index of small stocks contains about 10% of the dollar value of the 3,000 stock index. The 2,000 small stock index is particularly useful at the end of bull and the beginning of bear markets when such stocks show unusual activity.

Also called the "Russell 2,000."

U

U
Twenty-first letter of the alphabet used:
1. Lowercase in newspaper stock transaction reports to designate that an intra-day price was the new high for the year; for example, u67. Next day, the new high will replace the old high in the 52-week range.
2. Uppercase as the fifth letter in a NASDAQ/NSM symbol to designate an issue of units; that is, stock and some other distribution. For example, MOVYU is the symbol of New Star Entertainment units. Each unit is two shares of common plus a warrant to purchase a half share.
3. NYSE symbol for U.S. Air Group.

UK PROGRAMME TRADE
Unlike program trading in the United States, the U.K. Programme Trade is a package of securities that is offered to competing firms for their proprietary accounts. At the time it is offered in a blind auction, the competitors do not know the component stocks, only the package value based on their last trade price. The winner of the auction is speculating on its ability to reoffer the stocks at a price equal or greater than its last sale price.

UK STOCK EXCHANGE
A commonly used identifier for the International Stock Exchange of the United Kingdom and the Republic of Ireland. Before the "big bang" of October 27, 1986, this exchange was known as the London Stock Exchange.

"UMBRELLA DESIGNATION"
The NASD's description of a tagline, attached to the official name of a member to identify that member's market specialty, or to promote its

recognition. Thus, "ABC Corporation—Professional Marketmakers in Mortgage Securities" illustrates the official name plus the tagline.

UMBRELLA FUND
Name used for open-ended investment companies, domiciled outside the United Kingdom, that offer separate participations in one investment family's securities. Each fund is dedicated to a different specific objective and may encompass several currencies. Subscription is available to any or several of the subfunds, and exchanges can be made quickly, easily, and cheaply.

UNBUNDLED UNITS
Term applied to an idea sponsored by Shearson Lehman Hutton to discourage hostile takeovers. In exchange for their voting shares, the corporation would give the shareholders units composed of a 30-year bond, a preferred share(s), and an equity participation certificate (in effect, a warrant). Thus, in response to the issuer's tender offer, the holder of common stock would receive a package (the unit) of three different nonvoting securities, each with its own market value.

"UNCLE" SPOT, AN
American slang for the amount of money an investor is willing to lose either on a particular issue or in the market in general.

The derivation seems to arise from street fighting terminology where one opponent tries to get the other to say "uncle"; that is, "I give up." The dollar amount is the point where the investor cries "uncle."

UNDER REFERENCE
In the United Kingdom, the expression used by a marketmaker when the marketmaker is unwilling to make a firm bid or offer. In effect, it is the counterpart of the "subject" quote in the United States. It is usually given because the trader must contact a principal for authorization to trade at a specific price or over a specific quantity.

UNDERWATER OPTION
Slang for an option whose exercise is uneconomical. Although such an option is out of the money, the connotation is that the option is very deep out of the money. For example, an executive was granted a stock option exercisable at $28 per share. The stock is now selling at $19 per share. That would be an "underwater option."

UNIFORM TRANSFER TO MINORS ACT
See UTMA.

UNIVERSE OF SECURITIES
A general term for a group of issues having a common thread, or similar characteristics or business.

Similar in meaning to sector or industry.

UNLISTED SECURITIES MARKET
Popular abbreviation: USM.

The USM is a 1980 offshoot of the London Stock Exchange designed to meet the capital needs of young, small, growing companies in the United Kingdom. The USM provides offerings of these issues with a form of trading legitimacy in the English marketplace. The USM subjects them to exchange scrutiny, examination, and regulation normally afforded companies admitted to full trading privileges on the floor of what is now the ISE.

UNLISTED TRADING PRIVILEGES
A request by a regional exchange to the SEC to permit it to allow the trading of shares of a particular issuer even though the issuer has not requested such trading nor has it signed a listing agreement.

The NYSE does not permit unlisted trading, and the ASE has not permitted it since 1933.

UNREALIZED PROFIT AND LOSS
Also known as "paper" profit and losses. Thus, these represent capital transactions that are not yet completed by a sale, or, in the case of short sales, by a short cover. In most cases, for taxpayers who use the cash basis, there are no tax consequences for unrealized profits and losses. Certain commodity and option spread positions, however, must be "marked to the market" at year-end. Tax advice is needed. Tax advice is also needed for taxpayers, particularly corporations, who use accrual methods of computing tax responsibilities.

USM
See UNLISTED SECURITIES MARKET.

UTMA
Acronym: Uniform Transfer to Minors Act. UTMA is similar to UGMA and is common to all 50 states. There are two major differences, however. UGMA permits gifts of cash and securities; UTMA extends the gifts to real estate, paintings, royalties, and patents. UTMA also prohibits the minor from gaining control of the assets until 21 years of age (25 in California).

Under UTMA, custodial assets may be held in nominee name.

V

V

Twenty-first letter of the alphabet used:

1. As the fifth letter in a NASDAQ/NMS symbol to denote an issue that has recently paid a stock dividend, been through a reorganization, or distributed additional shares. For example, Smith-Collins Pharmaceutical Co., after a 1–8 reverse split, was symboled CUREV.
2. Uppercase with a j (example: Vj) in front of NYSE and ASE listed stocks to denote that the parent company has filed for bankruptcy.
3. Alone uppercase as the NYSE ticker symbol for Irving Bank (now merged with Bank of New York Company).

VALUE LINE COMPOSITE INDEX

A market indicator originated by Value Line, Inc., a SEC-registered investment advisor founded by Arnold Bernhard. The Value Line Index measures approximately 1,700 stocks traded on the NYSE, ASE, and NASDAQ/NMS and uses an equal weighting system rather than a straight price or capitalization weighting.

The index is widely followed and is the benchmark for a futures contract traded on the Kansas City Board of Trade and an index option contract on the Philadelphia Stock Exchange.

VAMPIRE STOCK

Tongue-in-cheek description of a rumored takeover stock. The stock is so called because the rumor cannot be traced, or even stopped, until someone—such as a well-known raider—"spikes" it through the heart with a formal tender offer or a denial.

VARIABLE COUPON RENEWABLE NOTE

See VCR.

VARIABLE RATE DEMAND OBLIGATION

See VRDO.

VARIABLE RATE MORTGAGE

See VRM.

VARIATION MARGIN

Term used most often in the futures industry to describe mark-to-the-market deposits required to supplement and collateralize open future contract commitments. In effect, both parties to the contract are properly secured on a day-to-day basis.

VAT

Acronym: Value Added Tax. VAT is popular in Europe and the United Kingdom as a form of national sales tax. VAT is levied upon most goods and services, based upon incremental increases in value at each stage of manufacture, distribution, or usage.

In the United Kingdom, VAT is also levied on commissions on securities transactions payable through inter-firm marketmakers, but not on orders placed with an in-house marketmaker.

VCR

Acronym: Variable Coupon Renewable Note. VCRs are a Goldman Sachs innovation designed to appeal to money market mutual funds. VCRs are a one-year note issued by a top-quality industrial company. The note is automatically renewable at the end of each quarter (91 days). The VCR is priced to float at 75 basis points above T-bills.

VCRs are putable (upon nine-month notice and a reduced yield).

VEGA

An analyst's expression used to describe the volatility of an equity issue. Specifically, vega measures the relationship between a stock's market price and the option premium it commands in the marketplace. In effect, vega is the inverse of DELTA.

VELDA SUE

Acronym: Venture Enhancement & Loan Development Administration for Smaller Undercapitalized Enterprises. Velda Sue is a U.S. government agency created to promote the funding of small businesses in the United States. It purchases and pools small business loans made by banks, securitizes them (in the same way as GNMA and FHLMC), and sells the security to large institutions as investments.

VENDOR PLACINGS

A somewhat inequitable British corporate finance technique used by some companies to acquire other companies. Recognizing that some shareholders may not want stock for their stock, the acquirer may intervene by placing such tendered stock with institutional holders in exchange for cash. It is inequitable in that all of the acquirer's shareholders do not get the same right to purchase new shares and maintain a proportionate interest in the company.

VENTURE ENHANCEMENT & LOAN DEVELOPMENT ADMINISTRATION FOR SMALLER UNDERCAPITALIZED ENTERPRISES
See VELDA SUE.

VIENNA STOCK EXCHANGE
One of Europe's smallest stock exchanges. Trading is conducted each weekday from 11 A.M. until 1 P.M., with no after-hour activity permitted.

Settlements are scheduled for the second Monday following each full business week, either in cash or by means of a special weekly clearing system known as *arrangement*.

VIP
Acronym: Value of Index Participation contracts. VIPs are the CBOE counterpart of the PHLX's Cash Index Participations (CIPs).

VIPs are a type of security whose value is tied to the performance of either of two stock indexes created by the CBOE. Like the CIP and the EIP (Amex), holders of this issue receive a proportionate share of the dividends paid to holders of the underlying stocks in the index.

However, unlike the other two products, naked (short) sellers can eliminate their liability (at the index value) by paying a small fee at cash-out time. That fee is paid to holders of the VIP as an extra dividend. They are now the subject of a court-issued injunction because of their similarity to futures contracts.

VISIBLE SUPPLY
The dollar value of municipal bonds that will come to market during the ensuing month. The value includes both competitive and noncompetitive issues.

Also called the "30-day visible supply" or the "calendar."

The visible supply gives underwriters an insight into the competitive risk they face from upcoming issues; thus, the underwriters of a marginal, small BBB-rated issue must so plan the offering that it does not compete head-on with a succession of AAA and AA offerings.

VOCON
Abbreviation for voluntary contribution.

Many participants in some employer-funded qualified pension plans are permitted to make voluntary contributions of after-tax dollars into such plans. Although the dollar contributions are after-tax, the internal growth of the contributed dollars is tax sheltered. This provides the principal benefit of VOCON contributions.

Following TRA 86, persons who are otherwise covered by qualified plans and who make above certain statutory amounts ($35K single, $50K married filing jointly) may make $2,000 annual IRA contributions that are similar in function to VOCON contributions.

VRDO
Acronym: Variable Rate Demand Obligation. VRDO is the generic name for a Shearson Lehman Hutton product similar to municipal commercial paper. VRDOs are tax-exempted debt whose interest rate is reset daily and which can be put back to the underwriter or municipality at par value if the rate is unacceptable to the holder.

VRM
Popular acronym for Variable Rate Mortgage, a real estate loan in which the interest rate is adjustable every six months for the 20 to 30-year life of the mortgage. Generally, the rate adjustments are limited to 1/2% changes, with both a floor and a ceiling applicable during the entire length of the mortgage.

VULTURE CAPITALIST
English euphemism for someone who contributes "seed money" to a new business but takes out so much in the early stages that the business is unable to succeed. In effect, a vulture capitalist is a venture capitalist with too little patience.

W

W
Twenty-second letter of the alphabet used:
1. As the fifth letter in a NASDAQ/NMS symbol to signify a warrant. For example, LUVSW stands for Southwest Airlines warrants, a security enabling the holder to buy common stock at $35 per share through 6/25/90.
2. Alone uppercase as the NYSE symbol for Westvaco Corp., a large manufacturer of paper products.

WABO/WASO
Acronym: We Are Buyers (Sellers) of. . . . Used by securities dealers in the United Kingdom as the heading for lists of securities that they are interested in buying (WABO), or are interested in selling (WASO). These lists are often circulated to salespersons and to other dealers prior to the opening of the market.

WAC
In real estate finance, this is the abbreviation for "weighted average coupon," the significant interest percentage applicable to a pass-through mortgage pool.

WAFFLE, TO

From the Scottish dialect, "to speak equivocally." Thus, in practice, the act of changing one's opinion or to be indecisive. In the financial industry, the actions of someone who is ambivalent about investing, or who fails to take a firm stance in the management of a portfolio.

WAG THEORY

Facetious market theory, which sounds pretentious, but, in reality, stands for "wild-ass guess."

See SWAG for a further explanation and example.

"WAIVER BY CONDUCT" DOCTRINE

Term used by U.S. regulators in their endeavor to obtain cooperation of foreign officials in the prosecution of persons violating U.S. securities laws from a foreign location. In effect, U.S. regulators endeavor to show that the activity mutually violates the laws of both countries; in this way, they are able to get help from foreign governments. Otherwise, foreign laws often block international enquiries and conceal identities of persons acting to violate U.S. securities laws.

WAIVING THE MARKET

A regulatory term used to describe this action: a market arbitrageur, who is long stock and short an index future, sells the stock in an endeavor to lower its price and thereby profit on the futures contract. Such an action has quasi-manipulative overtones because it can make both sides of the arbitrage profitable to the detriment of public investors.

"WALK-AWAY" MERGER

In some mergers, there is often a built-in time delay because of needed approvals from regulators. Because of this, there may be a drop in the price of the acquirer's stock (which is going to be used in part to pay for the merger). Thus, there is usually a stipulation in the consolidation agreement that permits the acquired company to cancel; that is, to "walk-away" from the merger if the acquiring company's stock falls below a predetermined price level.

"WALKING DEAD"

Stock market slang for an issue that does not react favorably to good news. In fact, such issues often do not react to any news—including the environment of a predominantly bullish market.

WALL

1. Verb phrase: going to the wall, or went to the wall. Used to signify a failure, or a defeat, for a corporation. For example, "They went to the

wall because of the failure of their most recent marketing campaign."

2. Used in the expression "Chinese wall", that is, the lack of communication of inside business information between the finance department of a broker/dealer (who have the information) and the sales and trading areas of the same firm (who do not have the information).

WALLFLOWER
A person who because of unpopularity or shyness remains without companionship at a party or dance. Thus, by metaphor, a stock, or indeed an entire industry, that is out of favor at the present time in the eyes of professional investors and portfolio managers. This unpopularity may be due to economic conditions or to lack of publicity about the company. For this reason, the role of the public relations expert for corporations has expanded dramatically in recent years.

WALLPAPER
As used in the securities industry, the term is derogatory and means a worthless certificate, either stock or bond. The inference is that the company became bankrupt and that no market exists for the security.

Do not confuse with the hobby of collecting old cancelled stock and bond certificates. Although these certificates have no stock or bond market value, they may have a great market value as collectors' items because of rarity or calligraphy.

See SCRIPOPHILY.

WAM
Acronym: Weighted Average Maturity. In the pricing of securitized real estate pools, both MBSs and CMOs, it is possible that there will be a premature paydown of unpaid principal balance. Thus, the average life may be less than the stated time to maturity. For this reason, it is the custom to price such securities in terms of their estimated weighted average maturity. It is not unusual that such prices be stated as a yield, as a dollar price plus 32nds, or as a number of basis points above Treasuries of similar anticipated maturity.

WAR BABY
See WAR BRIDE

WAR BRIDE
Also known as a "war baby," this is a reference to a company that was placed on an unusual footing because of its close connection to the government's war efforts in World War II. Such companies were immersed in defense contracting—hence the allusion—and many still are. General

Dynamics, Raytheon, and Lockheed were "war brides"—and they still are to a great extent.

WAR CHEST
A picturesque term used in corporate circles to designate a fund of money set aside by a company to defend itself against a hostile tender offer. These funds are set aside to pay for legal fees and other costs deemed essential to preserve the company's independence.

WARM
Acronym: Weighted Average Remaining Maturity. The acronym has the same meaning as WAM (q.v.).

WART
Acronym: Weighted Average Remaining Term. It has the same meaning as WAM (q.v.).

WASTING ASSET
1. Any asset that expires worthless at a particular time in the future; for example, a right, warrant, or option.
2. In particular, a long option; that is, the right but not the obligation to buy (call) or sell (put) a specified underlying. The specified underlying may be a stock, bond, currency, or index.

Because the option expires worthless at a specified time in the future, there is a "bias against its profitable exercise," and, therefore, long options are considered highly speculative and suitable only for speculative investors.

WATCHDOG (ON WALL STREET)
Tongue-in-cheek term for the Securities and Exchange Commission (SEC), the principal regulator of the securities industry in the United States.

WEAK HANDS
Wall Street term for investors who are easily frightened into selling by bad news about a company or the market, or who—in the first adverse financial fortunes in their private life—sell to provide adequate funds for day-to-day budgeting.

Also called "weak sisters."

Antonym: STRONG HANDS (q.v.).

WEAK SISTERS
See WEAK HANDS.

WEIGHTED AVERAGE COUPON
See WAC.

WEIGHTED AVERAGE MATURITY POOLS
See WAM.

WE OFFER RETAIL
See WOR.

WHISKEY
Popular nickname used by salespersons and floor traders for the common stock of Joseph Seagram & Sons, Ltd., a Canadian company listed on the NYSE.

The nickname is derived from the fact that Seagram's principal products are distilled spirits. Interestingly, the NYSE ticker symbol for Seagrams is VO, which also happens to be the name of one of its most popular brands of Canadian whiskey.

WHISPER STOCK
Descriptive term for a stock of a company that is rumored to be "in play"; that is, a company being purchased by arbitrageurs and speculators because they believe that the company will soon be the object of a friendly or hostile takeover. The allusion is to the fact that the name of the stock is "whispered" as though it were inside information; in fact, there is often more rumor than fact in the situation.

WHISTLE BLOWER
Term used in reference to the Insider Trading and Securities Fraud Enforcement Act of 1988. Thus, a whistle blower is anyone who informs the SEC about violators of the law. What is more, informants with facts or evidence, or both, of an illegal market transaction based on insider nonpublic information may be eligible for a bounty for their service to the country.

WHITE CHIPS
Colorful term for young, growing companies that are on their way to becoming "blue chips" as they mature and have stable earnings and markets.

WHITE-COLLAR WORKER
Generally accepted term for an administrative worker or a lower-level manager of a company. The allusion is to the uniform of accepted office wear: jacket, white shirt, and tie.

As a general rule, middle and upper management are so called and the term blue-collar worker is not used of them.

Antonym: BLUE-COLLAR WORKER.

See also STEEL-COLLAR WORKER.

WHITEMAIL

The opposite of "greenmail" whereby a company is forced to buy out a potential raider at above-the-market prices just to get rid of the raider.

In whitemail, the company sells sizeable amounts of new stock to a preferred customer at below-market prices to perpetuate existing management. This "protection" makes a takeover quite difficult because the raider has to buy a large amount of extra stock, often at inflated prices.

WHITE-SHOE FIRM

Tongue-in-cheek expression for a broker/dealer that does not get involved in hostile relationships; that is, for or against clients. The origin of the term is uncertain: it may go back to college fraternity unwritten rules that a "brother" would do nothing to jeopardize social relationships with another "brother"; or it may mean that the broker/dealer would not get its shoes dirty in a fight between companies.

WHITE SQUIRE

A corporate finance term for someone who protects companies from corporate raiders. For example, there are some public relations firms that warn companies of unusual activity in company stock.

Do not confuse with "white knight"; that is, someone who comes to the rescue of a company *after* an unwelcome suitor appears on the scene. The "squire" acts *before* the raid is public.

WIDOW-AND-ORPHAN STOCK

A colorful term for a blue-chip investment that has both steady (or rising) prices and a steady (or rising) dividend.

The analogy is to the fact that widows and orphans are persons who are least able to stand a surprise. Thus, this stock is as steady as a rock in good times and bad.

WILSHIRE 5,000

The cumulative dollar value of the common stock of 5,000 publicly traded companies listed on the NYSE and ASE or traded on NAS-DAQ/NMS.

The index was created by Wilshire Associates, a Los Angeles-based SEC-registered investment advisor. The index, in effect, represents the trend in value (capitalization times price) of the 5,000 most widely traded stocks in the United States. At the time of writing (early 1990), the value of the Wilshire Index was approximately $3.25 trillion—with a "t".

WINDOW DRESSING
Slang for the portfolio adjustments made by the managers of portfolios at the end of the quarter so their printed reports to participants (mutual funds need only make semiannual reports) will include well-known investment-grade securities.

In effect, the managers are "dressing up" their reports for popular consumption. Losers, in the meantime, were sold off, and "blue chips" were put in the portfolio to dress it up.

WINDOW TICKET
Industry term for a stamped receipt issued by a transfer agent to a broker/dealer for securities left with the agent for re-registration.

The term goes back to the old days when messengers physically delivered securities to banking windows and accepted receipts. Much of this work is now handled through depositories and is greatly simplified.

WINGGING
1. In the United Kingdom, a slang expression for doing something unethical or unprofessional in the financial industry. For example, "I feel that he is wingging the rules on suitability of customer recommendations."
2. Also in the United Kingdom, a constant complainer; that is, someone who blames his lack of financial success on outside manipulators of market prices.

WITHERING WITHDRAWAL PENALTY
Term used of no-load mutual funds, including 12b-1 funds, that have a diminishing fee for the early redemption of fund shares. The typical early redemption fee, known technically as a *contingent deferred sales charge*, usually disappears in about four to five years after purchase of the fund shares; thus, it may be 5% the first year, 4% in the second year, and so on.

Some no-load funds charge a flat redemption fee; that is, a fee that does not diminish over time.

WITHHELD ORDER
NASD term descriptive of the practice of failing to enter a customer's mutual fund order in a timely fashion in an endeavor to outguess the market.

The withholding of orders violates industry rules.

WONDER STOCK

Expression for a stock of a company that is involved in an exciting new technology and that, as a result, is expected to soar in price. Currently, stocks involved in AIDS research, pollution control, certain areas of high technology, robotics, and advanced communications are considered to be wonder stocks.

WOOLWORTH FIVES & TENS

Traders' reference to U.S. Treasury issues with 5-and 10-year maturities. Such bonds and notes are usually benchmarks for the pricing of other bonds in terms of yield spread. The designation is made to Woolworth's because that store was originally known as Woolworth's 5 and 10 Cent Store—a high-volume, lower-priced retailer.

WORLD GOVERNMENT BOND INDEX

A Salomon Brothers product designed to track the price performance of government securities in nine different international markets. Two government bonds (Japan and the United States) account for approximately three fourths of the index; the remaining countries are Great Britain, West Germany, France, Canada, the Netherlands, Australia, and Switzerland.

"WRAP ACCOUNT"

Term used of a customer's special brokerage account at a large diversified firm. The broker/dealer chooses a money manager for the customer, pays the money manager from the customer's assets, and executes the orders authorized by the investment advisor.

An annual fee is charged for the service. At year-end the broker/dealer is to monitor the performance of the advisor and report to the customer.

Y

Y

The 25th letter of the alphabet used:
1. As the generally accepted symbol for the Japanese yen. Generally, the Y is written with two horizontal lines through its downstroke; for example, .
2. As the fifth letter in NASDAQ/NMS symbols if the underlying is an American Depository Receipt. For example, Fisons, ADRs has the symbol FISNY.
3. Used alone uppercase as the NYSE symbol for Allegheny Corporation, a large title insurer and financial conglomerate.

YACKER
Term associated with high-pressure salespersons in a "boiler room" operation. Although there are few such boiler rooms around today, the counterpart is the high-pressure "penny stock" sales organization. The "yacker" is the front person who engages the prospective customer in idle chatter to determine if the prospect is interested; one or more salespersons may then take over for the actual sale (or follow-up sale).

YARD, A
Slang used in foreign currency transactions to signify "one billion." For example, "It is not unusual for large international money center banks to lay off 20 yards of currency transactions a day."

YB
NYSE specialist code name for "omnibus dealer accounts." It is a single contra party designation given up to floor brokers by specialists in lieu of a multitude of actual names on the opposite side of a particular transaction. Thus, in an active market, the specialist can give up YB as an omnibus designator, rather than take the time to designate each of the names. Eventually, the names will have to be given up for confirmation and clearing purposes, either to the contra broker or to the clearing house.

YBTO
Short identifier for Yield-Based Treasury Option, an index listed on the CBOE that is European-style and cash settled.

The excise price of this instrument is based upon the annualized yield to maturity of the underlying Treasury obligations.

YCA
See YIELD CURVE AGREEMENT.

YCAN
Acronym: Yield Curve Adjustable Note. YCANs are a Morgan Stanley product first employed by Sallie Mae as a five-year obligation whose interest-rate payments were keyed to LIBOR rates and reset semiannually until maturity.

YEARLING
Colloquial name in the United Kingdom for a bond with one year to maturity. Originally the term came from the weekly offering by English councils (governmental agencies not unlike our states and political subdivisions) under the auspices of the U.K. Treasury and the Bank of England.

Yearlings are issued in bearer form in the name of the individual councils. Their interest rate is set in common by the U.K. treasury as dictated by current money market rates.

YEAR OF THE JUBILEE
A biblical theory of economics. Thus, there is a long wave cycle of approximately 50 years. The excesses of previous years will be "purged" by a depression, and then a new business cycle—one of prosperity—will begin and will last for another "jubilee"; that is, about 50 years.

See also KONDRATIEFF CYCLE for a similar long-term wave or cycle.

YIELD CURVE ADJUSTABLE NOTE
See YCAN.

YIELD-BASED TREASURY OPTION
See YBTO.

YIELD CURVE AGREEMENT
Popular abbreviation: YCA. YCAs are arrangements between large investment banking firms and large institutional customers whereby the customer, on a semiannual basis, pays six-month LIBOR rates and receives in return the 10-year Treasury note yield minus 50 basis points. Thus, over the 10-year life of the YCA, the customer receives money every six months IF the spread between LIBOR and 10-year T-notes is wider than 50 basis points.

The term *large* is important: only large investment bankers can take the risk and only large institutional customers have the sophistication to make such an agreement.

YIELD CURVE NOTES
Term associated with certain issues of medium-term Student Loan Marketing Association securities. The interest rate on these notes maturing in 1990 is pegged to the LIBOR rate and will rise or fall semiannually as that benchmark rate reflects current interest-rate trends.

YIELD GAP
U.K. term for the average rate of return on gilts in relation to the yield on U.K. equities. Theoretically, the yield gap should be a function of risk, with the riskier equity investments yielding more than the blue-chip gilts.

Note: in this expression, the term *yield* when used of equities means *total return*; that is, a combination of growth and dividend income.

YMCA

Acronym: Young Married Career-oriented Accentuators. Tongue-in-cheek term for the group of college and business school graduates who descended on Wall Street and the investment banking industry during the bull market of the 80s intent on making it rich in a hurry. The allusion is to men of the YMCA (Young Men's Christian Association) who generally have loftier ideals.

YUPPIES

See DINKs.

Z

Z

Twenty-sixth and last letter of the alphabet used:
1. In stock volume listings to designate that the number is to be multiplied by 10 and not by 100. Thus, z55 is 550 shares traded, not 5,500.
2. In mutual fund listings to designate that the fund did not provide bid/asked prices by press time.
3. As the fifth letter in NASDAQ/NMS listings to designate closed end investment company shares, or "limited partnership" interests. For example, TPLPZ stands for Teeco Properties, LP.
4. Alone uppercase as the NYSE symbol for F. W. Woolworth Co., a major retailer in the United States.

Z-BOND

Z-bonds are the residual tranche (class) of CMOs. As the last part of a serialized mortgage obligation, the interest payable is not immediately distributed. Instead, it accrues and is added to principal. Then, at the time of redemption or maturity (whichever comes first), the holder is told how much of the final distribution is interest and how much is principal.

Also known as an "accrual bond."

ZAITECH

A Japanese term that aggregates the concept of "zaimer" (financial) and high technology; thus, ZAITECH.

It refers to the growing number of Japanese companies that have turned from manufacturing or product distribution to an investment of surplus funds into a multitude of financial instruments. Needless to say, the officials of these companies need superior financial sophistication to function profitably outside their original areas of expertise.

ZARABA TRADING
The method of trading that is used in the first session (9 to 11 A.M.) on the principal Japanese exchanges.

Zaraba trading is fast-paced. The auction system used is similar to the auction trading on the principal exchanges in the United States.

ZETA RISK
The prospective additional loss at each future contract price interval caused by a change in product volatility.

ZOMBIE BONDS
Slang expression for the debt obligations of near-bankrupt thrift institutions. Because no one knows whether or not these institutions will default, their debt sells at near-bankruptcy levels.

ZOMBIES
Nickname given to insolvent savings and loans that continue to function under the conservatorship of the FDIC. In effect, they are technically "brain dead" (hence the term zombie) institutions awaiting final Congressional decision on whether they will be saved or scuttled.

ZURICH STOCK EXCHANGE
The exchange is actually the Zurich, Geneva, and Basle exchanges linked together by computerized quotations.

There is one daily trading session from 10:30 A.M. until 1:30 P.M.—although after-hour trading is not prohibited. Settlement is made on the third business day after trade date by means of the Swiss Interbank Clearing System.

Eventually, trading on the exchange will be completely electronic.